Modern Materials Management

Modern
Materials
Management

Richard J. Tersine
John H. Campbell

NORTH-HOLLAND · NEW YORK
NEW YORK · AMSTERDAM · OXFORD

Elsevier North-Holland, Inc.
52 Vanderbilt Avenue, New York, New York 10017

North-Holland Publishing Company
P.O. Box 211
Amsterdam, The Netherlands

Library of Congress Cataloging in Publication Data
Tersine, Richard J
    Modern materials management.

    Bibliography: p.
    Includes index.
    1. Materials management. I. Campbell, John
Hardin, 1946-   joint author. II. Title.
TS161.T48   658.7   77-2291
ISBN 0-444-00228-6

Manufactured in the United States of America

To Dianne, Christine, and Laverne

Contents

Preface

The importance of materials in organizational performance has been known for several decades. Only recently, however, has the manager found it necessary to develop an organized body of knowledge on this subject. The resulting set of related disciplines is known as materials management. Spawned by commodity shortages, competition, and increasing costs, materials management is rapidly increasing in importance.

Materials management problems are common to all organizations. Profit-making manufacturing organizations were the first to recognize their importance as such, and more recently the nonprofit sector (government agencies, hospitals, universities, and prisons) has begun to realize their significance.

Because it is still in its infancy, the subject is suffering the pains of growth and identity. This book seeks to ease these pains by offering a refinement in conceptualization and approach. Materials management is concerned with the flow of materials to, within, and from an organization. The flow is regulated in relation to market demand, prices of materials, supplier performance on quality and delivery, the availability of materials, and so forth. Materials management does not add value to a product by physical transformation; value is added by virtue of existence, movement, and availability (the product undergoes no physical change).

Numerous planning and control activities formerly performed in a routine manner by clerical staff have evolved into more sophisticated functions with significant impact on organizational effectiveness. Materials management can be placed in this category of increased criticality. It is usually located in various parts of the organization, such as purchasing, production control, transportation, warehousing, materials handling, operations, receiving, and logistics. Identical activities are known by such titles as supply, material, procurement, and a variety of other names.

The book is geared to college students and practitioners in organizations. It can be used at the undergraduate and graduate level in operations management, production management, marketing management, industrial engineering, financial management, business administration, and materials management. In an organizational setting, it may be useful to personnel in production control, purchasing, inventory control, forecasting, accounting, material, supply, warehousing, and operations. Finally, as a supplemental text, it could be used in any of the functional areas. To support its value as an instructional tool, the book contains questions, problems, and cases at the end of each chapter. The book attempts to bridge the gap between theory and practice.

Appreciation is extended to the numerous peers and students who supplied helpful criticism. Thanks are also due to Edward Grasso, Walt Riggs, Sally Pruett, and Patricia Speakman who contributed their professional skills.

Chapter 1

Introduction

The role of management in any organization involves the acquisition, disposition, and control of factors such as labor, capital, material, and equipment. Although the factors are often referred to as factors of production, they are also applicable to non-production oriented organizations. This book specifically addresses the factor termed material. Without proper assortments of material, serious marketing problems can develop with respect to revenue generation and customer relations. Likewise, materials are critical to manufacturing, since shortages can stop operations or require processes to be modified. Just as shortages disrupt marketing and production, excessive materials create other serious cost problems. The management of material can be viewed as the attainment of a cost balance between shortages of stock and excesses of stock within an environment characterized by risk and uncertainty.

1

The management and control of material are common problems to all organizations in all sections of the economy. The problems do not confine themselves to profit making institutions. The same type of problems are encountered by social and nonprofit institutions. Material is common to agriculture, manufacturers, wholesalers, retailers, hospitals, churches, prisons, zoos, universities, and national, state, and local governments. Indeed, material is also relevant to the family unit in relation to food, clothing, medicines, toiletries, and so forth. On an aggregate national basis, the total investment in material (inventory) represents a sizable portion of the gross national product. The average manufacturing firm spends over half of its sales revenue on purchased parts, components, raw materials, and services; a larger portion of the sales dollar of wholesalers and retailers is a materials cost. Manufacturing organizations usually have from 25 to 30% of their total assets invested in inventories, while wholesalers and retailers may have as much as 75% of their assets in inventories.

Designing a product, financing the venture, manufacturing the product, and marketing the product have long been recognized as important organizational activities. Recently another major activity has joined the group. This new activity looks at the total flow of materials and parts from suppliers to production and the subsequent flow of the product through distribution centers to the customer. Materials management plans and controls the total flow as an integrated system.

Materials management is responsible for planning, acquisition, storage, movement, and control of materials and final products so as to optimize the utilization of personnel, facilities, and capital while providing customer service in line with organizational goals. Materials management attempts to provide the right goods at the right price at the right time to maintain a desired service level at minimum cost. It is a systematic integrated approach to the control of materials to, through, and from the organization. The subject and purpose of materials management is the effective control of material throughout its flow cycle.

Materials management deals with several activities or functions which are very important in organizations, but are in many cases neglected. It cuts across the classical functional boundaries, so that integrated control frequently comes into conflict with traditional management principles. Nevertheless materials management is administratively rational for an organization when material costs are a significant part of total costs or the product line is very complex and diversified.

Traditionally, materials management has been neglected because of the nature of cost accounting systems. Many of the materials management costs are buried in overhead or indirect charges. Direct or variable costs are usually highlighted to a greater degree and receive more management attention. Today, the more highly trained and sophisticated manager is more aware of all the cost contributions, and he is looking beyond the traditional limitations of accounting systems.

Why has materials management become important? Historically, more analysis and control has been placed on the expenditure of monies for personnel, plant, and equipment than on materials. But for manufacturing organizations, materials related costs have grown to be the largest single expenditure. Because of increased specialization, organizations are making less and less while buying more and more of their inputs. Inputs are no longer basic raw materials, but consist of complex parts and subassemblies. Some organizations have become pure assembly operations with virtually no production of the components for their products. The quantity and variety of items purchased have increased, which has resulted in a larger portion of expenditures on material inputs. The purchasing function has become much more critical because of the increase in expenditures; it also requires more highly trained professionals, since the quantity and complexity of items have increased substantially.

The control of materials has become considerably more complicated because of the purchase of a greater portion of what goes into the product as components and subassemblies rather than as raw materials for conversion in the plant. It is not uncommon for organizations to have thousands of input materials from hundreds of suppliers. In addition to the financial burden of the increased number of items, many more supplier accounts must be managed. The systematic storage of many more items and the processing of many more pieces of paper are required.

With more specialized inputs having specific uses, mismanagement of materials results in inventories that are not naturally depleted as a function of time. With the purchase of raw materials only, large inventories would eventually be depleted. Raw materials usually have many uses and provide a measure of flexibility, while specialized components have fewer uses and less flexibility.

The movement from basic raw materials to more highly processed components has made materials management a sophisticated organizational function. The decade of the fifties saw a great leap in production capability for the industrialized nations. In the sixties the major emphasis shifted to selling and marketing. But to make more and sell more is not enough. The decade of the seventies rediscovered the need for resource conservation. It brought a realization that commodity shortages have a severe impact on profitability, and that the impact will continue in the foreseeable future.

In addition to creating more risk and uncertainty, commodity shortages tend to extend the planning horizon of an organization. In a complex and interdependent economic environment, the influences of shortages may be amplified through several market sectors. Today management is turning toward the better utilization of material and human resources. The effective utilization of resources is the major theme of this book.

It is no accident that wasted resources are usually concerned with materials. The share of organizational funds required for materials is so large that it must be a primary management concern. Every problem associated with the acquisition, storage, movement, and delivery of materials comes within its scope. Tremendous increases in manufacturing efficiency (technology) have reduced the cost of manufacturing a product to such an extent that in many cases it is far less than the cost of materials that go into the product. As a result, the most fruitful potential sources of further cost savings in many products come under materials management. It is these forces that have buoyed the management of materials to a prominent organizational status. More and more organizations are coming to the realization that materials management is the next frontier.

CONCEPTUALIZATION

Materials management can begin as a cycle with market analysis providing a base for production planning, which in turn establishes material requirements. Materials are purchased, delivered to the plant, inspected, and transferred to stores. Materials are withdrawn from stores, transferred to manufacturing, and processed through various stages into a finished product. The product may go into temporary storage, then to the shipping department, and then be transported to branch warehouses, to wholesalers and/or retailers, and finally to the customer. Although the flow cycle can vary from organization to organization, the basic functions performed are essentially the same.

As a body of knowledge, materials management is a difficult subject to internalize. Compared with accounting, engineering, or personnel administration, it is not characterized by relatively distinct and clear boundaries. In fact, materials management is actually a set of interrelated activities which can be and often are treated as discrete areas. In a world of specialization and high technology, each activity of materials management has become more and more complex. In turn, the interrelationships among activities have become more intense and subtle, requiring materials management to become extremely sophisticated.

A clear analysis of materials management reveals that it does not start with the purchase of goods and end with production. It follows the total flow of material, from the forecasting of future demand to physical distribution. All the subsystems of materials management are viewed as individually important, but at the same time it is recognized that they do not exist in isolation.

STRUCTURAL APPROACHES

Concepts are mental models and ideas that establish a framework for thought. They are required to insure an understanding of a complex subject such as materials management. Still, mere conceptualization is not enough to provide techniques for investigating the subject. That calls for articulating the concepts in the form of a highly developed structure. Because materials management is a set of interrelated activities, each with its own inherent complexity, it must be approached in a manner conducive to appreciating both its discrete and its aggregate aspects. Historically, two popular approaches have been (1) the evaluation of individual activities or functions in isolation, and (2) the viewing of all activities collectively as a system. While the merits of each approach are recognized, neither offers a sufficient foundation responsive to the study of materials management. It will be seen that a third approach is necessary.

ACTIVITIES APPROACH

The twentieth century introduced a plethora of technological innovations accompanied by extensive interest in numerous areas of organizational endeavor. With the advent of modern electromechanical capabilities and the attendant specialization in job design, efforts were focused on individual tasks to achieve maximum efficiency. The resulting approach is illustrated in Figure 1.1. Applications were first made in the manufacturing areas which were particularly amenable to the analytical principles of the scientific method.

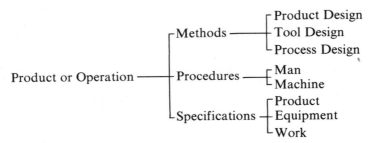

FIGURE 1.1. The activities approach to manufacturing.

The activities approach requires that each activity or function be exploded and evaluated with respect to its component elements or steps. Many organizations operate within well-defined functional boundaries. Each function is administered as a separate entity, and its performance measured by its own efficiency and effectiveness. This micro approach provides a detailed view of each individual organizational activity. Unfortunately, it is rather static in a dynamic environment. The activities approach treats each activity in isolation without considering the interactions among the various other activities. Emphasis is on internal analysis as opposed to synthesis.

SYSTEMS APPROACH

Increasing technological intensity has added to the complexity of existing activities and introduced new activities. Rapid change has not only been manifested in modified and new activities, but also has resulted in more sophisticated relationships among existing activities. Activities are categorized into homogeneous groupings. Finally, the larger groupings are seen as interactive components of a larger entity called a system.

Thus, it is realized that the micro view of the activities approach ignores the influences of other related activities. Today, we characterize the dynamism of activity relationships as *sensitivity* (the tendency for activities to influence and be influenced by other activities). The degree and complexity of sensitivity will vary with the situation. Accommodating the sensitivities among organizational activities has been a major accomplishment of the systems approach.

The systems approach counters the micro view of activities with a macro orientation. The flow of materials is viewed as a single integrated system from the raw materials source through the many stages of processing to the distribution of the finished product. While this approach is a valuable management tool, unbounded enthusiasm for it leads to oversimplification of problems and decisions. The convenience of systems conceptualization is achieved at the expense of decoupling micro and macro influences. Depicted in Figure 1.2, the systems approach can either distort or ignore the detail contained in the individual activities of a system. The systems approach accounts for the sensitivities existing *among* activities, but has a tendency to ignore the complexity *within* each activity.

The division of labor, specialization, and complexity generated by technology obviously demands the use of an activities approach. Simultaneously, the complex environment of modern organizations requires a systems approach. Neither of the approaches represents a single suitable method for problem solving; both appear to be based on sound reasoning.

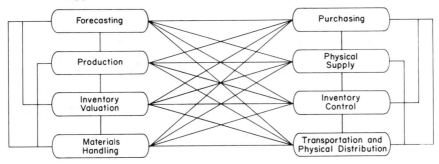

FIGURE 1.2

This dilemma suggests a need for a modified orientation—an approach which can get around the limitations of an activities or a systems view. Such a modified approach to materials management is developed herein and is termed the integrated functional approach.

INTEGRATED FUNCTIONAL APPROACH

A valid approach to materials management must consider both micro details and macro relationships, with a synthesis of the activities and systems approaches. That synthesis results in an integrated functional approach as shown in Figure 1.3.

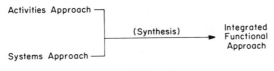

FIGURE 1.3

The functional approach considers the detailed workings of each activity. It depicts an activity as an open system, constantly interacting with its environment inputs are continually being transformed into outputs. Mathematically, it can be written as

$$\text{Output} = f(\text{inputs}) = f(X_1, X_2, \ldots, X_n).$$

Figure 1.4 serves as a point of reference for discussing individual functions. Inputs, restraints, factors, and outputs are generic headings for groups of elements common to each function. *Inputs* initiate action in an activity which necessitates the making of decisions. *Restraints* are those forces which act to modify the decision environment. *Factors* are technical

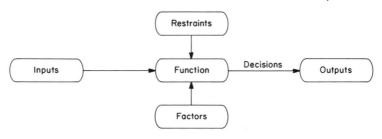

FIGURE 1.4

characteristics uniquely pertinent to a specific function. Finally, *outputs* are the final result of decisions within the function which support organizational objectives.

Restraints limit the number of feasible solutions or alternative plans of action. They establish boundaries within which a solution must be found. Restraints may be technical (limitations on the knowledge about the state of the art), economic (the money available or the cost restrictions on a particular solution), political (legal restrictions), social (restrictions imposed by religious, work, or informal organizations), and temporal, (the need to find a solution within a predetermined time frame).

At this point the reader is cautioned against the limitations of models. Although a conceptual model is useful in establishing a framework of thought, no model has universal applicability. The structure of a model is necessarily rather static, while the realities it attempts to mirror are dynamic. Realities or situations cannot be made to fit models. Conversely, models should be selected on the basis of their similarity to a given situation. Thus, you will notice that some of the materials management functions require modifications to the basic model.

The integrated functional approach treats each activity of materials management as a dynamic function. The set of functions is characterized by a high level of sensitivity, since each function influences and is influenced by all others. Thus, changes in one function may be related to changes in others, depending on the degree of sensitivity. Figure 1.5 illustrates the functional set for manufacturers, distributors, and retailers.

The materials manager in a manufacturing organization is usually responsible for purchasing, production and inventory control, physical supply, materials handling, transportation, and physical distribution. His responsibility is to have material available on time and in sufficient quantity so that a product can be produced and then shipped to a customer or controlled in storage for later shipment. Characteristically, the demand for a finished product (end item) is usually independent of any other demand and must be forecasted. However, once the production

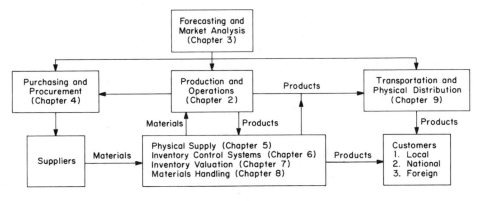

FIGURE 1.5

schedule for end items is established, the dependent demand for components, assemblies, parts, and raw materials can be established by exploding the bill of materials.

As illustrated in Figure 1.5, forecasting and market analysis indicate to the manufacturing organization its demand potential for the upcoming planning horizon. The organization via its master production schedule outlines its supply plan for how it hopes to satisfy its customers. From forecasts and the master production schedule, purchasing contracts with suppliers for the basic materials required. When the materials arrive, they are stored or made available to production. After production, the final products are stored or prepared for movement to the customer either directly or through distribution channels. All physical movements within the organization involve materials handling and various physical supply (storage) activities. Movements to and from the organization involve transportation and physical distribution. Of course, all movements involve the generation of paper and other documentation.

Materials management for distributors or retailers is simpler than for manufacturers. With distributors and retailers, the activities are the same, but the product does not undergo any physical change. Therefore, materials management activities are the same as in Figure 1.5 except that the production activity in nonmanufacturing organizations is referred to as operations. The materials manager in distributing or retailing organizations is usually responsible for operations or purchasing, inventory control, physical supply, materials handling, transportation, and physical distribution.

The structure, philosophy, and logic of this book are contained in Figure 1.5. Chapter 2 is production and operations, Chapter 3 is forecasting and market analysis; Chapter 4 is purchasing and procurement; Chapter 5 is physical supply; Chapter 6 is inventory control systems; Chapter 7 is inventory valuation; Chapter 8 is materials handling; and Chapter 9 is transportation and physical distribution. Thus, the integrated functional approach emphasizes the specific activities or functions while not neglecting the relationships among them. Any form of study less than an integrated functional approach tends to be simplistic and dysfunctional.

MATERIALS MANAGEMENT FUNCTIONS

Materials management can be more of a concept or philosophy than an organizational form. Its application is not tied to any specific structure. It is systems-oriented, yet it takes account of functional dependence, with organizational structure as a secondary consideration. It is an integrated approach as opposed to a partial, activities approach.

Materials management is addressed in this book as a set of eight integrated activities or functions. The functions consider the entire flow of material through an organization. The form utility of material is enhanced through manufacturing or fabricating in *production and operations*. *Forecasting and market analysis* is responsible for projecting the behavior of the product market over a temporal horizon. *Purchasing and procurement* is involved with the acquisition of material to satisfy other functional requirements.

Physical supply is charged with the responsibility of providing mechanisms to insure material accessibility, while *inventory control* and *inventory valuation* are concerned with material availability and worth. Finally, movement of material throughout its flow cycle is the concern of two functions, *materials handling* and *transportation and physical distribution*. Each of these functions will be briefly discussed in the remainder of this chapter.

PRODUCTION AND OPERATIONS

Materials management is often considered a part of production and operations. However, the management of material requires control throughout its entire flow cycle, which is often beyond the scope of production and operations. Similarly materials management does not exhaust the entire subject of production and operations. Thus, the relationship between materials management and production and operations can be described as the intersection of two sets, as depicted in Figure 1.6. There are elements common to both sets, such as production control and materials handling. However, it is difficult to grasp the full implications of

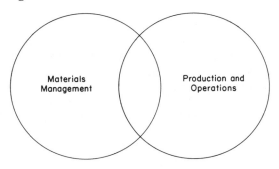

FIGURE 1.6

materials management when the subject of production and operations is omitted. Production and operations has pronounced and unavoidable sensitivities with other materials management functions. To account for those sensitivities, production and operations is approached as a key consideration in materials management. Extensive technical treatment of production and operations is not our purpose, nor could the subject be so covered in a single chapter. Chapter 2 does, however, address major considerations pertinent to materials management.

FORECASTING AND MARKET ANALYSIS

All organizations need to know something about the future. Whether he realizes it or not, the manager makes decisions based on forecasts. The forecasting techniques used may be scientific, heuristic, or a combination of both. The purpose in either case is to minimize risk and uncertainty. Forecasting and market analysis is responsible for projecting the behavior of markets over a temporal horizon. Chapter 3 covers this function and provides the rudimentary tools necessary for effective forecasting and market analysis.

PURCHASING AND PROCUREMENT

This function is responsible for the acquisition of material to satisfy other functions. Purchasing and procurement has received substantial attention over the past few years because of availability difficulties and rising costs. Given an unsettled economic environment, that attention will no doubt continue. Chapter 4 offers an evaluation of the purchasing and procurement function with methods for insuring operating effectiveness at an acceptable cost.

PHYSICAL SUPPLY

The responsibility of ensuring the accessibility of materials to the organization is often associated with warehousing, but that term has connotations which severely limit the general notion of material accessibility. Physical supply is the entire part of materials management charged with providing mechanisms to ensure material accessibility. It is covered in Chapter 5.

INVENTORY CONTROL SYSTEMS

While physical supply is concerned with material accessibility, inventory control is concerned with material availability. Influences on other functions are extensive. Those influences are especially prominent in times of rising costs, commodity shortages, and consumer awareness. Aspects of inventories and methods of economic control are covered in Chapter 6.

INVENTORY VALUATION

Any material held for later use or sale has a value associated with it. Popular accounting methods for determining value are discussed in Chapter 7. The subject of inventory valuation does not lend itself to input-output evaluation. Therefore, our conceptual functional model is ignored in this chapter.

MATERIALS HANDLING

Materials handling is a function which causes the physical movement of material throughout its flow cycle within the organization. As such, it is not confined in activity to a single physical location. It is apparent in several of the other functions. The high cost of materials handling gives it a prominent position in materials management. Chapter 8 evaluates the growing importance of materials handling and describes several handling alternatives and methods.

TRANSPORTATION AND PHYSICAL DISTRIBUTION

An accurate definition of the transportation and physical distribution function has been the subject of debate for several years. Two orientations are common. From the production viewpoint it is primarily concerned with the movement of incoming material to the organization. From the marketing viewpoint it is concerned with movement of finished goods in support of sales. It is not unusual for an organization to have incoming and outgoing movements under two distinct responsibility centers. Proper treatment has also been hampered by the number of popular terms applied to the function, including transportation, traffic, physical distribution, and logistics. Chapter 9 treats transportation and physical distribution as the function responsible for the flow of material external to the organization.

CONCLUSION

Managements have been plagued with expanding backlogs, deteriorating customer service, vendor problems, increasing inventories, and control difficulties. Lack of effective materials management systems results in an inability to react positively to either good or bad economic conditions. The performance of a materials management system can be measured by the customer service level, the magnitude of the inventory investment, and the cost of plant operations. Ratios are the most commonly used management control tools. They are used for goal setting, trend monitoring, and performance measurements.

Materials management is a relatively new field. It exists because managers have begun to realize that material considerations play a major role in organizational performance. Ignored, material considerations can lead to unnecessary costs and inefficiency. Properly managed, their beneficial features can be optimized while restraining characteristics can be controlled.

Aggregate materials management is "a look at the forest and not each tree." An organization is an open system, since its constituents have contact not only with each other, but also with the external environment consisting of suppliers, customers, competitors, the community, and other interested parties. Material flow to, inside, and from an organization requires a panoramic view.

The significance, relevance, and organizational stature of materials management will increase in the future. Numerous forces are dictating changes in this direction. One force is the trend towards increasing the number of highly specialized and complex products. As a result of this development, more organizations will make fewer and buy more of their material requirements. Consequently, materials will represent an increasing percentage of total product costs, and their control will be even more important than it is today. A second major force is the increasing trend towards automation. An uninterrupted flow of material is required for an automated facility. A third major force is the burgeoning cost of materials. An expanding world population with an almost insatiable demand for goods and services is creating shortages in supply which are causing costs to skyrocket. The days of cheap and abundant raw materials appear to be past. For these reasons and many others, the management of materials is no longer a trivial matter relegated to lower managerial levels.

QUESTIONS

1. Identify four factors of production.
2. What is materials management?
3. How does the flow of material influence an organization?
4. Why do cost accounting systems tend to neglect materials management?
5. Why is materials management difficult to internalize?
6. Define and discuss the significance of sensitivity analysis.
7. Distinguish between the activities approach and the systems approach.
8. List and describe the elements of the functional approach.
9. Discuss the limiting effect of restraints, and list the different types.
10. What is the primary significance of the integrated functional approach?
11. What are the materials manager's usual responsibilities in a manufacturing organization?
12. Compare and contrast materials management as it applies to manufacturers and to distributors and retailers.
13. Give three reasons for the expected increase in the importance of materials management in the future.

Chapter 2

Production and Operations

Production and operations is concerned with the creation of goods and services. The subject involves productive systems and their management. The function of a productive system is to transform a set of inputs into desired outputs. The inputs may be some combination of men, materials, money, machines, and methods. The transformation may be physical as in manufacturing, locational as in transportation, storage as in warehousing, exchange as in retailing, or more abstract as in services. A service system does not usually produce a physical product, whereas a manufacturing system does. Service industries such as universities, hospitals, governments, and prisons are frequently not thought of as productive systems by the uninformed. Rising costs and deteriorating performance are dramatically correcting this myopic view. Production and operations may occur in factories, schools, banks offices, warehouses, retail stores, or any type of organized human endeavor. It is applicable whether the organization is profit or nonprofit, private or public; whether the output is tangible or intangible, a physical product or a service.

It is management's responsibility to make decisions that determine the future course of action for the organization over the short and long term. These decisions have to do with every conceivable aspect of organizational affairs or activities. In making decisions, management selects from a set of alternatives what is considered to be the best course of action. To determine the optimum strategy from a set of alternatives requires criteria along with forecasts of performance of the alternative strategies. The decision criterion or value system must weigh the desirable and undesirable features of each strategy. The maximization of utility is a frequently sought after goal for organizations. It may be further subdivided into profit maximization, cost minimization, time minimization, and so forth.

Since the making of decisions implies action, it is usually necessary to forecast future conditions under which the organization will function. Models are developed as a synthetic aid in making decisions. Models frequently combine the forecast of future events with a value criterion in helping to select desirable strategies. Although there are numerous types of models, they represent no more than an abstraction of reality. That is necessary if the decision making process is to be rendered manageable. Ideally, it would be desirable to construct a single model to outline and depict all organizational activities and their interactions. If the model could predict the impact of any change, it would be priceless. Such a prediction model is beyond our scope of knowledge at this time. However, a simplified descriptive model can at least indicate the scope of the production or operations function.

Given the complexity of modern organizations, it is virtually impossible to view the segments of the production function as a group of separate independent entities. Indeed it is common for the interrelationships among functional areas to be of paramount importance. The behavior of a system tends to be determined more by the interaction than by the things that interact. It becomes necessary to develop a conceptual framework or philosophy that unites all the functional efforts, contributions, and knowledge within an organization. A conceptual understanding of an organization permits managers to solve problems rather than treat local symptoms. The systems concept outlines the scope of an organization in the abstract in order to define, analyze, and control it in an effective manner.

To depict the production function, a conceptual systemic model will be developed which outlines the functions that must be performed by an organization in getting a successful product to market. The systemic functional model can be subdivided into five interdependent categories—policy decisions, product decisions, process decisions, plant decisions, and operations decisions (see Figure 2.1). These categories give answers to the questions of why make it, what to make, how to make it, where to make it, and when to make it:

Why	Policy Decisions
What	Product Decisions
How	Process Decisions
Where	Plant Decisions
When	Operations Decisions

These generally recognized decision levels must be addressed, formally or informally, in order for an organization to survive.

The systemic functional approach follows the progress of a productive system from its inception to its conclusion while reflecting the true breadth of the activity. The approach does not indicate who conducts the functions but only those functions that must be conducted—that is, the emphasis is on what must be done and not on who should do it. Thus the model does not infringe on the functional prerogatives of any departmental boundaries. However, the domains of the functional areas have become less independent under systems design, which requires more integrated decision making.

A general system model must bring together, in an ordered fashion, information on the numerous dimensions of an organization. The concept of a function (input-transformation-output) is used to characterize systems performance. Outputs can be defined tangibly as goods or services, or intangibly as levels of satisfaction to the various interest groups. Emphasis on outputs is necessary so they can be precisely related to the essential inputs and the required combinations of inputs during the transformation (combination) phase.

POLICY DECISIONS

As shown in Figure 2.1, policy decisions begin with the statement of the broad long range objectives of the organization. Policy decisions establish the purpose for the organization. Objectives amount to a "statement of

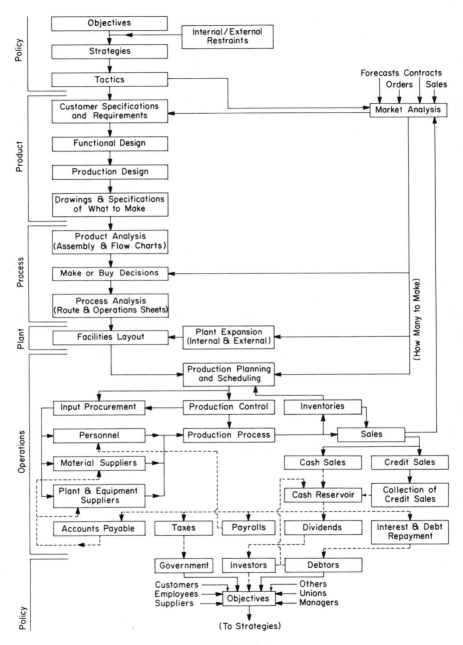

FIGURE 2.1

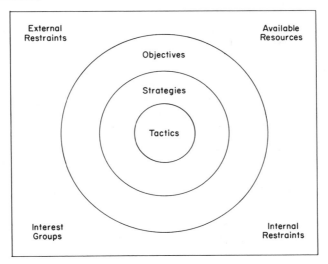

FIGURE 2.2

purpose"; they are the goals of the organization as a whole. The establishment of organizational objectives is the basic requirement for all subsequent decisions to be made on a lower level. Since there are many different types of organizations in a society, objectives are diverse. (Typical examples are growth, survival, market share, social responsibility, profit maximization, return on investment, product leadership, and so forth.) The objectives indicate why the organization exists. They are not subject to frequent revision, but are guideposts to direct the movement of the organization over time (the future) which is characterized by risk and uncertainty.

Policy decisions include the overall organizational objectives, strategies, and tactics. As illustrated in Figure 2.2, policy decisions are a progressive movement from objectives to strategies to tactics under various influences. The most prevalent influencing factors are special interest groups, available resources, external restraints, and internal restraints. After tactics are promulgated, they are usually subjected to some type of market analysis to determine feasibility.

OBJECTIVES

Policy decisions are made in order to determine where an organization is going and how well it is doing. An objective is a desired condition or state that an organization seeks to achieve. Objectives are goals or ends that explain the reason for the organization's existence. Objectives tend to be directional, while not being specific in magnitude. It is generally more meaningful to refer to a set of organizational objectives than to a singular objective. Since organizations are subject to complex influences from various groups, objectives are rarely simple and straightforward.

An organization is a coalition of individuals and groups seeking to improve or maintain their interests. In any organization it is important to identify the major coalition members. Coalition members include managers, stockholders, workers, suppliers, unions, and so forth. With diverse individuals and groups, internal conflict is inevitable. Conflict is resolved through consensus. Conformity to objectives is purchased by payments (wages, interest, status, dividends) to coalition members. Agreement on objectives usually requires a broad level of ambiguity to satisfy the various interests. Objectives become aspirational levels rather than optimal. Changes and adjustments usually involve bargaining among the major coalition members. Coalition members are not all of the same stature, and some may be passive most of the time. Past bargains become precedents for future bargains, and the process can become informally institutionalized. For an organization to be successful, it is necessary to identify the needs of each interest group, to establish some balance among them, and to designate policies which permit the satisfaction of needs.

People at the helm of an organization have explicit or implicit aspirations and values. The personal value orientations of those in "control" have a significant bearing on future directions. A personal value system can be considered a permanent perceptual framework which shapes and influences the general nature of an individual's behavior. Values are similar to attitudes, but are more ingrained and stable. The power of personal values to select, filter, and influence what an individual sees, hears, and does is an important behavioral phenomenon. Personal values influence decisions throughout an organization.

In systems analysis the efficiency of transfer from inputs to outputs is paramount, and for this purpose the most common measure of value is profit. When profitability is not relevant, control of cost is substituted. Although profit is a necessary objective of a profit making organization, it is not sufficient when conglomerate influences of different parties are influential. Survival of the organization is perhaps the predominant influence that unites heterogeneous groups. When survival is not in doubt, other objectives become conspicuous.

Every organization develops traditions, habits, and a character distinct from its constituents'. The individuality of an organization is complex and multifaceted. Financial analysis deals with only a portion of organizational activities. Although it reflects many objectives, it does not deal with the substantive activities underlying monetary data. Financial analysis is only one view of a complex organizational domain; it neglects many other human and institutional aspects.

Every organization has limits on its resources (amount and sources of capital, number and quality of key personnel, physical production capacity, etc.). The relevant issue is how to use these limited resources to best advantage. Over a period of time an organization develops a character with distinctive competences in various areas. To stray far from the common areas of expertise involves special risks.

An organization is part not only of a market but also of an industry, economy, community, nation, and other systems. An analysis of its environment involves the examination and detection of international, national, political, social, economic, and technological trends. Risks as well as opportunities must be assessed.

The broad organizational objectives must be modified to account for internal and external restraints operating on the organization. These are limiting factors such as technology, financial resources, market conditions, sources of capital, the size of the organization, competitor actions, weaknesses of the existing organization, and so forth. Broad and celestial objectives must be brought down to terrestrial organizational realities. The redefinition of objectives to a nearer time frame in line with the capabilities of the organization results in strategies.

An organization must be analyzed both externally and internally to determine its special competences and weaknesses so strategies can be developed for new and better goal attainment. External restraints can be classified as social, political, technological, and economic.

Internal restraints are determined by the resource and technical capabilities within the organization. An organization can determine its "sphere of competence" by analyzing its internal operations. An appraisal of the areas of finance, sales, production, engineering, and personnel will reveal strengths and weaknesses. A review of the mix and performance of an organization's assets (human and nonhuman) indicates future potentials. A detailed assessment of performance in internal operations provides data for the development of strategies.

Financial analysis consists of studying the history of income figures, operating statements, and balance sheet relationships. It is implicitly assumed that future performance is based on trends and experiences of the past. For stable organizations without substantial change, financial analysis can be very meaningful. However, for growth or high technology organizations the past helps little for prognostication. Although financial analysis may indicate the results, it may not indicate the underlying causes. However, financial analysis is a very important starting point even though it is neither adequately comprehensive nor oriented to the future.

To adequately evaluate an organization, it is necessary to look at the present and future as well as the past. From a product *point of view*, it is necessary to analyze products, product lines, markets, distribution channels, and the competitive position. From a *technological point of view*, it is necessary to analyze research and development, equipment, processes, quality, and manufacturing capabilities. From a *financial point of view*, it is necessary to analyze liquidity, cash flow, working capital, capitalization structure, sources of funds, and operating efficiency. From a *managerial point of view*, it is necessary to analyze the composition, age, talent, background, and capabilities of management. Overall, the evaluation of an organization requires clinical judgment of the highest order.

STRATEGIES

Strategies provide direction to the activities of an organization and the people associated with it. They must be formulated, implemented, and evaluated. Strategies should be committed to paper and made explicit. This lessens the danger of their being incomplete or misunderstood, and it simplifies delegation and coordination. The formulation of strategies requires an analytical view with a conceptual and integrative ability to visualize the potential and direction of the organization.

After an organization has assessed its strengths, weaknesses, and restraints, it can develop its marketing strategy, financial strategy, operating strategy, organizational strategy, and personnel strategy. Strategies must be developed for its entire environment and sphere of interest. Strategies integrate the functional purpose with desired aspirational levels, and they can be based on the following:

1. Retrenchment
2. Stability
3. Growth
4. Combinations

Retrenchment is a regressive mode based on reduction of operations, sale of the organization, or captive combination with a stronger organization. Retrenchment may be best when there is little hope of achieving success with other strategies because of inadequate resources and little likelihood of obtaining the resources. It may be chosen by default when there is no other way to attain objectives. It may be chosen as a temporary action until resources are obtained and growth is pursued. Reduction retrenchment cuts cost via personnel layoffs, elimination of all but the most profitable products, elimination of product variety, reduction in marketing expenditures, emphasis on purchasing and production efficiency, and so forth. During recessions and depressions, retrenchment is common. The ultimate retrenchment is the sale or abandonment of the organization.

Stability is a status quo mode based on maintaining the present course or direction. The organization continues to do what it has been doing, the way it has been doing it, with only minor modifications or changes. It can be very effective in unchanging or very slowly changing environments.

Growth is an aggressive mode of expansion by internal or external means. Growth can be set at a rate measured by some indicator such as assets, sales, product line, profit, and so forth. Several avenues for growth are available: vertical or horizontal integration, diversification, multinationalism, or conglomeration. Growth can occur through internal expansion of present products and services or externally through merger and acquisition. Mergers and acquisitions are a means of achieving growth through synergism by better utilization of physical facilities, new product lines, additional distribution channels, more technical expertise, a stronger financial position, geographic penetration, and so forth. Growth addiction can be harmful; bigger is not always better.

Combinations of retrenchment, stability, and growth are adapted to meet particular needs. It is possible for an organization to retrench on one product, stabilize on another, and grow with another.

In different time periods and life cycles an organization may change its strategies in view of environmental realities. Strategies are more subject to change than objectives because they apply to an intermediate time frame (longer than the short term, but shorter than the long term). Strategies redefine and make more realistic the objectives in view of environmental conditions. Strategic planning involves constant surveillance of the environment so that potential opportunities, threats, and problems can be identified and the necessary strategies formulated to exploit opportunities and neutralize threats. Even though drastic modifications to strategies may be unnecessary, frequent incremental changes may be warranted to keep abreast of the times. From strategies, specific tactics can be developed to exploit market opportunities. Each strategy can lead to numerous tactics, a few or all of which may eventually be implemented.

TACTICS

Tactics involve the further definition and implementation of strategies. Tactics or plans deal with the specific allocation of resources. While strategies are paths to objectives, tactics are paths to strategies.

Strategies set the direction for the organization; tactics are needed to implement strategies. Tactics develop the details of how strategies will be implemented. Tactics spell out the meaning of strategies to the subsystems or lower levels of an organization. A tactic is a guide for carrying out a strategy.

Tactics must be developed for every major function (operations, finance, marketing, etc.) but are crucial in the following areas:

1. Products and markets
2. Sources and uses of funds
3. Operations and resource utilization
4. Personnel utilization

Quantitative and/or qualitative tactics can be developed for the affected functions and crucial areas.

Because of their generality, the development of objectives and strategies involves few quantitative techniques. Tactics, being more short term and specific, are more amenable to such analysis. Analytical techniques can be of great value in developing tactics although vision, imagination, and keen judgment remain essential.

The need for tactics arises from change, which may be of internal as well as external origin. The tactics are inputs to market analsis, which must determine the feasibility of plans. Market analysis will determine what goods or services the public wants and whether the organizational plans will receive favorable market acceptance. Market analysis is the testing grounds for new products or services; it determines which tactics should be pursued and which discarded.

PRODUCT DECISIONS

Product decisions determine the goods and services an organization will provide to society. They entail the systematic gathering of a number of project proposals and the selection of those products that satisfy the objectives of the organization. A product by definition is the output of a productive system made available to some customer. Demands arising from customers, new technology, and competition, continually increase the number of different products, options, and special features. Product decisions are a never-ending task in a dynamic economy. Proposals for new and improved products must be evaluated, and final selection based on a cost-benefit or incremental analysis.

The reason for the constant concern about product decisions lies in the fact that a product tends to have a life cycle. Product decisions manifest themselves in entirely new products, major modifications to existing products, and minor modifications (improvements) to existing products. Competitive marketplace pressure exists to provide higher quality and better performance products without an increase in price. The final design of a product is never fully frozen in an organization. Thus, organizations, unlike individuals who inevitably age and die, can maintain an ageless vigor and vitality by the continual development of new products and services.

Product decisions usually begin with general or customer specifications from market analysis which indicate customer requirements. Internal research, employee suggestions, or suppliers may also be sources of new product ideas. Periodically all new products and projects are subjected to a feasibility study to examine their economic and technical feasibility. Infeasible products and projects are discarded, and feasible selections are sent to preliminary design.

In preliminary design the specifics of the products are tentatively established, and the development effort may be aided by prototype testing of various design possibilities. After the initial development effort, the product is subjected to a detailed design (functional design, form design, and production design). The detailed design will result in blueprints and specifications that will completely define the product and its characteristics. An outline of the flow of effort for product decisions is contained in Figure 2.3.

General or customer specifications are usually quite vague and lacking in detail. From the general specifications, technical specifications must be formulated that will define the product in much greater detail. Technical specifications are established by a sequential process of applied research and product development (preliminary design and prototype testing). The technical specifications are the basic input to detailed design that comes from the preliminary design effort. The detailed design will draw heavily on inputs from marketing and several branches of engineering.

The detailed design, sometimes referred to as final design, comprises functional design, form design, and production design. Functional design is concerned with how the product works (performance). Form design is concerned with how the product looks (appearance). Production design is concerned with how the product will be produced (cost). All of the detailed design efforts are coexisting or parallel activities.

FUNCTIONAL DESIGN

Functional design is concerned with the performance of the product. Management must be concerned with the relationships among market

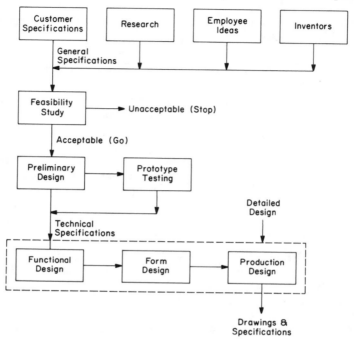

FIGURE 2.3

quality level, reliability, and cost in terms of technical specifications. Through various research means, management can determine market quality level and reliability relative to competitive products, and relate these factors to cost. Market surveys and other means can determine how the market for a given product is structured.

The various market segments may demand various quality levels of the product.[1] Management may be able to make product policy decisions in reference to the market segments it wishes to serve. A product may serve high, moderate, and low quality markets. These market quality levels will be reflected in the materials used for production and in the reliability of the final product. Likewise, production costs will vary with the market quality level. Functional design will establish specifications for the product in terms of these variables. In some cases, process decisions will be affected to a greater or lesser extent by specified market quality and reliability standards.

---

[1]Market quality levels and production quality levels are sometimes confused. Market quality level relates to the type of market segment desired. A high market quality level usually indicates a higher price product with features not included in a lower market quality level product. Production quality level relates to the ability of the manufactured product to meet its design specifications.

Functional design can include packaging decisions. Although this may be primarily a marketing function, the product designer must be included. If the product will be packaged, then any decisions he can make that will aid this requirement will be helpful in the production phase.

FORM DESIGN

Form design relates to the physical appearance of the product. Asthetic features enter into the physical shape of the final product which may have little to do with functional requirements. For consumer goods, form design is much more important than for industrial goods. With consumers, the features of color, style, and fashion may be more important than function. Personal identification and image may be significant factors to a consumer. The packaging of a product may be an extension of the form or shape of the product and contribute to its acceptance.

PRODUCTION DESIGN

Production design is concerned with the economics of production. The available modes of production can affect the final cost of a product. Production design is the conscious effort to consider how a product will be built during the design phase. If no consideration is given to production during design, the cost of the item will frequently be excessive. Production design does not determine how the product will be manufactured, but it does consider such modes in establishing the final product design.

Functional design should result in something which functions according to specifications. Once the functional design has been accomplished, there are usually alternative designs which will meet functional requirements. At this point, production design takes over. The goal is to select a detailed design that meets requirements while minimizing production cost.

The final release of engineering drawings and specifications of what to make terminates product decisions. The drawings and specifications completely define the product. The specifications indicate the functional characteristics of the item and how it should perform. The engineering drawings or blueprints will indicate the following information:

1. Materials
2. Material standards
3. Dimensions
4. Tolerances
5. Surface finishes

Engineering drawings contain a bill of materials or parts lists to identify each item composing the product and the quantity required. The bill of materials for each product will be a basic production planning document to determine what parts, supplies, and components must be available before production can be scheduled.

It should be mentioned that product design and development (product decisions) rarely follow the concise, discrete sequences suggested herein. Typically, there are frequent recycling loops to prior steps, and certain activities that may be out of sequence or performed concurrently. The extent of formalization varies from organization to organization and depends on the type of product or service being developed.

PROCESS DECISIONS

Whereas product decisions determine what will be produced, process decisions establish how the product or service will be produced (or supplied). Process decisions, also referred to as process planning, take over where product decisions leave off. The outputs of product decisions (drawings and specifications), along with quantity forecasts from market analysis, are the inputs to process decisions. The aim is to devise the best production techniques and work methods consistent with capital, equipment, and manpower availability.

Process decisions are concerned directly with the transformation of inputs into outputs. The introduction of new products, product improvements, and model changes make it mandatory that adequate organization be provided for process decisions. Every time a new output is designed or an existing output is redesigned, process decisions are undertaken. Additionally, existing processes are reviewed when technological advances are available. During product decisions, preliminary consideration for process decisions are made during production design.

Process decisions begin with a product analysis that extends to every subassembly, component, or raw material going into the item. In view of the quantity demanded and the resources available to the organizations, a make or buy decision is made on each material or component required by the finished product. A buy decision means the purchase of components from external suppliers; a make decision means internal production. Make or buy decisions are influenced by the following factors:

1. Idle plant capacity
2. In-house capabilities
   a. Personnel
   b. Equipment
   c. Future capabilities

3. Economic advantage
    a. Incremental cost
    b. Overhead allocation
4. Reliability of supply
5. Trade relations (reciprocity)
6. Employment stabilization
7. Alternative resource uses

The decision to purchase or build in house resolves the issue of internal versus external supply. Internal supply will require additional process decisions on the production processes as well as the steps and procedures necessary to produce the item. In some circumstances, there may be no alternative but to make. This occurs when the technology is unavailable elsewhere or when the process involves "trade secrets". Process design, operation design, and job design will be required for all internal production. Process decision relationships are schematically represented in Figure 2.4.

Process design decides the general process to adopt in providing the product. There are usually several good ways to make a product, and process design attempts to select the most desirable one in the light of quantity requirements. Methods of manufacture can vary widely based on the volume to be produced. A process may be automated, semi-automated,

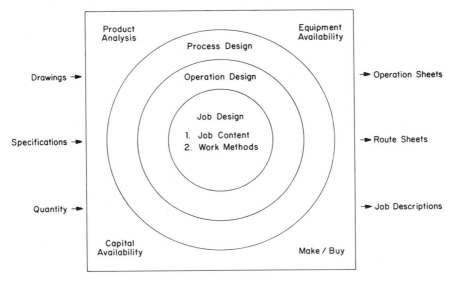

FIGURE 2.4

or manual. Once a process is chosen, it tends to limit the scope of the operations contained within it. A process is comprised of several operations; operation design determines the best procedures for each operation making up the selected process. Job design involves the integration of the human element into the production environment. Specific personnel job content and work methods are established during job design.

PROCESS DESIGN

Process design, or the selection of the overall plan for producing a product, will be affected by volume (quantity), quality, and cost. These control aspects are paramount factors in process design. If the expected volume of processing economically justifies it, a fully automated system may be warranted. Otherwise a manual or man-machine system is used. There are usually several alternatives available within each of these choices.

Process design will select the work stations and work flow system. Work stations are composed of equipment and machines to be included in the process. The work flow system will govern the flow of work between the work stations. It can be continuous, intermittent, or a combination of both. In work station selection, the dimensional requirements, surface finishes, and other characteristics of items to be provided must be matched to the available machines and methods (technology).

A process planner will question all the details of a proposed process. He will attempt to eliminate operations, combine operations, or develop a better sequence of operations. He will try to minimize transportation and storage. The output from process design will be a *route sheet* for the product. It will specify the sequence of operations in a process by name, number, location, and any other descriptive information required.

OPERATION DESIGN

Process design concentrates on the set of operations as well as their interrelationships. Operation design concentrates on the aspects of each operation in the process, but not the interrelationships among operations. Operation design is composed of operation content and operation methods. Process design, in meshing operations, will tend to dictate their content but not their methods.

After process design is accomplished, operation design is next. It specifies the content and performance method of each operation in the process. The content of an operation will include a combination of inputs such as material, manpower, work station, and tools required to produce or process a product. (It is sometimes difficult to separate content and method, since they interact.) By subdivision of the content of each operation, alternative methods of performance can be ascertained. The objective is to determine the least cost method of performing the operation. Operation design involves both technology and economics in establishing production methods and procedures. The final output from operation design will be *operation sheets* at each work station that delineate the exact methods and procedures required to process a product.

JOB DESIGN

Man is still a predominant factor in production systems. Even in automated and computerized systems, labor is necessary in a surveillance role. In manual, semi-automated, man-machine, and automated work systems job design is important to the overall effectiveness of operations. Job design will determine the role of the human element in production systems. Whereas process design and operation design tend to be product-oriented, job design is human-oriented. Man is the most complex of all factors of production. His physiological, psychological, and sociological characteristics as well as his capabilities and limitations must be considered in job design.

Just as process design limits the alternatives for operation design, operation design in turn limits the alternatives for job design. Operation design determines what operations (human and nonhuman) are necessary at each work station. Job design is only concerned with the human operations specified in operation design.

A *job* is the aggregate of all the work assignments a worker may be asked to perform. Job design should provide the worker with a carefully planned work station where he can perform at peak effectiveness with maximum comfort, and whatever guidance or instructions he needs to do his work. The basic content of many jobs (usually trade, professional, and skilled) is established by tradition and customs. Union contracts may also define job content.

Job content and work methods comprise job design. While job content defines what must be accomplished, work methods specify how the worker should perform his assignments. Operation design will essentially dictate job content at each work station or area. Constraints and objectives of an organization will also influence job content, as shown in Figure 2.5. Division of labor and job enrichment are opposing factors in establishing job content. The greatest degree of freedom in job design is in the selection of work methods to accomplish a given job content. Job design is based on both economic and noneconomic needs, and particular organizational

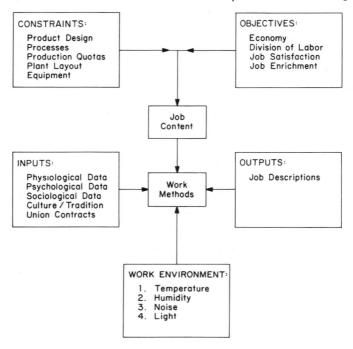

FIGURE 2.5

philosophies greatly affect how jobs are designed. Job design is not a science, so considerable latitude and judgment are involved.

The final output of job design will be *job descriptions* delineating the number and type of personnel required by the production system. The work methods established will supplement or improve the procedures outlined on the operation sheets. Job descriptions outline the role of man and how he will be integrated into production operations.

The outputs from process decisions are *operation sheets*, *route sheets*, and *job descriptions*. Operation sheets specify in detail how to perform each operation of a process. The operation sheets are maintained at the work stations so technicians can refer to them for direction. The route sheets show the physical flow of the product through the different operating departments or work stations. Route sheets determine what shall be done, where, and how, by establishing the operation, their sequence, and manpower and equipment requirements. The route sheet is essentially a map for guiding the product through production. Job descriptions will include the job requirements, duties, and a brief description of working conditions as well as personal qualifications required to give the highest probability of success. The personnel department can use the job descriptions in its recruitment of personnel.

PLANT DECISIONS

While product decisions determine what will be produced, and process decisions how the product will be produced, plant decisions determine where the product will be produced as well as the physical plant layout. Plant decisions begin with a decision to utilize unused plant capacity, expand existing plant capacity, or build a new plant to accommodate the product. If an existing plant is operating at less than full capacity, the product may be integrated into the present facility. If market analysis indicates a potential demand that exceeds existing facilities, either internal or external expansion may be warranted. Internal expansion means building onto the existing facility at the current site. External expansion will involve a plant location study to determine the site of a completely new facility. After the expansion decision has been made, the layout of the physical facilities is necessary, including work station location and the selection of materials handling equipment.

Plant location and layout are the major problem areas for plant decisions. If existing facilities can be employed, the location decision is very simple. For a new plant, on the other hand, it is of paramount importance. The layout consideration is a tradeoff among capacity (quantity), quality, and cost. The basic inputs to plant decisions are the forecasts from market analysis and the operation and route sheets from process decisions.

PLANT LOCATION

The location of the plant or warehouse is significant because of its influence on cost. Modes of available transportation and the costs of labor, taxes, land, construction, and fuel, as well as many other factors, contribute to the overall competitive position of an organization. The addition of a new plant is not a matter of determining a location independent of existing plants. Each potential location results in a new allocation of capacity to market areas; the solution from the economic viewpoint is one that minimizes costs for the network of plants rather than for the additional plants being considered.

There is usually no such thing as a plant location that is clearly superior to all others. There are many tangible and intangible factors which are not readily quantifiable. A selection must be made involving tradeoffs among the different locations. A comparative cost analysis of various locations may point toward settling in one community, but an appraisal of intangible factors may result in a decision to select another.

Plant location involves the selection of a region, then the selection of a community, and finally a selection of a site. A site five times the actual plant area is considered minimal to meet the needs of future expansion, parking spaces, and so forth. An outline of basic location factors is as follows:

1. Selection of region
    a. Market proximity
    b. Raw material proximity
    c. Transportation costs
    d. Public services (power, water, fuel)
    e. Climatic conditions
2. Selection of community
    a. Labor supply
    b. Wage scales
    c. Tax structure and ordinances
    d. Living standards
    e. Financial inducements
3. Selection of site
    a. Land availability
    b. Transportation access
    c. Zoning restrictions
    d. Services (power, sewage)

Usually the closer a product moves to the ultimate consumer, the greater the transportation cost it has accumulated. A material when first extracted from nature has a negligible transportation cost. From this point on the basic material cost is the same, but each successive move adds labor and other costs, so the total transportation cost in the product continually increases. In general, a product which experiences a weight gain should be produced near the market (assembly industries). Likewise, a weight-losing product should generally be produced near the source of supply (extracting industries).

Plant location is far from being a scientific exercise. Because of the uncertainties associated with the analysis, there is no such thing as the best plant location. An organization must guard against a poor location and attempt to select one that is good enough. A thorough analysis of the plant location factors listed above will identify potential locations as acceptable or unacceptable. The final selection can be made from those in the acceptable category.

PLANT LAYOUT

The major objective of plant layout is to develop a productive system that meets the requirements of capacity and quality in the most economical fashion. Plant layout furnishes the internal configuration for the building to house the physical facilities. The drawings and specifications of what to make, combined with the operation sheets and route sheets of how it is to be made and with the market analysis of how many to make, become the basis for developing the plant layout. Layout must integrate machines, support services, work places, manpower, logistical subsystems, and storage areas so that feasible production schedules can be formulated. The major subdivisions of plant layout are capacity levels and layout types. The major layout factors are schematically represented in Figure 2.6.

Capacity levels fix the maximum output for the productive system. They relate to the number of work shifts, overtime outputs, growth capacity, subcontract capabilities, and seasonal sales levels. The resolution of the capacity problem will depend on forecasts of future demand. It will determine total plant investment and future operating costs for the facility.

In general, plant layouts can be classified as either process or product oriented. Continuous production systems are product oriented, while intermittent production systems are process oriented. A process layout results in equipment of the same functional type being grouped together. It is employed when the same facilities must be used to fabricate and assemble a wide variety of products or when product designs are not stable. With the process layout, the facilities and equipment are set up so they can be

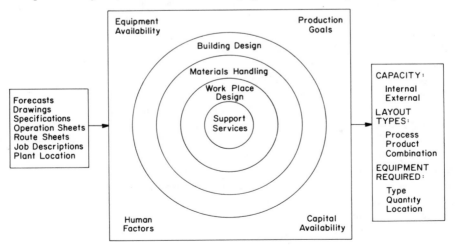

FIGURE 2.6

used on numerous products, the production rate for each product being greater than the consumption rate. The location of departments or machine centers with a process layout is based on minimizing materials handling costs.

A product layout has equipment arranged according to the sequence of operations to be performed on a product. Assembly lines are product layouts where specialized equipment is arranged so as to assemble large quantities of product. With a product layout, the best configuration of tasks assigned to work stations is obtained by balancing the line. Balance refers to the equality of output of each successive work station in sequence along the line. Tasks are assigned to work stations so that each takes the same amount of time to complete its work effort.

The outputs from plant decisions are the capacity levels, the layout type, equipment designations, and the location of the physical facility. The configuration of the plant, including all its equipment, is known and spatially defined. The planning of the product, processes, and plant are complete. The next major decision involves activation of all the prior decisions or a "scrub" of the project.

OPERATIONS DECISIONS

Up to this point, with the exception of prototypes, no resources (plant, men, material, or equipment) have been procured for production. Operations decisions will make the go or no-go decision on the product or project. A no-go decision will scrap the complete undertaking. A go decision will necessitate activation and organization to implement all the prior planning (product decisions, process decisions, and plant decisions). With activation, operations decisions will determine when and how many units of the product to produce.

Production planning and scheduling is the link between design and manufacture. It plans for and controls the utilization of facilities, manpower, and materials. The activation phase is initiated by production planning and scheduling's release of orders for the acquisition of men, materials, plant, and equipment. Once the installation is operational and the manpower is on board, the operation and control of the production system is the paramount consideration. The major areas for operations control are forecasting, planning and scheduling, procurement, manufacturing, plant engineering, inventory control, manpower control, quality control, and production control (see Figure 2.7).

The system operates from forecasts and firm orders which are transmitted to the "brain center," planning and scheduling. This central decision area determines what must be done to meet the expected demand. It

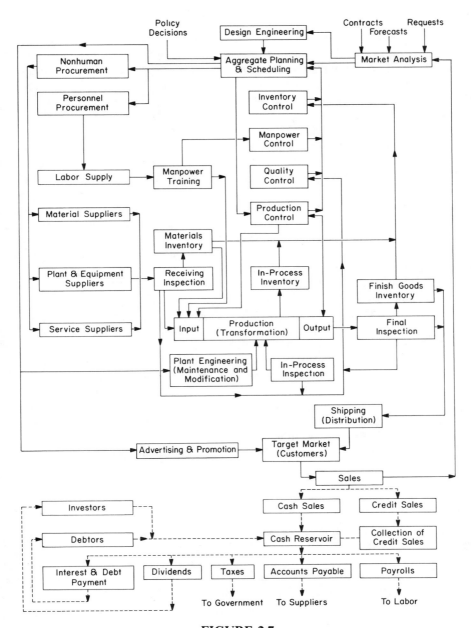

FIGURE 2.7

establishes the type and mix of required inputs and schedules them for the production process. Personnel and procurement obtain the desired mix of human and nonhuman inputs. Manpower is hired and trained before entry into the input stream. Materials and other nonhuman resources are purchased and subjected to quality inspection before entry into the input pool. Production control provides the short term (day to day) scheduling of the resources into the production system. Manufacturing takes the inputs and processes them into the finished product. Quality control assures the quality standards of the inputs, processes, and finished outputs. Manpower control through the personnel department assures the proper quantity and type of human inputs to the system. Inventory control assures that the proper quantities of materials, in-process goods, and final products are available to manufacturing and sales. Plant engineering maintains, modifies, and installs new plant and equipment. The sales function, through advertising and promotion, provides for the successful interaction of the customer with the output products of the organization.

The production process generates inventories of products which, in turn, are depleted by sales. Sales, as well as investors and creditors, generate an inflow into the cash reservoir of the organization. Many parties have claims on this cash reservoir—employees, investors, creditors, governments, suppliers, and so forth. Objectives are met when these claims are balanced with expectations. Any party able to modify this balance, in turn, influences the objectives of the organization. From the cash inflows and outflows a general idea of the groups, people, and parties who have an influence on the objectives of the organization can be ascertained. At this point the systemic functional model (see Figure 2.1) reflects a full circle return to the objectives in policy decisions.

Because of the many and various groups of human beings affected by modern organizations, they are thrust into the role of social institutions. Corporations have been undergoing significant changes that are modifying their historical role. Some of these changes are as follows:

1. The separation of management and ownership has affected corporate structure and relationships among the different subgroups. Although stockholders elect directors, the latter tend to be a self-perpetuating body. Due to dispersion and lack of organization, stockholders are almost without power to bring pressure on management.

2. Certain groups other than stockholders are better situated to exert influence on management. These groups include customers, governments, unions, employees, creditors, and the general public (all of which make demands on the corporation).

3. Subject to the various demands, management tends to be less and less responsive to the owners, and more and more responsible to the corporation as a whole. Management attempts to satisfy the needs of all groups, not just those of the owners.

4. The first task of management is to create a successful product with widespread use and salability. The second task is to divide the proceeds of success among those responsible for it. All of the groups compete for as large a share of the "success pie" as possible. The groups do not all have equal influence, and stockholders frequently are far from being the most powerful.

CONCLUSION

Each organization must be designed as a unique system. All activities revolve around the system with its objectives. The functions are executed only as a means to this end. In this capacity, the organization is viewed as a set of flows of information, men, materials, and behavior. The systems approach represents a movement from independent operating units to coordinated functional units. The nature and size of an organization may affect production and operations, but the fundamental activities that must be performed are almost identical in most organizations.

Individual systems should not be developed and implemented without some consideration of other interfacing or interacting systems. Each system or subsystem should not be developed as an island unto itself without bridges to other systems. Organizations are combinations of socio-economic-technical systems, and any approach which does not give attention to the conglomeration is suboptimal. The systems approach as outlined herein provides management with the means to recognize the relationships necessary for a realistic synthesis of production and operations.

QUESTIONS

1. What are the five broad interdependent decision categories associated with a functional analysis of an organization?

2. What are policy decisions?

3. Name four influences that act as external restraints on the objectives of an organization.

4. What are the different modes that strategies may follow?

5. Indicate the time frame of objectives, strategies, and tactics.

6. What are product decisions?

7. From what sources may product ideas emanate?

8. Detailed product design is usually composed of what other design activities?

9. What information is contained in engineering drawings or blueprints?

10. What are process decisions?

11. Process decisions are composed of what three design activities?

12. What are plant decisions?

13. Name the two major classifications of plant layout.

14. What are operations decisions?

15. Indicate the inputs and outputs from each of the broad decision categories (policy, product, process, plant, and operations).

PROBLEMS

1. An organization has forecasted sales for the upcoming time period of $87,000 for a given product. The forecast was based on a selling price of $12.50 per unit. Soon after the forecast was made, management decided to increase the price by 10%, with the result that dollar sales are expected to increase by 6%. What impact will the price increase have on the production level for the period?

2. The Slippery Shoe firm manufactures shower clogs at a variable cost of $2.10 per pair. The fixed costs for a month are $90,000. If the clogs are sold to a distributor for $3.00 per pair, how many pairs must be produced monthly for the firm to break even?

3. A single-product company operates at 100% capacity with annual sales of $2,400,000, fixed costs of $800,000, and variable costs of $1,200,000. The product sales price is $80 per unit. Plant capacity is scheduled to increase by 30% through the purchase of additional equipment which will increase fixed costs by $200,000 with no change in the variable cost per unit. At what percentage of plant capacity must the expanded plant operate to maintain the same return on sales (assume sales price is constant)?

4. The Sputter Company has an order for 450 two-cylinder lawnmower engines. Each piston requires two piston rings, which are made at the company's Waybelow Casting Works. Currently there are 50 engines in stock which can be applied to the order. Additionally, Waybelow needs to supply 700 rings to its service outlets. The standard time to produce the ring is 2.85 minutes with a 15% scrap loss and a 0.90

labor efficiency. What is the work load in hours for the piston ring department for the upcoming period?

5. A proposed assembly line is to have an output of 2,000 units per week. The route sheet for the product indicates that a milling operation is required that will take 0.072 hours per unit. If the line will operate 40 hours per week, how many milling machines should be purchased?

6. A specific department is to be laid out on a process basis. The equipment to be located in the department will require 950 square feet of floor space. An analysis of a similar layout of a department reveals that it occupies a total space of 48,000 square feet, of which 12,000 is utilized by equipment. In general, the department does not appear to be congested, nor does it seem to contain wasted space. What might be a good estimate of the total space requirement for the department under consideration?

7. Materials are being moved continuously from one location in the plant to another. The quantity to be handled is such that equipment can be assigned solely to the transportation of material. The two locations are separated by a distance of 0.2 mile. The materials are stacked on pallets, and one loaded pallet weighs 500 pounds. A fork lift truck is being considered for this activity. Its load capacity is two loaded pallets per trip, and its average speed would be 5 miles per hour. This average was obtained by taking into account the speed under load, the speed without load on the return trip, delays, and down time for repairs and maintenance. If 105 tons of material are to be moved from one location to the other during an eight hour day, how many fork lift trucks should be acquired?

8. Castings loaded on skids are to be moved continuously from one department to another by means of a truck. The departments are separated by a distance of 660 feet. Each casting weighs 20 pounds, and 30 such castings can be loaded on one skid. The trucks to be used for this activity can carry one skid per trip at an average speed of 2 miles per hour. If 24,000 castings are to be moved from one location to the other during a 40 hour week, how many trucks will be required for this activity (neglect loading and unloading time as well as down time per truck)?

Case 1: Centralized versus Decentralized Storage

The Solar Heater Company has been a manufacturer of water heaters for a number of years. At present all operations are conducted in a number of small plants in the

Hampton Roads area. Recently a decision was made to build a new plant of sufficient size to house all manufacturing operations as well as company offices. Considerable time and effort has been put into the design of the new plant, in order to make it as efficient as possible.

One of the innovations under consideration for the new plant is the elimination of all central storage area for incoming materials. Instead, at each work area, storage space will be provided for the incoming material needed for that particular operation. For example, sheet steel for heater shells is to be stored near the machine used for cutting the plates to the correct size. The same would be true for all other materials that are used in the product line. The only central storeroom would be used for maintenance supplies as well as for tools and dies.

Owing largely to differences of opinion among the executives as to the value of this system for storing materials, work has not started on construction of the new plant.

1. What advantages can be claimed for the new system?
2. What problems would be created by it?
3. What approach should be used to resolve the problem?

Case 2: Another Stockout

The Morrell Machinery Company is a producer of specialized pulverizing equipment. Almost all of its products are made to customers' special order, and vary from small units suitable for making face powder to huge machines used to pulverize rocks.

The company uses in its machines a number of bearings that are relatively expensive and that must be ordered from three to six months before the date they are needed. Because of the required lead time it has been the practice to keep a considerable inventory of bearings on hand. Under the circumstances it is almost impossible to predict future usage, but the general intent is to keep a five months' supply of bearings on hand at all times. This considerable investment in bearings, however, still has not prevented the delay of a number of orders as a result of an inadequate supply of the right kind of bearing for a specific job.

One difficulty seems to stem from the fact that frequently, when the storeroom clerk is busy with other work, the machine assemblers help themselves to the bearings needed. The assemblers, being more interested in machine assembly than in paperwork, will seldom leave requisitions for the bearings they take.

1. What steps can be taken to ensure that bearings will be on hand when needed?
2. Is there any way the investment in bearing inventory can be reduced?
3. How would you resolve the problem?

Case 3: A Personal Decision

Ben Brown is an operations supervisor for a large national firm. He joined the company after receiving his undergraduate degree from State University. During his three year tenure, he has progressed from trainee to operations supervisor with twelve people reporting to him. This rate of advancement is what could be expected in the company.

Since Ben wished to advance within the company as fast as possible, he has been attending night school and recently received his MBA from State University. Being anxious to apply the tools and techniques he learned while obtaining his degree, Ben has spent several hours after work designing programs to improve the effectiveness of the organization. All of his proposals have been sent to his department head, who reviews them and refers them to higher level management. With each proposal, the proper company officer personally talks with Ben and indicates appreciation for his initiative and suggestions. To date, not any of Ben's ideas have been implemented.

Yesterday, Ben resigned. Al Ewing, the personnel manager, and Bob Willis, the department head, were shocked. They had had no idea Ben was unhappy with the company. In an effort to encourage him to reconsider, they held a conference with him and indicated how important he was to the organization. As an additional inducement, Ben was offered a $2,000 annual salary increase. A similar position with a local company was available if Ben wanted it. His income there would be approximately 10% less than his increased salary at the national firm. He has 24 hours to reconsider.

1. Should Ben Brown reconsider and stay with the national firm?
2. What advantages might there be with the local firm?
3. Are Ben's efforts to increase operational effectiveness a likely path to advancement?

Case 4: Tough Times

The Business Equipment Corporation is a manufacturer of office equipment and supplies. The equipment line consists of steel filing cabinets, storage cabinets, desks, and tables. The supplies are principally paper products such as folders, cards, and printed forms. The firm does about $10,000,000 in business volume, and approximately two-thirds of it is in the equipment line.

Selling is done through retail branches in the larger cities and also through independent dealers in the smaller centers. All retail outlets specialize in service to offices. Some very large customers, like the federal and state governments, are served directly from the main office of the company.

Manufacturing is carried out in two divisions, one for the metal products and another for the paper and printed goods. The Metal Products Division includes departments for the following kinds of work: sheet metal cutting and forming, welding, enameling, and assembling. The Paper Division does paper cutting and folding, printing, tabbing, celluloid forming, and bookbinding. Up to this time the concern has confined its output to high-grade products, and it has built a national reputation for quality. Workers have become accustomed to high quality standards, and the sales force has emphasized quality in its selling effort.

At this time, a period of business depression combined with keen competition has reduced annual sales below the breakeven point. The greatest loss of business is in the metal products. Management is therefore concerned with increasing business volume by extending the product lines, and it appears that a break with tradition will be necessary to improve the situation. Among the product proposals under consideration are the three described below:

  a. Introduction of a line of low-priced office furniture. The market for quality goods has declined more than that of cheaper products, a condition which has stimulated considerable pressure from the sales organization. The proposed new line would require some new dies and welding fixtures, but all the existing machine tools and most of the present accessory tools can be used.

  b. Introduction of a line of "safety papers" based on the patent of the Research Engineer. This is the kind of paper used in checks and important documents to reveal efforts at forgery. It has an international market. Manufacture involves lithographing and chemical treatments for which special equipment would have to be provided.

  c. Manufacture of household devices made from sheet metal—dustpans, baking tins, wastebaskets, etc. These products can be made by the existing machines, but special dies and fixtures will be required.

1. If at least one of the proposals is to be adopted, outline the list of considerations necessary to reach a reasonable conclusion.

2. Assume only one of the proposals is to be adopted. Which proposal would you select? Why?

Case 5: New Plant Location

A group of men connected with the furniture industry has decided to pool resources and establish a manufacturing business. The group includes a noted furniture designer, a production man, a sales expert, and a businessman. These men expect to furnish about half the required capital, the other half to be derived from the sale of stock and by borrowing as necessary. The objective agreed upon is to manufacture fine furniture for homes, hotels, clubs, and offices. Most of the anticipated sales will be to retail establishments, such as department stores and dealers in home furnishings.

The raw materials for fine furniture are varied in character and source. The American hardwoods like birch, maple, and walnut will come from the northern states and Canada. Mahogany and other tropical woods will be obtained mostly from importers. No softwoods will be used except for a few novelties and for crating. Most upholstering fabrics can be obtained from eastern and southeastern mills. Some fabrics will be imported.

Although the plant is to be mechanized, there will be many skilled hand operations. Workers will include cabinetmakers, upholsterers, wood carvers, and finishers; also, unskilled or semiskilled labor for machine operations, sanding, packing, and similar jobs.

The production man hopes to store and season much of the lumber outdoors and in unheated sheds. Kiln drying will also be required. The finished furniture will be stored in heated space. The varnishing and enameling operations are not exceedingly critical as to temperature conditions, but trouble is expected during hot, humid weather. Shipment in and out of the plant will be made principally by railroad and truck.

The founders plan to start operations with not more than 100 employees in a plant of about 20,000 square feet. They envision rapid growth and hope to justify a plant at least five times that size within a few years. They have established a committee within their group to work on the problem of plant location. A consulting firm may be called in after they have completed a preliminary investigation.

Assume that you are a member of the committee. For personal reasons, you would like to locate the plant in an industrial community near your present home. To support this objective, proceed as follows:

1. Study the geographic area or metropolitan district in which you live and make a list of the factors pro and con that will affect the location of your plant.
2. If the above analysis seems reasonably favorable, select a vacant plant site or a suitable suburban area and continue the pro and con analysis.

Chapter 3

Forecasting and Market Analysis

The Forecasting Function
Time Series Analysis
    Last Period Demand
    Arithmetic Average
    Moving Average
    Regression Analysis
    Exponentially Weighted Moving Average (EWMA)
    Overview of Time Series Analysis
Soliciting Opinions
Economic Indicators
Econometric Models
Conclusion
Questions
Problems
Cases

Most organizations are not in a position to wait until orders are received before they begin to determine what production facilities, processes, equipment, manpower, or materials are required and in what quantities. Few consumers would be willing to wait over such a time horizon. Most successful organizations forecast the future demand for their products and translate that information into factor inputs required to satisfy expected demand. The better management is able to estimate the future, the better it should be able to prepare for it. For a business to survive, it must meet its customers' needs at least as quickly as its competitors. The future is rarely assured, and some system of forecasting is necessary, whether it be implicit or explicit. Forecasting is the estimation of the future on the basis of the past.

Many factors influence the demand for an organization's products and services. It is never possible to identify all of the factors or to measure their probable effects. It is necessary in forecasting to identify the broad, major influences and to attempt to predict their direction. Some major environmental factors are:

1. General business conditions and the state of the economy
2. Competitor actions and reactions
3. Governmental legislative actions
4. Marketplace trends
    a. Product life cycle
    b. Style and fashion
    c. Changing consumer demands
5. Technological innovations

A forecast is an estimate of the future level of demand. Organizations may use many different forecasting bases. Sales revenue, physical units, cost of goods manufactured, direct labor hours, and machine hours are common forecasting bases. The selection of a forecasting base is dependent upon plans for establishing the necessary factor requirements. In many organizations, sales forecasts are used to establish production levels, facilitate scheduling, set inventory levels, determine manpower loading, make purchasing decisions, establish sales conditions (pricing and advertising), and aid financial planning (cash budgeting and capital budgeting).

Top-down forecasting and *bottom-up forecasting* are general demand forecasting patterns. Top-down forecasting begins with a forecast of general economic activity (GNP, national income, etc.) for the geopolitical unit where the organization resides. Industry forecasts are developed from the general economic activity forecast. The organization's share-of-the-market forecast is predicted from the industry forecast, and specific product group forecasts are developed from it.

Bottom-up forecasting begins at the product level. Forecasts are made for each product or product group and are summed to obtain the aggregate organizational forecast. The aggregate forecast can be modified in relation to the general business outlook and the competitive situation. Advertising and promotion may necessitate an additional forecast revision.

Forecasting, as we are referring to it here, is a short-run tool for establishing input-output levels. In the short run products, processes, equipment, tooling, layout, and capacity are essentially fixed. All statistical forecasting techniques assume to some extent that forces that existed in the past will persist in the future. A forecast is the link between the external, uncontrollable environment and the internal, controllable affairs of an organization.

THE FORECASTING FUNCTION

Adequate forecasting procedures can go a long way toward eliminating many organizational problems. Frequently, forecasting is considered as a group of procedures for deriving estimates of future activity, with the major emphasis on the type of forecasting technique. It is desirable to focus on the forecasting function rather than the specific forecasting techniques or models. The forecasting function includes techniques and models, but it also highlights the significance of inputs and outputs (see Figure 3.1).

To develop the forecasting function, it is necessary first to determine the outputs and the intended uses of the forecast. This chapter has already mentioned numerous uses for forecasts in organizations. When the users obtain the outputs, specific actions will be taken to assure that future demand will be satisfied. The precision and accuracy of forecasting outputs should be conveyed, along with the intended uses, during the development of the forecasting function.

The initial specification of outputs can simplify the selection of the forecasting model, but the forecasting function is not complete without the input considerations. No matter how long a system is studied, only a small number of the many inputs can be isolated. Fortunately, most systems are relatively insensitive to a majority of inputs. The size of the problem must

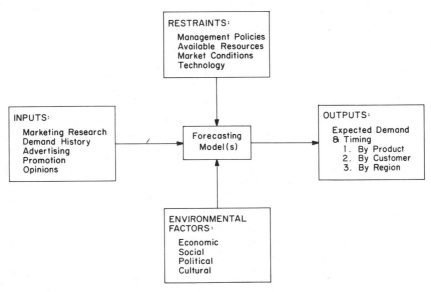

FIGURE 3.1

be reduced by only including the most significant inputs in the forecasting models. These are the inputs that will be closely observed for changes.

By knowing the desired outputs and the significant inputs or variables that affect the demand, a forecasting model is selected. The selection of the forecasting model will involve considerations such as cost, precision of the model, availability of the input data, and so forth. Sometimes a specific model will be indicated. When a single model is not apparent, many may be tested and the most accurate one adopted.

In most organizations, a small percentage of the material requirement represents a majority of the investment. These high cost or high usage items should receive the greatest degree of forecasting attention. There are also a great many low cost or low usage items that represent a small percentage of the total investment (although a high percentage of the number of items). Very little effort should be devoted to making forecasts for them; crude forecasts supplemented with large safety stocks are sufficient.

There are four basic demand forecasting techniques—*time series analysis*, *soliciting opinions*, *economic indicators*, and *econometric models*. These are short-range forecasting devices, and their value diminishes as the time horizon increases. Many of the techniques are based on extrapolation into the future of effects that have existed in the past.

The forecasting approaches to new products and established products are dissimilar. For established products, the forecasting techniques of time series analysis, economic indicators, and econometric models may be appropriate. For new products with little or no history of past demand, soliciting opinions is more suitable.

There is no single technique which is clearly superior for new product forecasting. The direct survey approach of asking prospective customers their buying intentions is frequently used. An indirect survey approach may also be employed, where information is obtained from people (salesmen, wholesalers, jobbers) who know how the customer responds. If a comparable or substitute product exists, comparisons with similar products can be made. Finally, a limited market test of the new product can indicate a product acceptable to potential customers.

There is no single forecasting technique that is superior in all cases. An organization might use one method for some of its products, a second for others, and a third for still others. It is difficult to ascertain the effect of changes in selling price, product quality, marketing methods, promotion, and economic conditions on demand. Regardless of the method adopted, the results provide the decision maker with nothing more than a starting point for making the final forecast. No organization should make an annual forecast and adhere to it for the entire year without a periodic review. The final forecast usually requires input from judgment, intuition, and experience.

TIME SERIES ANALYSIS

Time series analysis predicts the future from past internal data. This may work, but the forecaster should be alert to factors that may cause severe abruption from the past. External factors frequently have a pronounced effect. Time series analysis tends to neglect them.

A time series is a set of time ordered observations on a variable during successive and equal time periods. In time series analysis, historical data are analyzed to determine temporal patterns. Usually, the analysis of time series is accomplished by decomposing the data into five components—*level of demand, trends, seasonal variations, cyclical variations,* and *random variations.* Trend represents the long term movement in the variable, while seasonal variations consist of similar periodic patterns that occur each year. Cyclical variations represent the recurrent undulations of a variable over a number of years, and random variations are the sporadic movements of the time series related to chance events that last for only a short time. Figure 3.2 displays typical trend, seasonal, and cyclical time series components.

Projections of trends may be an inadequate short term forecasting method because of the presence of seasonal and cyclical effects. Seasonal variations refer to recurring events in a time series that manifest themselves each year. Seasonality is present when demand fluctuates in a similar pattern within each year. The twelve month periodicity may be related to weather patterns, tradition, school openings, vacations, taxes, bonuses,

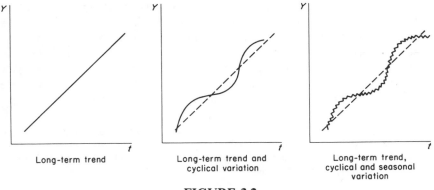

Long-term trend

Long-term trend and
cyclical variation

Long-term trend,
cyclical and seasonal
variation

FIGURE 3.2

model changeovers, or calendar oriented customs (Thanksgiving, Christmas). Examples of products with a seasonal pattern are antifreeze, soft drinks, ice cream, toys, snow tires, grass seed, textbooks, air conditioners, and greeting cards.

Before seasonal corrections are included in a forecast model some conditions should be met. There should be some known reason for the periodic peaks and valleys in the demand pattern, and they should occur at essentially the same time every year. For the seasonal modification to be included, it should be of a larger magnitude than the random variations, or the seasonal demand will not be discernable from random variations.

Cyclical variations are long term oscillations or swings about a trend line. The cycles may or may not be periodic. An important example of cyclical movements are the business cycles representing intervals of prosperity, recession, depression, and recovery. Cyclical fluctuations vary as to the time of occurrence, the lengths of the phases, and the amplitude of the fluctuations. Unfortunately, there are no generally reliable methods for handling cyclical variations which can be applied conveniently. The available methods are involved and beyond the scope of this section.

Random variations represent all the influences not included in trend, seasonal, and cyclical variations. They include such things as measurement errors, floods, fires, earthquakes, wars, strikes, and unusual weather conditions. Many times an erratic occurrence may be isolated and removed from the data. There are no specific techniques for measuring or isolating random variations. An averaging process will help eliminate their influence. Random variations are often referred to as noise, residuals, or irregular variations.

There are many techniques for time series analysis. Some of the most common are last period demand, arithmetic average, moving average, regression analysis, and the exponentially weighted moving average. All of the techniques assume some perpetuation of historical forces on future occurrences. An objective function frequently employed in determining the best technique to apply to a variable with historic data is the smallest mean absolute deviation (*mean* is the statisticians' term for average; *absolute* means the plus or minus sign is ignored; and *deviation* means the difference between the forecast and the actual demand).[1] The mean absolute deviation (MAD) is determined by dividing the number of observations

---

[1] Sometimes the minimum sum of squared deviations is applied. (This criterion is justified if the cost of making an error is proportional to the square of its size: small errors do not cost much but big errors are expensive.) For a normal distribution, the standard deviation is closely approximated by 1.25 times the MAD. The relationship between the standard deviation and the MAD is important in determining confidence limits for forecasts and in establishing inventory safety stock levels via computer routines.

into the sum of the absolute deviations. Each technique is applied to the historical data, and the one with the smallest MAD is selected as the forecast instrument.

LAST PERIOD DEMAND

The last period demand technique simply forecasts for the next period the level of demand that occurred in the previous period. No calculations are required, and forecasted values lag behind actual demand by one period. Mathematically,

$$\overline{Y}_t = Y_{t-1},$$

where

$\overline{Y}_t$ = forecasted demand for period t,

Y_{t-1} = actual demand in the previous period.

The last period demand technique responds fairly well to trends; it does not compensate very well for seasonals; and it overreacts to random influences.

ARITHMETIC AVERAGE

The arithmetic average simply takes the average of all past demand in arriving at a forecast. Mathematically,

$$\overline{Y}_t = \frac{1}{n} \sum_{i=1}^{n} Y_i,$$

where

$\overline{Y}_t$ = forecasted demand for period t,

Y_i = actual demand in period i,

n = number of time periods.

The arithmetic average technique, unlike the last period demand technique, will smooth out random fluctuations; it will not adequately respond to trends in demand; and it neglects seasonals. Smoothing refers to the damping of random fluctuations and is synonymous with averaging.

The basic objection to the arithmetic average is that it takes too little account of recent data and is not responsive enough to changes in demand pattern. The arithmetic average works well in a stable situation where the level of demand does not change. It takes little account of variations around the forecast, which indicates that it is not disturbed by random fluctuations in demand.

MOVING AVERAGE

The moving average technique generates the next period's forecast by averaging the actual demand for the last n time periods. The choice of the value of n should be determined by experimentation. The objective of the moving average is to include a sufficient number of time periods for random fluctuations to cancel, but few enough periods so irrelevant information from the distant past is discarded. Mathematically,

$$\overline{Y}_t = \frac{1}{n} \sum_{i=1}^{n} Y_{t-i},$$

where

$\overline{Y}_t$ = forecasted demand for period t,

Y_{t-i} = actual demand in period $t-i$,

n = number of time periods included in moving average.

This technique gives more weight to the more current time periods. How many periods to use in the average depends on the situation. If too few are used, the forecast fluctuates wildly, influenced by random variations in demand. If too many are used, the average is too stable and current trends are not detected. If there is a trend in demand, the moving average will always lag behind it. If the number of periods in the average is short, the lag will be small, and vice versa.

The moving average technique is a compromise between the last period demand and the arithmetic average technique, with the advantages of both and the disadvantages of neither. If the demand rate is steady, the moving average will respond with fairly constant forecasts, as does the average method. However, when the average demand does change, the moving average forecast, like the last period demand forecast, responds fairly quickly to the change, but without the extreme fluctuations that are characteristic of the last period demand forecast. Increasing the number of periods in the moving average will produce forecasts like the average forecasts. Decreasing the number of periods will produce forecasts like the last period demand forecast. The moving average dampens random effects, responds to trends with a delay, and does not compensate for seasonals.

*   *   *   *   *

EXAMPLE 1.   The monthly demand in units for the last two years is listed below in Table 3.1. Evaluate the forecasts with the last period demand, arithmetic average, and two month moving average techniques. Utilizing the mean absolute deviation (MAD) as a criterion, determine the most desirable of the three forecasting techniques. What is the forecast for the 25th month with each of the three techniques?

Table 3.1

MONTH	DEMAND	MONTH	DEMAND	MONTH	DEMAND
1	34	9	38	17	58
2	44	10	44	18	54
3	42	11	36	19	46
4	30	12	46	20	48
5	46	13	42	21	40
6	44	14	30	22	46
7	56	15	52	23	52
8	50	16	48	24	54
				Total	1080

Table 3.2 compares the three forecasting techniques.

The arithmetic average has the smallest mean absolute deviation, 5.92 (142/24); the two month moving average has a mean absolute deviation of 6.82 (150/22); and the last period demand has the largest MAD of 8.00 (184/23). The arithmetic average technique is the most desirable of the three techniques evaluated, and its forecast for the next month is 45 units.

*   *   *   *   *

REGRESSION ANALYSIS

Regression analysis establishes the temporal relationship for the forecast variable. The variable to be predicted (demand) is called the dependent variable, while the variable used in predicting (time) is called the independent variable. A cause-effect relationship is implied. The simplest type of relationship is a linear association. Regression analysis by the least squares method will fit a straight line to a plot of data where the independent variable is time. The line fitted by the method of least squares will be such that the sum of squares of the deviations about the line is less than about any other line. The regression line will encompass the trend effect, but not the seasonal effect. The basic equation for a straight line that expresses demand (Y) as a function of time (t) is

$$\overline{Y}_t = \alpha + \beta t,$$

Table 3.2

Month	Demand	Last Period Demand Forecast Demand	Last Period Demand Absolute Deviation	Arithmetic Average Forecast Demand	Arithmetic Average Absolute Deviation	Two-Month Moving Average Forecast Demand	Two-Month Moving Average Absolute Deviation
1	34			45	11		
2	44	34	10	45	1		
3	42	44	2	45	3	39	3
4	30	42	12	45	15	43	13
5	46	30	16	45	1	36	10
6	44	46	2	45	1	38	6
7	56	44	12	45	11	45	11
8	50	56	6	45	5	50	0
9	38	50	12	45	7	53	15
10	44	38	6	45	1	44	0
11	36	44	8	45	9	41	5
12	46	36	10	45	1	40	6
13	42	46	4	45	3	41	1
14	30	42	12	45	15	44	14
15	52	30	22	45	7	36	16
16	48	52	4	45	3	41	7
17	58	48	10	45	13	50	8
18	54	58	4	45	9	53	1
19	46	54	8	45	1	56	10
20	48	46	2	45	3	50	2
21	40	48	8	45	5	47	7
22	46	40	6	45	1	44	1
23	52	46	6	45	7	43	9
24	54	52	2	45	9	49	5
25		54				53	
			184		142		150

where α is the intersection of the line with the vertical axis (when $t=0$) and β is the slope of the line. The parameters α and β are estimated from the following formulas:

$$\beta = \frac{n \sum_{i=1}^{n} t_i Y_i - \left(\sum_{i=1}^{n} t_i \right) \left(\sum_{i=1}^{n} Y_i \right)}{n \sum_{i=1}^{n} t_i^2 - \left[\sum_{i=1}^{n} t_i \right]^2} = \text{slope},$$

$$\alpha = \bar{Y} - \beta \bar{t} = \frac{\sum_{i=1}^{n} Y_i - \beta \sum_{i=1}^{n} t_i}{n} = \text{intercept},$$

where n is the number of periods of demand data included in the calculation.

If the relationship between variables in regression analysis is not perfect, there will be a scatter or variation about the regression line. The greater the scatter about the regression line, the poorer the relationship. A statistic that indicates how well a regression line fits the observed data is the correlation coefficient. The degree of linear association of the forecast variable with the time variable is determined by the correlation coefficient, which ranges between -1 and $+1$. A high absolute value indicates a high degree of association, while a small absolute value indicates little association between variables. When the coefficient is positive, one variable tends to increase as the other increases. When the coefficient is negative, one variable tends to decrease as the other increases. (Figure 3.3 illustrates

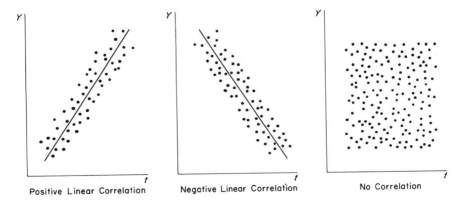

Positive Linear Correlation   Negative Linear Correlation   No Correlation

FIGURE 3.3

typical scatter diagram correlations.) The following formula is used to compute the correlation coefficient.

$$r^2 = \frac{(\Sigma xy)^2}{(\Sigma x^2)(\Sigma y^2)}$$

where

$r =$ simple correlation coefficient,

$x = t - \bar{t}$,

$y = Y - \bar{Y}$.

The following table represents a general rule of thumb for interpretation of the coefficient of correlation.

Absolute Value of Correlation Coefficient	Interpretation
.90–1.00	Very high correlation
.70– .89	High correlation
.40– .69	Moderate correlation
.20– .39	Low correlation
0– .19	Slight correlation

In linear regression analysis, it is assumed that demand is a normally distributed random variable whose mean is the Y coordinate on the regression line at that point in time. By knowing the standard deviation of the distribution, probability statements can be made about the reliability of the forecasts. It is assumed that the standard deviation S_r can be determined from the following formula:

$$S_r^2 = \frac{1}{n-2} \left[\sum_{i=1}^{n} \left(Y_i - \bar{Y} \right)^2 - \frac{\left[\sum_{i=1}^{n} \left(t_i - \bar{t} \right)\left(Y_i - \bar{Y} \right) \right]^2}{\sum_{i=1}^{n} \left(t_i - \bar{t} \right)^2} \right].$$

Once the linear regression line and the standard deviation have been determined, control limits can be established at one, two, or three standard deviations from the mean. When the actual demand occurs, it can be compared with the control limits to determine if the demand is what could be reasonably expected. If the demand falls outside the control limits, there is reason to wonder if the cause system has changed. If it has, a new forecasting model should be developed to replace the inadequate model.

Frequently, time series data are autocorrelated or serial correlated. Autocorrelation occurs where one observation or data point tends to be correlated with the next. Autocorrelation violates the condition for a valid regression estimate: each observation on the data in regression analysis should be totally independent of any other observation. Time series data do not usually meet this condition, since most observations in the series can be forecasted as the last observation plus or minus a small change. This is especially true where a strong trend exists. Regression analysis requires that errors about the regression line be small and unrelated to each other and that their expected value be zero.

In some cases a high demand in one period may be an indication of a low demand to follow (the high demand could be due to advanced stocking for some reason). This condition implies negative autocorrelation. In other cases, a high demand can arise from a cause which will also increase the following periods demand. This condition implies positive autocorrelation.

If autocorrelation exists, regression will underestimate the true variance and result in confidence limits that are too narrow. Many time series with autocorrelation will exhibit no autocorrelation of residuals from a regression in the form of first differences. With first differences, the observed datum Y_t is replaced with its first difference, $Y_t - Y_{t-1}$. Autocorrelation can be determined by the Durbin-Watson statistic or the von Neumann ratio, which are treated in advanced statistics books.

* * * * *

EXAMPLE 2. Annual sales for the last seven years for an organization are given in Table 3.3. Determine (a) the linear least squares regression line; (b) the standard deviation of the regression; (c) the correlation coefficient; (d) the forecasted demand for next year; and (e) the two standard deviation control limits for next year.

Table 3.3

YEAR	ANNUAL SALES
1	$1,760,000
2	2,120,000
3	2,350,000
4	2,800,000
5	3,200,000
6	3,750,000
7	3,800,000

Table 3.4

YEAR	DEMAND			x	x^2	y	y^2	xy
t	Y (10^6)	tY	t^2	$(t-\bar{t})$	$(t-\bar{t})^2$	$(Y-\bar{Y})$	$(Y-\bar{Y})^2$	$(t-\bar{t})(Y-\bar{Y})$
1	1.76	1.76	1	−3	9	−1.07	1.14	3.21
2	2.12	4.24	4	−2	4	−0.71	0.50	1.42
3	2.35	7.05	9	−1	1	−0.48	0.23	0.48
4	2.80	11.20	16	0	0	−0.03	0.00	0.00
5	3.20	16.00	25	1	1	0.37	0.14	0.37
6	3.75	22.50	36	2	4	0.92	0.85	1.84
7	3.80	26.60	49	3	9	0.97	0.94	2.91
28	19.78	89.35	140		28		3.80	10.23

Table 3.4 develops the pertinent data. We have

$$\bar{t}=\frac{28}{7}=4.0, \qquad \bar{Y}=\frac{19.78}{7}=2.83.$$

(a)

$$\beta=\frac{n\sum_{i=1}^{n}t_iY_i-\sum_{i=1}^{n}t_i\sum_{i=1}^{n}Y_i}{n\sum_{i=1}^{n}t_i^2-\left(\sum_{i=1}^{n}t_i\right)^2}=\frac{7(89.35)-(28)(19.78)}{7(140)-28^2}=0.365,$$

$$\alpha=\bar{Y}-\beta\bar{t}=2.83-(0.365)4.0=1.37,$$

$$\bar{Y}_t=\alpha+\beta t=(1.37+0.365t)\times10^6=1,370,000+365,000t.$$

(b)

$$S_r^2=\frac{1}{n-2}\left[\sum_{i=1}^{n}\left(Y_i-\bar{Y}\right)^2-\frac{\left[\sum_{i=1}^{n}\left(t_i-\bar{t}\right)\left(Y_i-\bar{Y}\right)\right]^2}{\sum_{i=1}^{n}\left(t_i-\bar{t}\right)^2}\right]=\frac{1}{5}\left(3.80-\frac{(10.23)^2}{28}\right)$$

$$=0.0125,$$

$$S_r=0.112\times10^6=\$112,000.$$

(c)

$$r^2 = \frac{\left(\sum xy\right)^2}{\left(\sum x^2\right)\left(\sum y^2\right)} = \frac{10.23^2}{28(3.80)} = \frac{104.65}{106.40} = 0.9836,$$

$$r = 0.992.$$

(d) $\overline{Y}_8 = 1,370,000 + 365,000(8) = \$4,290,000.$

(e) $\overline{Y}_8 \pm 2S_r = 4,290,000 \pm 2(112,000) = \$4,290,000 \pm 224,000.$ The two standard deviation control limits are from \$4,066,000 to \$4,514,000.

*   *   *   *   *

EXPONENTIALLY WEIGHTED MOVING AVERAGE (EWMA)

The exponentially weighted moving average is a special kind of moving average that does not require the keeping of a long historical record. The moving average technique assumes that data have no value after n periods. However, some value (although possibly very little) remains in any datum, and a model that uses all the data with appropriate weightings is superior to a model that discards data.

Like most forecasting techniques, the EWMA uses historical data as its prediction basis. In the EWMA, however, past data are not given equal weight. The weight given to past data decreases geometrically with increasing age of the data. More recent data are weighted more heavily than less recent ones. The major advantage of the EWMA is that the effect of all previous data is included in the previous forecast figure, so only one number needs to be retained to represent the demand history.

The simplest model estimates the average forecast demand ($\overline{Y}_t$) by adding to the last average forecast demand ($\overline{Y}_{t-1}$) a fraction of the difference between the actual demand (Y_{t-1}) and the last average forecast demand ($\overline{Y}_{t-1}$):

New forecast = (old forecast) + a (actual demand − old forecast)

$$= a \text{ (actual demand)} + (1 - a)(\text{old forecast}),$$

$$\overline{Y}_t = \overline{Y}_{t-1} + a\left(Y_{t-1} - \overline{Y}_{t-1}\right) = aY_{t-1} + (1 - a)\overline{Y}_{t-1},$$

where

$Y_{t-1} - \overline{Y}_{t-1} = $ error in previous forecast,

$a = $ exponential smoothing constant between 0 and 1.

For example, suppose you are attempting to obtain the forecast of June sales by the EWMA. The relationships would be as follows:

$$\overline{Y}_t = aY_{t-1} + (1-a)\overline{Y}_{t-1},$$

June forecast $= a$ (May actual) $+ (1-a)$(May forecast).

The smoothing constant a lies between zero (no weight to recent actual data) and 1.0 (all weight to recent actual data). Small values of a put greater weight on historical demand conditions and have a greater smoothing effect (maximum stability with minimum sensitivity). Large values of a put greater weight on current demand conditions (maximum sensitivity with minimum stability). The appropriate value of a for a given set of data is determined by trial on a sample of actual past demand (retrospective testing). It is common to develop forecasting models on the first half of historical data and then test them on the second half.

Guideline values for a range from 0.1 to 0.3. Larger values of a may be used for short time periods when anticipated changes will occur, such as a recession, an aggressive but temporary promotional campaign, introducing a new product, or discontinuing some products in a line. The value of a should allow the forecast model to track major demand changes while averaging the random fluctuations.

The general formula for the exponentially weighted moving average model is as follows:

$$\overline{Y}_t = a\left[Y_{t-1} + Y_{t-2}(1-a) + Y_{t-3}(1-a)^2 + \cdots + Y_1(1-a)^{t-2} \right]$$

$$+ (1-a)^{t-1}\overline{Y}_0,$$

where

$$\overline{Y}_t = \text{forecasted demand for period } t,$$

$$\overline{Y}_0 = \text{forecasted demand for period } 0,$$

$$Y_{t-1} = \text{actual demand for period } t-1.$$

The EWMA attributes part of the difference between actual demand and forecasted demand to a real cause and the remainder to chance causes. The EWMA assigns weights to the demand values of the previous periods in such a way that the weights decrease exponentially (exponential decay) as the demand data get older and farther removed from the present (thus the name exponentially weighted moving average). The weight of past demands decreases exponentially because the fraction $1-a$ is raised to a power. Exponential smoothing is based on the assumption that the future is more dependent upon the recent past than on the distant past.

A general formula for expressing the weight of an actual demand on a future forecast is as follows:

$$\text{Weight} = a(1-a)^{n-1},$$

where n is the number of time periods removed from the existing period. For example, if $a = 0.2$ and the latest available actual demand is for May, the May demand will have a weight of 0.2 for the June forecast, a weight of 0.16 for the July forecast, a weight of 0.128 for the August forecast, and so forth. The above formula illustrates the lessening importance (exponential decay) of past data as they are further removed from the forecast period. The weights were obtained as follows:

$$\text{June weight} = 0.2(1-0.2)^{1-1} = 0.2,$$

$$\text{July weight} = 0.2(1-0.2)^{2-1} = 0.16,$$

$$\text{August weight} = 0.2(1-0.2)^{3-1} = 0.128.$$

With the EWMA you can forecast more than one period into the future, but the more distant estimates are the same as the current estimate. The relationship to forecast n periods into the future when you are at the beginning of time t is as follows:

$$\overline{Y}_{t+n} = \overline{Y}_t.$$

Of course, the above relationship assumes that there are no trend, seasonal, or cyclical effects in the data (only random effects need correction).

The exponential smoothing model without a trend correction reacts slowly to a big change in demand, since the change may be only a random variation. If the change reflects an actual increase or decrease in demand, it will continue in subsequent periods, and the exponential smoothing system will track the actual demand and respond to it. The size of the smoothing constant a will determine the sensitivity of the response to changes in demand. Surges in demand can be satisfied by safety stock when a small value of a is used in the forecast system.

There is a direct relationship between the moving average technique and the EWMA without trend or seasonal effects. Just as the sensitivity of a moving average decreases as the number of time periods in the moving average increases, the sensitivity of an EWMA decreases as a decreases. In fact, there is a relationship between n (number of periods in moving average) and *a* which is expressed as follows:[2]

$$a = \frac{2}{n+1}, \quad \text{or} \quad n = \frac{2-a}{a}.$$

Thus, if *n* is equal to 7, that is equivalent to $a = 0.25$ in the EWMA model without trend or seasonal influences.

*   *   *   *   *

EXAMPLE 3.   From the data in Table 3.5, determine the best forecasting method by using the smallest mean absolute deviation. Evaluate the last period demand, three month moving average, and EWMA with $a = 0.3$. (Assume $\overline{Y}_0 = 185$.)

Table 3.5

MONTH	1976 DEMAND	1977 DEMAND	1978 DEMAND
1	180	215	225
2	186	208	225
3	179	195	215
4	170	200	225
5	170	194	210
6	165	185	200
7	155	180	204
8	150	180	195
9	170	181	210
10	192	205	220
11	195	225	240
12	205	235	250

Table 3.6 (pages 66–67) compares the three forecasting methods, with fractions rounded to whole numbers. The last period demand has the smallest mean absolute deviation, 9.30 (335/36); the EWMA has a MAD of 14.05 (506/36); and the three month moving average has the largest MAD, 14.27 (471/33).

*   *   *   *   *

OVERVIEW OF TIME SERIES ANALYSIS

In selecting a forecasting technique, it is common to apply numerous techniques to historical data and determine which one best fits the data. A common criterion is to select the technique with the smallest mean ab-

[2]See Robert G. Brown, *Statistical Forecasting for Inventory Control*, New York: McGraw-Hill, 1959, pp. 58–62.

solute deviation. The errors or deviations for each period are obtained by subtracting the actual demand from the forecasted demand. The *absolute* sum of deviations is used in place of the *algebraic* sum of deviations because it is possible to obtain zero as the sum of algebraic deviations even when the individual deviations are large. This situation is remedied by using the absolute deviation without regard to its sign. Once the specific technique is adopted, the algebraic sum of errors is also used to measure its effectiveness.

The error in the forecast is defined as the difference between the forecast demand level and the actual demand level. If the error terms are plotted for a large number of forecasts, a frequency distribution is generated. The dispersion (variability) of the error about the mean error (the mean error should be zero if our forecast errors are normally distributed) can be expressed in a common form such as the variance, standard deviation, or mean absolute deviation. The distribution of forecast errors should approximate the normal distribution.

The forecasting model having the lowest MAD over a period of time is the most desirable. Concurrently, the algebraic sum of errors should cancel out (be at the zero level) over a period of time, so that no bias remains in the distribution of forecast errors. The algebraic sum of errors helps to indicate how well the forecasting system is estimating demand. When the forecast fails to respond to changes in demand, it grows larger and larger in a positive or negative direction. Negative errors indicate that demand is rising faster than the forecast. A positive sum of errors indicates a decreasing demand.

Demand patterns for items are subject to change over a product's life cycle. This situation dictates a revision of the forecasting model. While there are many tests which can indicate a permanent change, usually a plot of the demand will reveal the need for a revision. There are usually external environmental conditions that cause demand changes and managers are well aware of them.

Sales promotions as well as other factors influence a forecast to such an extent that predictions based on intuitive judgments and experience may override a statistical extrapolation of past data. Forecasts cannot properly estimate future demand when promotional activities are involved. When past data contain unusual promotional effects, it is a good idea to "depromotionalize" the data to a normal level.

When the forecast is for many periods ahead, time series analysis can be perilous. The use of a short term forecasting technique for a long time ahead implies a stability which may not occur. The longer the projection, the less reliable the forecast becomes.

Time series analysis is best suited to items which have continuous

Table 3.6

Month	Actual Demand	Last Period Demand		Three Month Moving Average		EWMA	
		Forecast Demand	Absolute Deviation	Forecast Demand	Absolute Deviation	Forecast Demand	Absolute Deviation
1	180	185	5	—	—	185	5
2	186	180	6	—	—	183	3
3	179	186	7	—	—	184	5
4	170	179	9	182	12	182	12
5	170	170	0	178	8	178	8
6	165	170	5	173	8	176	11
7	155	165	10	168	13	173	18
8	150	155	5	163	13	168	18
9	170	150	20	157	13	163	7
10	192	170	22	158	34	165	27
11	195	192	3	171	24	173	22
12	205	195	10	186	19	180	25
13	215	205	10	197	18	187	28
14	208	215	7	205	3	195	13
15	195	208	13	209	14	199	4
16	200	195	5	206	6	198	2

17	194	200	6	201	7	199	5
18	185	194	9	196	11	197	12
19	180	185	5	193	13	193	13
20	180	180	0	186	6	189	9
21	181	180	1	182	1	186	5
22	205	181	24	180	25	184	21
23	225	205	20	189	36	190	35
24	235	225	10	204	31	200	35
25	225	235	10	222	3	210	15
26	225	225	0	228	3	214	11
27	215	225	10	228	13	217	2
28	225	215	10	222	3	216	9
29	210	225	15	222	12	219	9
30	200	210	10	217	17	216	16
31	204	200	4	212	8	211	7
32	195	204	9	205	10	209	14
33	210	195	15	200	10	205	5
34	220	210	10	203	17	206	14
35	240	220	20	208	32	210	30
36	250	240	10	223	27	219	31
37		250		237		228	
			$\overline{335}$		$\overline{471}$		$\overline{506}$

demand. For items with discrete or lumpy demand, this mode of forecasting is inadequate. Demand is lumpy when it is so low that it is quite likely to be zero. For such items a probabilistic approach based on expected demand or marginal analysis is more appropriate.

SOLICITING OPINIONS

A subjective approach to forecasting involves the solicitation of opinions concerning future levels of demand from customers, retailers, wholesalers, salesmen, and managers. Through interviews and market research, estimates of future demand can be obtained from customers, wholesalers, and retailers. There are difficulties to this approach, since customers do not always do what they say, and it is not uncommon to obtain a broad spectrum of conflicting opinion.

If a sufficient history of past demand is not available, then forecasts must be based on market potential studies, general surveys, and whatever parallel experiences are available. These factors are then combined with selected experiences, insights, and intuitions. Internal opinions can be secured from salesmen and managers. Each salesman may be asked to estimate future volume in his territory, and the estimates of all salesmen added to obtain a forecast for the entire company. This collective opinion approach is frequently used for new products with no sales history, but it becomes less effective as the length of the forecast horizon is increased.

This less elaborate and less technical approach makes use of the qualitative knowledge of people in the field and home office. Forecasts of this type tend to be heavily influenced by immediate events. When an estimate is developed from collective opinion, the final result may reflect opinions of a few influential or persuasive individuals rather than of those of the group from which it was drawn. Judgment forecasts normally tend to overreact to immediate circumstances.

The Delphi technique is designed to remedy some of the problems which arise in consensus forecasts. The technique attempts to maximize the advantages of group dynamics while minimizing the problems caused by dominant personalities and silent experts. An iterative procedure is employed to develop forecasts from forecasters (experts) on an individual by individual basis. Each expert develops his forecast of a well-defined event individually without contact with other experts. The responses are statistically summarized and returned to the experts. The experts revise their forecasts, and the procedure is repeated until consensus is achieved. The Delphi technique has been used mainly in forecasting future technological events, but it has also been adapted to short term forecasting problems.

ECONOMIC INDICATORS

Economic indicators are frequently used to predict future demand. The knowledge of one variable is used to predict the value of another (prediction by association). The decision maker searches for an economic indicator (gross national product, personal income, bank deposits, freight car loadings, etc.) which has a relationship with the forecast variable. A cause-effect relationship is implied. The simplest type of relationship is a linear association. Regression analysis by the least squares method will fit a straight line to a plot of data from two variables. The line fitted by the method of least squares will be such that the sum of squares of the deviations about the line is less than the sum of the squares of the deviations about any other line. A linear function has the form

$$Y = \alpha + \beta \chi,$$

where

Y = dependent variable (variable to be forecasted),

χ = independent variable (economic indicator),

α = intercept,

β = slope.

The parameters α and β are estimated from the following formulas:

$$\alpha = \bar{Y} - \beta \bar{\chi} = \frac{\Sigma Y - \beta \Sigma \chi}{n},$$

$$\beta = \frac{n(\Sigma \chi Y) - (\Sigma \chi)(\Sigma Y)}{n \Sigma \chi^2 - (\Sigma \chi)^2}.$$

With the simple regression analysis, the forecaster seeks to discover those variables which have the greatest correlation with the forecast variable. What linear regression analysis does is compute a line which comes closer to connecting the observed points than any other line which could be drawn. It may be used to estimate the relationship between any two or more variables. A statistic that indicates how well a regression fits the observed data is the correlation coefficient.

The degree of linear association of the forecast variable and the economic indicator is determined by the correlation coefficient, which ranges between -1 and $+1$. A high absolute value indicates a high degree of

association, while a small absolute value indicates little association between variables. When the coefficient is positive, one variable tends to
increase as the other increases. When the coefficient is negative, one
variable tends to decrease as the other increases. We have

$$r^2 = \frac{(\Sigma xy)^2}{(\Sigma x^2)(\Sigma y^2)},$$

where

$$r = \text{simple correlation coefficient,}$$
$$x = \chi - \bar{\chi},$$
$$y = Y - \bar{Y}.$$

The decision maker can verify the statistical significance of any derived
simple correlation coefficient by using standard statistical tests found in
many texts. A simple t-test can be used to verify if a correlation coefficient
differs significantly from zero.

*   *   *   *   *

EXAMPLE 4.   Find the least squares regression line and the coefficient of
correlation of Y on χ from the following data:

Y	68	66	68	65	69	66	68	65	71	67	68	70
χ	65	63	67	64	68	62	70	66	68	67	69	71

The data are reduced in Table 3.7. We have

$$\alpha = \frac{\Sigma Y - \beta \Sigma \chi}{n} = \frac{811 - 0.476(800)}{12} = 35.85,$$

$$\beta = \frac{n(\Sigma xY) - (\Sigma x)(\Sigma Y)}{n \Sigma x^2 - (\Sigma x)^2} = \frac{12(54,107) - (800)(811)}{12(53,418) - (800)^2} = 0.476,$$

$$Y = \alpha + \beta \chi = 35.85 + 0.476 \chi.$$

The calculations leading to the coefficient of correlation are shown in

Table 3.8. We have

$$r^2 = \frac{\left(\sum xy\right)^2}{\left(\sum x^2\right)\left(\sum y^2\right)} = \frac{(40.34)^2}{(84.68)(38.92)} = 0.4938,$$

$r = .7027 =$ coefficient of correlation.

Table 3.7

Y	X	x^2	xY	Y^2
68	65	4225	4420	4624
66	63	3969	4158	4356
68	67	4489	4556	4624
65	64	4096	4160	4225
69	68	4624	4692	4761
66	62	3844	4092	4356
68	70	4900	4760	4624
65	66	4356	4290	4225
71	68	4624	4828	5041
67	67	4489	4489	4489
68	69	4761	4692	4624
70	71	5041	4970	4900
$\sum Y = 811$	$\sum X = 800$	$\sum x^2 = 53,418$	$\sum xY = 54,107$	$\sum Y^2 = 54,849$

Table 3.8

Y	X	$x = X - \bar{X}$	$y = Y - \bar{Y}$	x^2	xy	y^2
68	65	-1.7	0.4	2.89	-0.68	0.16
66	63	-3.7	-1.6	13.69	5.92	2.56
68	67	0.3	0.4	0.09	.12	0.16
65	64	-2.7	-2.6	7.29	7.02	6.76
69	68	1.3	1.4	1.69	1.82	1.96
66	62	-4.7	-1.6	22.09	7.52	2.56
68	70	3.3	0.4	10.89	1.32	0.16
65	66	-0.7	-2.6	0.49	1.82	6.76
71	68	1.3	3.4	1.69	4.42	11.56
67	67	0.3	-0.6	0.09	-0.18	0.36
68	69	2.3	0.4	5.29	0.92	0.16
70	71	4.3	2.4	18.49	10.32	5.76
$\sum Y = 811$	$\sum X = 800$			$\sum x^2 =$	$\sum xy =$	$\sum y^2 =$
$\bar{Y} = 67.6$	$\bar{X} = 66.7$			84.68	40.34	38.92

*   *   *   *   *

An economic indicator for a given year will be known only after the year has ended, and that is too late to permit its use to predict sales for that year. An ideal indicator is one which leads the forecast variable. If no lag exists, a forecasted value of the economic indicator can be used for prediction. This approach assumes that the relationship that existed in the past will exist in the future.

Multiple linear regression deals with the relationship between the dependent variable (variable to be predicted) and two or more independent variables (variables used to make the prediction). The difference between a simple linear regression and a multiple linear regression is in the number of independent variables used in the analysis. For example, for two independent variables X_1, X_2 the linear regression equation would be

$$Y = \alpha + \beta X_1 + \gamma X_2.$$

In multiple linear regression analysis, more than one independent variable is used to forecast the dependent variable. An F-test is conducted on the multivariable model to determine if the model significantly forecasts the dependent variable.[3] In multiple linear regression analysis, the simple correlation coefficient is replaced with *partial correlation coefficients*. These indicate the influence of each individual independent variable on the dependent variable while all other independent variables are held statistically constant. The significance of each independent variable is determined by a t-test.[3] An insignificant t-test means that an independent variable does not significantly aid in the forecast of the dependent variable. A *multiple correlation coefficient* is analogous to the single correlation coefficient except it contains the contributions of several independent variables. In determining the multiple correlation coefficient, only those independent variables that have a significant partial correlation coefficient should be included.

With multiple regression analysis, the problem of multicolinearity can arise. Multicolinearity is the situation where there is intercorrelation between independent variables. When two or more of the independent variables are highly correlated, you are in effect using the same variable twice. In this situation, the forecaster simply deletes one of the related variables.

In many cases, the relationship between variables is nonlinear or curvilinear and a more complex type of analysis is required. Straight lines, polynomials, and logarithmic functions are frequently used when trends or

---

[3]The F-test and t-test determine if the regression coefficients are significant. The F-test determines if $\beta_1 = \beta_2 = \beta_3 = \cdots = \beta_n = 0$, and the t-test individually determines if $\beta_1 = 0$, $\beta_2 = 0$, $\beta_3 = 0, \ldots$, and $\beta_n = 0$.

growth patterns are present; trigonometric functions (sines and cosines) can be used when cyclic tendencies are present.

It is seldom practical to use economic indicators for item forecasts. They are usually used to forecast product groups or aggregate dollar demand for an organization. Time series analysis is much more practical for item-by-item forecasting.

ECONOMETRIC MODELS

An econometric model is usually a set of simultaneous equations which represent the interactions of variables involved in a business situation. The models attempt to show the relationships between relevant variables such as supply, demand, prices, and purchasing power of the consumer. The models can become quite complex, since they are supposed to include the causative forces operating on the variable to be predicted. Usually they require forecasts of a number of structural variables.

The structural relationships of econometric models can be grouped into four categories—behavioral, technical, institutional, and identities. Behavioral relationships include supply curves, demand curves, and other curves that reflect the behavior of particular economic units (consumers, business firms). Technical relationships are mainly production functions that show input-output relationships as constrained by technology. Institutional relationships are specified by law or regulatory agency and indicate the boundaries of acceptable social behavior (taxes, minimum wages). Identities specify balance relationships such as the gross national product (GNP), which is by definition equal to the sum of personal consumption expenditures, gross private capital formation, government purchases of goods and services, and net foreign trade.

A variant of econometric analysis is input output forecasting models. These models consider intraperiod dependences between sectors of the economy as well as the interperiod dependences. Econometric textbooks are devoted to model development in this area.

In order to capture all the interactions, the econometric model must have many equations. As more equations are added, the model becomes cumbersome in terms of both the initial estimation and the required maintenance. However, once a model is developed, its entire structure is known and its assumptions are in full view. Over a period of time, the model can be refined by new research.

A possible way to estimate future product demand is to first determine the customers, their uses of the product, how much they need for each use, and when they will order the product. A mathematical model could then be built relating all the relevant factors. Because of the number and complexity of factors, a complete model is seldom possible. However, approximate models can be built which are worth while.

A difficulty with this approach is the cost as well as the time consumed in model development. Econometric analysis usually requires a highly technical and professional staff as well as a computer. Thus, it can be a very expensive forecasting approach. Usually only a large organization with vast resources can afford the luxury of such a specialized staff. Of course, the selection of a forecasting technique should not be based on cost alone, but on a cost-benefit analysis. Econometric models are not economically feasible for controlling inventories of individual items. They are more appropriate for forecasting aggregate demand.

CONCLUSION

New analytical capabilities and techniques are providing better tools for forecasting. Forecasting is predicting, projecting, or estimating some future event or condition which is outside of an organization's control. While forecasting is not planning, it is an indispensable input into planning. Planning sets goals and develops alternative strategies to attain them. Forecasting deals with matters outside of management's control. Organizations forecast so they can plan and help shape their future. Based on forecasts of future conditions, plans and policies can be developed to respond to future opportunities and react to future problems.

A demand forecast is the link between external factors and internal affairs. The determination of the types of forecasts required and the establishment of procedures governing their generation are fundamental steps in the structure of a well-conceived organization. Forecast techniques depend very much on the number of items being controlled and on the type of operating system. Forecasts need to be made on a routine basis, so the techniques must match the available staff skills and computing facilities.

The forecasting of independent demand items is required for supply to be maintained in anticipation of demand. A forecast is important when an advance commitment (to procure or to manufacture) has to be made. From the forecasts, operational plans are developed. The less flexibility there is in subsequently modifying original plans, the more important are the dependability and accuracy of the forecast. If it is easy to modify operational plans, the accuracy of the forecast is not so important. There has been a substantial increase in the availability of sophisticated forecasting techniques, but increases in forecasting effectiveness have not been as pronounced. Unfortunately, poor forecasts are often a fact of life. Refinements in forecasting techniques are frequently less important than the development of operational flexibility to be able to live with poor forecasts.

Forecasting should not be viewed in isolation. The importance of forecasting is its usefulness in planning. Forecasting techniques should be chosen with that in mind, particularly with regard to the degree of accuracy required.

The essential steps necessary to satisfy the forecasting function are:

1. Select forecasting technique(s).
2. Select the forecasting base (units, gallons, dollars).
3. Determine the time increment (week, month, quarter).
4. Prepare the data.
5. Make forecasts.
6. Report and interpret forecast deviations.
7. Revise forecasting model(s) as required.

A forecast is only an estimate of expected demand. Actual demand and forecasted demand cannot be expected to agree precisely. Forecasts are only "ballpark" figures that permit the planning function to commence. Feelings of frustration should not result from the inability to predict the future precisely. One may be far more confident about a range of values rather than a single point forecast, and usually that is all that is needed.

With a properly designed forecasting system, uncertainty is kept to a measurable minimum. A good forecast usually includes not only an estimate of the demand itself, but also an estimate of the magnitude of likely deviations as a guide to reliability. Deviation is usually specified by stating the best single estimate (expected value) and then establishing limits above and below that indicate the range of likely variation.

The tracking (scrunity of errors) of a forecast model is necessary to verify the continued integrity of the model. Forecasting models do not ensure reliability in perpetuity and must be revised when they are no longer appropriate. The tracking of a model can provide numerous benefits to management, such as:

1. Indicating the reliability of the existing model
2. Providing the criterion for forecast model selection
3. Facilitating selection of parameters (months in moving average, or exponentially weighted smoothing constant)
4. Assisting in establishing safety stock levels

Reducing forecast errors requires increasing expenditures on forecasting techniques. Expenditures of large amounts of money to improve forecasting accuracy reaches a point of diminishing return, and a perfect forecast is an impossibility. Frequently, a much better investment is the development of operational and production flexibility which permits a rapid redeployment of resources in the light of market changes.

Forecasting is an ongoing processs that requires maintenance, revision, and modifications. The most obvious time to revise a forecast is when it is in error. Some techniques have built-in warning signals that indicate a divergence from some predetermined tolerance range. Other techniques require personal surveillance to give the signal. Either way, the existence of the error should be communicated along with the reasons if known.

It is impossible to design decision rules and forecasting models that will cover every eventuality. Design is primarily concerned with routine, repetitive situations. Unusual situations which cannot be anticipated must result in a managerial override or interrupt. The computer can handle the routine occurrences and man (manager) can devote his skill and experience to the nonroutine situations.

The techniques outlined herein are not intended to be exhaustive, but only to summarize prevalent categories. The imagination and ingenuity of a forecaster are vital ingredients in the design of forecasting systems. Although precise mathematical formulas give the impression that forecasting is a science, it still remains an art with a tenuous scientific superstructure.

QUESTIONS

1. What is a forecast?
2. Name the four basic demand forecast techniques.
3. What is a time series?
4. Name five components into which time series data are usually decomposed for analysis.
5. Name five of the most common time series analysis techniques.
6. What are the basic limitations of the arithmetic average for forecasting?
7. Which exhibits a greater degree of linear association, a correlation coefficient of $+1$ or a correlation coefficient of -1?
8. What does it mean when time series data are autocorrelated?
9. Why does the exponentially weighted moving average (EWMA) not require the keeping of a long historical record?

10. What is a common criterion for selecting a forecast technique?
11. Name two difficulties associated with the solicitation of opinions for forecasting.
12. Give four examples of economic indicators which might be used to predict future demand.
13. What is an econometric model?
14. Into what four categories can the structural relationships of economeric models be grouped? Give examples of each.
15. Name some forecasting techniques which might be used for established products.
16. What are some of the considerations in the selection of a forecasting model?

PROBLEMS

1. From the data in the table, determine the sum of absolute deviations for the last period demand forecasting method. What is the forecast for month 13?

Table for Problem 1

MONTH	DEMAND UNITS	FORECAST	ABSOLUTE DEVIATION
1	500		
2	510		
3	480		
4	600		
5	600		
6	660		
7	590		
8	700		
9	680		
10	740		
11	790		
12	760		

2. From the data in Problem 1, determine the sum of absolute deviations for the three month moving average forecasting method. What is the forecast for month 13?

3. From the data in Problem 1, determine the sum of absolute deviations for an EWMA with $a = 0.1$ (assume forecasted demand for month 1 is the same as actual demand). What is the forecast for month 13?

4. If $\overline{Y}_{t-1} = 40$ and $Y_{t-1} = 30$, show the effects of the smoothing constants $a = 0.1$, 0.5, and 0.8 on the new average forecast.

5. Determine the linear regression equation for the data given below:

MONTH	1	2	3	4	5	6
DEMAND	30	40	40	50	55	60

What is the forecast for month 7?

6. From the data given in Problem 5, determine the standard deviation of the regression line. What is the correlation coefficient?

Case 1: Rocky Road

The Hill Company is a manufacturer of weatherstripping and related products. The company was formed in 1961 to exploit a patent on an improved type of steel-bound weatherstripping invented by George Hill. The company is managed by George Hill and his son, Walter. Until recently, their major product was limited to special, high-efficiency applications.

The company has 20 employees, and operations are balanced throughout the year. Traditionally, 70% of sales occurred in the fall of the year. Inventories increase during the off seasons and are depleted in the fall. Monthly production quotas have been figured by multiplying last year's sales by 1.1 and dividing by 12. The 10% growth factor has worked fairly well in the past.

Recently, the rising cost of energy has increased the demand for Hill's products significantly. With new building structures requiring better insulation, sales are no longer highly seasonal. Sales in the off seasons have increased substantially. The work force has been expanded to 30 employees and the single shift operation has been maintained.

The firm was not prepared for the increase in business. Stockouts in both raw materials and finished goods have occurred and production delays encountered. Walter has attempted to adapt his planning to the new conditions, but he has not been very successful. Customers have been willing to accept the inconvenience because there was very little competition available. However, another small firm in the area has started to produce competing products. The sales of the Hill Company by season for the last four years are as follows:

YEAR	TOTAL SALES	SPRING SALES	SUMMER SALES	FALL SALES	WINTER SALES
1974	$230,000	$10,000	$10,000	$160,000	$50,000
1975	250,000	10,000	20,000	170,000	50,000
1976	450,000	50,000	110,000	200,000	90,000
1977	640,000	70,000	200,000	240,000	130,000
1978	800,000[a]				

[a]Forecasted by Walter Hill: (1.25) (1976 sales).

Walter is very concerned because the patent on their major product will expire in a few years. Costs are increasing dramatically and must be subjected to tighter control. George has asked his son to evaluate other forecasting approaches. He believes inadequate forecasts have made planning and control impossible. Walter believes there are other more basic difficulties facing the firm.

1. What are the major problems facing the firm?
2. What forecasting techniques might the Hill Company consider?
3. What impact will growth and competition have on the firm?

Case 2: Go or No-Go

Cannon Controls Corporation has just developed a new integrated circuit design which represents an advance in the state of the art. The new product has wide market application in the electronics industry. It will be sold at a higher price than conventional design circuits, but it offers significant advantages in size, stability, and reliability. A patent has been applied for by the firm.

Market research and test marketing of the product have just been completed in a single test market in one geographic area. The market research was aimed at determining if a breakeven sales volume of four million units per year could be attained. The research indicated with a high level of confidence that at least four million units would be sold. For reasons independent of the market research, marketing officials believe that the market will be in the range of six to twelve million units.

The two distinct industrial markets for the product are manufacturers of consumer products and manufacturers of industrial products. The consumer products market will be in radios, televisions, timing devices, and microwave ovens. The industrial products market will be in power generation equipment, calculators, X-ray equipment, measuring devices, and military weapon systems. The industrial products market will account for approximately 70% of sales. General economic conditions will have an important influence on the consumer product's market.

Mr. Lewis, the marketing manager, has recommended that a ten million unit production facility be built. Mr. Harris, the controller, has requested that the product be market tested in other geographic areas. Additional market testing will take five months and cost $150,000. After plant capacity is decided, it will take another six months before the plant is operational. The capital costs for the different size facilities under consideration are as follows:

PRODUCTION PLAN	PLANT CAPACITY (UNITS)	ESTIMATED CAPITAL COST
A	4,000,000	$15,000,000
B	6,000,000	20,000,000
C	8,000,000	24,000,000
D	10,000,000	26,000,000

If the plant is expanded after it is built, the cost will significantly exceed the initial plant costs listed above.

1. Would you recommend that the plant be built at this time? If you do, what plant size would you recommend? Why?

2. If additional market forecasting is necessary, what specific techniques and approaches would you prescribe?

3. Why is Mr. Harris not satisfied with the market test data?

Case 3: The Numbers Game

Four major retailing firms, which compete with each other, traditionally make annual industry sales forecasts. From its industry sales forecast, each company estimates its own sales and related market share. Each company makes a number of basic forecasting assumptions concerning the general condition of the national economy.

At the end of the current year, total industry sales were $8.5 billion. Using this figure as a starting point, each of the firms will forecast industry-wide sales for the coming year. Each firm bases its industry-wide forecast on the following three factors:

1. An overall economic growth rate of 6% in GNP

2. Consumer income rising by 7%

3. An increase in consumer credit

Even though industry forecasts were based on the above factors, there were significant differences in the forecast of each firm. Sales projections were as follows:

Firm A: $10 billion
Firm B: $9 billion
Firm C: $10.5 billion
Firm D: $9.5 billion

1. Why are the forecasts different?

2. What influence do forecasting errors have on an organization?

3. If actual sales are $10.5 billion, will Firm B experience operational difficulties?

4. If actual sales are $9 billion, how will it affect Firm C?

Chapter 4

Purchasing and Procurement

Every organization to varying degrees depends on materials and services supplied by other organizations. Therefore, purchasing and procurement are common functions of every organization. Purchasing is the exchange of money for goods or services, while procurement is the total responsibility for acquiring goods and services. The changing supply scene, with cycles of shortage and abundance complicated by varying prices, lead times, and availabilities, has buoyed purchasing and procurement to a prominent organizational position.

The great majority of U.S. industries spend from 40 to 60% of their revenues for materials and services from outside sources. It has been estimated that U.S. industries purchased materials totaling over $350 billion per year in the early 1970s. For the same period, capital expenditures amounted to another $20 billion and year-end inventory exceeded $100 billion. The magnitude of these figures emphasizes the importance of purchasing and procurement on the U.S. economy as well as to individual organizations.

As organizations have increased in size and complexity, many of the activities performed by the owner or foreman have gradually been taken over by specialists. In particular, purchasing and procurement have been removed from their earlier location and realigned as a separate and important organizational function. By this means economies of scale were obtained. A trained buyer familiar with the details of a large number of items could usually do a better job than a foreman. Also, as more organizations became specialized, they produced fewer and fewer of their parts. This change in production operations has significantly raised the dollar value not only of raw materials, but also of complex components and subassembly units. Whereas buyers of raw materials had needed only simple skills, buyers now had to be much more sophisticated. Thus, purchasing has been transformed from an insignificant repetitive subfunction of production or sales to a primary business function.

Procurement or purchasing can make a substantial contribution to the efficiency and effectiveness of an organization. To attain maximum benefits, it is necessary that it be treated as a functional area along with finance, production, and marketing. The purchasing function is vital to any organization. The ability of the purchasing department to obtain the required materials, equipment, services, and supplies at the right prices and at the right times is a key to successful operations. These expenditures usually account for more than half of an organization's total expenditures.

Because purchasing involves large sums of money, even a small percentage saving can amount to a large dollar figure. Any reduction in material costs exerts a high leverage on profits. Since many items are purchased repetitively, any saving tends to accrue year after year. A simple example will illustrate how profits can be increased in a variety of ways. In a small manufacturing organization, the following major relationships exist:

$1,000,000 total sales
   500,000 purchased goods and services
   300,000 labor and salaries
   150,000 overhead
    50,000 profit

To double profits to $100,000 the following actions could be taken:

1. Increase sales 100%.
2. Increase prices 5%.
3. Decrease labor and salaries $16\frac{2}{3}\%$.
4. Decrease overhead $33\frac{1}{3}\%$.
5. Decrease purchase costs 10%.

A review of the above figures reveals the leverage potential of purchased goods and services. Every 1% decline in purchased goods and services results in a 10% increase in profits. It is frequently difficult (if not impossible) to increase prices, substantially increase labor productivity, or reduce overhead. Thus, a major opportunity for reducing costs and improving profit lies in purchasing and procurement.

Purchasing has the responsibility of procuring the kinds and quantities of materials authorized by requisitions issued by engineering, maintenance, production control, inventory control, or any other entity requiring materials. Purchasing means procuring goods and services from outside the organization in return for a price. The evaluation of the total cost must include quality, quantity, and time considerations. These are usually specified for the purchasing department, but its decisions then largely determine the price and source.

Purchasing can be viewed in terms of the purchasing cycle, which is a series of recurring events in almost all purchases (see Figure 4.1). To initiate the cycle, purchasing usually receives purchase requisitions from other functional areas of the organization. The requisitions are reviewed for authorization, for proper description, and to determine if available cheaper resources could do the job. Before writing the purchase order, suppliers must be selected on the basis of price, quality, and delivery schedule. Then the purchase contract is signed and shipping dates confirmed. When the order arrives, it is inspected to verify quality and

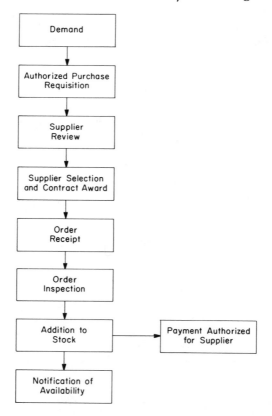

FIGURE 4.1

quantity stipulations. Supplier invoices for the acceptable order are transmitted to purchasing and to the requisitioner of the order. The acceptable
order is placed in stores and becomes inventory until consumed in a
production process or sold to a customer. With the fulfillment of the
contract, purchasing must review the invoice, adjust it as needed and
agreed, and process it for payment, considering any discounts. The
purchasing cycle stretches from the receipt of purchase requisition to the
point at which the order is available to the requisitioner and payment is
authorized to the supplier.

From this point of view it may appear that purchasing is a simple,
straightforward function. This appearance can be very deceptive for those
with little purchasing experience. To help dispel simplistic notions,
purchasing should be viewed in terms of the purchasing function as
detailed in Figure 4.2. Here we describe purchasing in an input-decision-

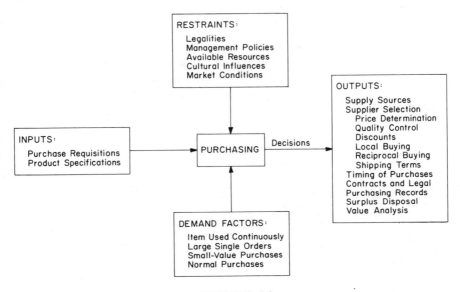

FIGURE 4.2

output framework with organizational restraints and demand factors influencing the final outputs.

The relevant inputs to the purchasing function are outputs from other organization sources or functions. Inputs include purchase requisitions (authority for procurement) and product specifications. Purchasing is limited by organizational restraints (limitations imposed by the organization) and market factors. Restraints differ from entity to entity; some common ones are legalities, management policies, available resources, cultural influences, and market conditions. Demand factors (both current and expected) influence the quantity, amount, and type of purchase that will be made. For example, an impending unit price rise for a component might economically justify a larger purchase for an item with a continuous demand. The outputs of purchasing include the specification of approved supply sources, supplier selection, timing of purchases, contracts and legal work, purchasing records, surplus disposal, and value analysis.

The significance of studying purchasing as a function is in the total (systems) perspective obtained. A more shallow analysis would treat inputs, organizational restraints, demand factors, and outputs as independent unrelated influences. But since the dependence is readily apparent, it is worthwhile to study it. The resulting analysis of the purchasing function can result in economical, rational, logical, consistent, and uniform policies for all the activities of the purchasing department. It permits the role of purchasing to be more readily integrated into overall organizational purposes and goals.

Purchasing is in transition from a largely clerical activity to a demanding analytical and intellectual function. A purchasing agent is no longer merely a clerk who receives requisitions from managers and catalogs from suppliers, simply selecting the lowest price alternative. Purchasing's role in organizational effectiveness requires that it not be perceived as an independent isolated activity of negligible significance.

PURCHASING INPUTS

The inputs to purchasing come from outside the purchasing department. They are required before action can be initiated by purchasing personnel. The most important inputs are purchase requisitions and their accompanying product specifications.

PURCHASE REQUISITIONS

A purchase requisition describes the needed item(s) and is the legal basis for action. This multicopy form is signed by the requisitioner, other authorized signatures often being required to avoid irresponsible expenditures. The originator of a purchase may be in any operating department or functional area. Most organizations use a standard requisition form, but the format varies considerably with the communication pattern. The three most common forms are: (1) standard purchase requisition, (2) traveling purchase requisition, and (3) bill of materials. Most organizations use standard purchase requisitions, but for special categories of repeat items, the traveling purchase requisition or the bill of materials may be used.

The *standard purchase requisition* is standard only within a given organization. There is no standard form in common use. Although various formats can be developed, a requisition should provide space for the following:

1. Purchase Requisition Number (identification)
2. Originator
3. Date of request
4. Account to be charged
5. Description and quantity of items
6. Date items are needed
7. Purchase order number

8. Delivery date
9. Shipping instructions
10. Buyer's name

A *traveling purchase requisition* is used to procure recurrently needed materials and standard parts that originate from stores or the inventory control section. It takes the form of a card maintained continuously for each item stocked. Since the information is on a single card which can be reused many times, the entire transaction can be handled without delay and with a minimum of paperwork. When the stock level drops to the reorder point or a replacement order is initiated from stores, the card is sent to purchasing (no new purchase requisition need be made each time). The card contains information on the item, potential sources, usage, order quantities, and so forth from which the purchasing agent can make out his order. To indicate that the item has been requisitioned, a colored signal slip is attached to the inventory record card by stockroom personnel. When the purchase order is placed, the card is returned to the stockroom for reinsertion into the stock files until another order is signaled. Upon receipt of the order, the colored signal clip is removed and the cycle can start over again. Automated systems may function with different procedures, but the end result is the same.

A *bill of materials* is a list of all items incorporated into a finished product that the organization produces. The bill of materials is prepared at the time engineering drawings are made, and it is usually an integral part of the engineering drawings. The bill of materials and the upcoming production schedule are sent to purchasing, which ascertains the quantities of all the needed production materials. The bill of materials indicates how much of each material is needed to produce a single finished product. By multiplying the production schedule quantity by the bill of materials, the size of the purchase order for each item is obtained. This procedure eliminates the necessity of typing numerous purchase requisitions for production items. The bill of materials procedure is primarily applicable to the purchase of standard production items.

PRODUCT SPECIFICATIONS

Specifications are a detailed description of the characteristics and features of an item. Product specifications perform three main purposes:

1. Further describe items on the purchase requisition
2. Let the supplier know exactly what the buyer wants
3. Permit verification of items upon order receipt

There are many different types of specifications used to describe and grade products. Some common types are blueprints, market grades, commercial standards, material specifications, performance specifications, and so forth.

A *blueprint* or engineering drawing can accompany a purchase requisition. It is most appropriate where close tolerances or a high degree of mechanical perfection is required.

Market grades are a common method of specifying the quality of commodities such as wheat, cotton, tobacco, lumber, and meats. Trade associations, commodity exchanges, and governmental agencies establish and regulate market grades.

Commercial standards have been developed for widely used items above the commodity level. All nuts, bolts, pipes, motors, and electrical items are made to standard specifications as dictated by governments, trade associations, or engineering societies. Without commercial standards, mass production systems would be virtually impossible.

Material specifications usually outline the physical or chemical properties desired in an item. Items such as metals (aluminum, steel, copper), drugs, oils, and paints are examples of products with material specifications.

Performance specifications do not describe an item physically or chemically, but in terms of what the item is to do (how it is to function). The supplier is told the performance that is required and not its content or how it should be manufactured. Performance specifications are based on the principle that the product should pass tests which indicate its performance in service. They are common for complex systems where function and reliability are paramount, as in military, space, and other sophisticated equipment.

Product specifications may emanate from (1) individual standards developed by the buyer, (2) standards established by private agencies (either other users, suppliers, or professional societies), and (3) government standards. Individual standards can be arduous and expensive to establish. Standard specifications for many items have been developed by nongovernmental private agencies such as the American Standards Association, American Society of Mechanical Engineers, American Society for Testing Materials, American Institute of Electrical Engineers, and the Underwriters Laboratories. Governmental agencies such as the National Bureau of Standards, the General Services Administration, and the Defense Department also develop standards.

Many products cannot be adequately described by a single type of specification. In such cases, a combination of specifications may be used. If a nonstandard product is desired, engineering must compose in detail its own particular specification. Of course, the preparation of specifications for small-lot purchases can be economically prohibitive. Buying by brand or trade names can be very economical for low-cost purchases. It indicates a reliance upon the integrity and reputation of the supplier for consistent quality.

RESTRAINTS

Restraints limit the alternatives available to a purchasing manager in making his decisions. These limiting factors narrow the decision space of acceptable solutions. Organizational restraints can be many and varied, and are not the same from organization to organization. Organizations are restrained by legal considerations (statute and common law), management policies, resource limitations (money, machines, manpower), cultural influences (holidays, operating hours, operating days), market conditions, and so forth.

LEGALITIES

Although a legalistic approach to purchasing is in most cases unnecessary, the purchase contract is a legal document and the organization must be protected from legal problems. All purchasing agents must deal with the Uniform Commercial Code, which has been adopted by all but one of the states. It determines rights and obligations on the basis of fairness and reasonableness according to accepted business practice. However, there are variations in interpretations of laws by various states. When legal problems arise, the purchasing agent must understand basic legal concepts well enough to detect potential problems before they arise.

The Uniform Commercial Code covers most of the transactions involving the purchase and sale of goods and services. Federal and state laws also control purchasing activities to varying degrees. Antitrust legislation forbids any business practice which hinders competition or restrains trade. A buyer should possess an understanding of the basic principles of commercial law.

MANAGEMENT POLICIES

Management policies influence the effectiveness of the purchasing department. The organizational structure within which procurement activities take place can limit its efficiency. However, there is no one best form of organization. Structure is usually shaped by tradition and the operating needs stemming from the nature of the organization. Management may choose between centralized or decentralized methods. Centralized purchasing has economic advantages for multiplant organizations, since greater buyer specialization and input standardization can occur. Centralization tends to be slow, rigid, and rule-bound, and is very costly for low-value purchases. To overcome these shortcomings, mixtures of centralized and decentralized techniques are adopted.

Centralization is worth while when an organization uses generally related products in several locations. The advantages of centralization are lessened when a multiplant organization has broad unrelated items and its plants are widely scattered. Advantages of centralized purchases include:

1. The development of specialized purchasing skills
2. Quantity and cash discounts resulting from the consolidation of order quantities
3. Better control over inventory investment
4. Less overlapping and duplications of purchasing effort
5. Uniform quality and standardization of materials

RESOURCE LIMITATIONS

Resource limitations can seriously alter purchasing activities. The most apparent resource limitation involves finances. Purchasing must operate with the working capital and cash flow positions developed by the finance department. The right time to buy based on price is not always the right time to buy from the standpoint of the organizational treasury. If purchasing places orders to take advantage of unusually low prices but neglects the financial situation, the organization can find itself paying for the purchases with funds needed for other purposes. Purchasing must strive for overall organizational goals, and this means that it must sometimes subvert its own optimum subgoals. Other resource shortages such as available manpower, storage space, and handling equipment can also place limitations on the purchasing department.

CULTURAL INFLUENCES

Cultural influences comprise the time-honored methods and procedures by which organizations conduct their business. Usually these influences are not even thought about, since they are ingrained in a society. When interfacing with organizations in foreign countries, the cultural differences become very apparent. Typical differences relate to attitudes toward work, hours of operation, holidays observed, methods of payment for services, and approaches to contract settlement.

MARKET CONDITIONS

Market conditions are short term situations that are influenced strongly by supply and demand as well as the state of the national economy. For example, during periods of shortage of strategic items, reliable supply may be more important than price. The purchasing agent must function in a changing environment and be able to change his strategies as prevailing market conditions dictate. What was sound judgment in a previous period may become irresponsible, or vice versa. Purchasing is frequently influenced by situational dynamics.

DEMAND FACTORS

The type of purchase procedure adopted depends upon the type of demand that exists for the product. Quite obviously, the procedure for high volume, continuously used products will be different from that for one time, single purchases. Products can be grouped into four basic categories based on demand—items used continuously, large single orders, small-value purchases, and normal purchases (items not falling into any of the first three categories). Different categories will receive substantially different treatment by the purchasing agent.

ITEMS USED CONTINUOUSLY

Items that are used continuously for production and for which there is a fairly predictable demand can be handled under a blanket purchase order. Blanket purchase orders, also referred to as open-end purchase orders, permit the requisition to go directly to the supplier without being processed by the purchasing department. Individual purchase orders need not be written for each order. Purchasing negotiates a contract for a fixed period of time (perhaps a year) with delivery dates, quantities, and prices open. If the price is not specified, it is the price in effect when the quantity is purchased. Notification of delivery dates and desired size of shipments is sent to the supplier by the production control department. The purchasing agent is not involved in placing individual orders, but he does negotiate the basic contract.

With blanket purchase orders, discounts are usually obtained from the supplier, based on the total annual purchases. The size of such a discount can be substantial. The use of such orders also makes purchasing during the year a routine matter that can be delegated to less technical personnel. This conserves the time of the purchasing agent and his staff for more important duties.

LARGE SINGLE ORDERS

Large single orders usually apply to the purchase of special machinery or other unique types of capital goods (computers, vehicles, new buildings, military hardware, spacecraft). Many months of planning and evaluation are involved in the effort. Suppliers usually are requested to submit bids for the special order which include the cost of any design work. These types of purchases are negotiated on a one-time basis.

SMALL-VALUE PURCHASES

At the opposite end of the spectrum from the large single orders are the small-value purchases, that is, purchases of low-cost items that are used infrequently. It is not uncommon for the process cost of such a purchase order to exceed the cost of the item. To reduce the cost of these purchases, petty cash accounts or open-end orders with suppliers are established. Open-end orders are authorizations for functional departments to purchase infrequently used, low-cost items directly from a supplier. Notice that purchasing does not do the actual buying, but only establishes the condition and monitors the system.

NORMAL PURCHASES

Purchases that do not fit into any of the above categories are termed normal purchases and are handled by the normal purchasing routine, that is, the purchasing cycle previously delineated. The purchasing agent does all the buying, and he coordinates the total activity from purchase requisition to delivery of goods.

PURCHASING DECISIONS

Taking into account the purchasing inputs from other functional areas, the organizational restraints from the environment, and the demand factors, the purchasing manager must make a host of decisions. These decisions will functionally, operationally, or financially have an impact on every department in the organization. The decisions will ultimately result in the establishment of purchasing policies and procedures for the future. These decisions are transfer functions that take data and information and transfer them into actions necessary to acquire goods and services.

PURCHASING OUTPUTS

From purchase requisitions, the purchasing department will generate purchase orders. Purchase order forms vary as to their format and routing through the organization. The purchase order is essentially a legal document. It should contain at least the following:

1. Purchase order number (identification)
2. Date of issue
3. Name and address of supplier receiving the order
4. Quantity and description of item(s)
5. Required delivery date
6. Shipping instructions
7. Price and terms of payment
8. Conditions governing the order

Outputs of the purchasing function do not just select the supplier and award the contract. They establish policies, data, and procedures for future purchases made by the department. Each contract award provides additional information to a data bank for improving future purchasing activities. The data bank (purchasing records) has many useful purposes, such as:

1. A list of supply sources for future purchases
2. An appraisal of supplier performances
3. A source of cost and price data
4. A data base for make-buy-lease decisions
5. An evaluation of purchasing agent effectiveness

SUPPLY SOURCES

There are two primary sources of supply for an item: internal (the organization itself) and external (outside suppliers). The make or buy decision is one of internal versus external supply. In one case (make), the organization supplies itself, and in the other (buy), the source is another organization. The make or buy decision can involve numerous factors, but a major factor must be an incremental cost analysis.

The make or buy decision is multidimensional, and most organizations are faced with it continually. Most organizations do not have a consciously expressed policy with reference to this issue, but prefer to decide each separate incident on its own merit. Pursued as a policy, the "make" decision leads to largely independent and self-sustaining industrial entities that are vertically integrated. Being one's own supplier presents an opportunity for diversification. The "buy" decision leads to largely dependent industrial entities that are horizontally integrated.

Information on external sources of supply can be obtained from numerous references. Industrial advertisements of suppliers appear in many periodicals. Supplier catalogs that are quite comprehensive in product listings are often available upon request. Supplier salesmen and trade journals provide information on new products and processes. Trade directories or trade registers, such as *Thomas' Register of American Manufacturers*, give listings of suppliers for different product classifications. The yellow pages of telephone directories list local suppliers. Records of an organizations's past purchases indicate supply sources and their capabilities.

International trade widens supply horizons to foreign sources. Industrial buyers tend to seek domestic sources of supply when possible, but licensing agreements, joint ventures, acquisitions, and mergers have led many organizations into world-wide operations. Competitive pressures also force organizations to consider new and lower cost sources of supply.

Suppliers are the "outside shop" managed by the purchasing department. Their products are brought into the organization as materials and are its livelihood. Few organizations can operate without them. If materials are not properly available, costs escalate and profits cascade.

Though all suppliers and orders are important, it is wise to classify suppliers into the traditional ABC categories based on the dollar volume of orders and relative importance of each supplier. Usually 10 to 20% of your suppliers represents 80% of your purchases. It pays to establish special communication with the top 20% of your suppliers.

SUPPLIER SELECTION

When selecting a supplier, the buyer is trying to find an organization that will meet his needs in quality, quantity, and timing at the lowest cost. The purchasing agent must determine who the potential suppliers are for a given item or family of items. Compiling a list of organizations that can make the needed item is only a starting point. The relative proficiency of each potential supplier must be assessed. Only sources which meet satisfactory performance standards are acceptable. Purchasing departments should compile a list of acceptable suppliers for each class of item procured.

When a purchase requisition is received, the purchasing agent can choose a few likely candidates from the approved supplier list. After contacting them, the final selection can be based on comparative quotations of price and delivery. The development of an approved supplier list is a cumulative process. With each purchasing transaction, additional data are developed for inclusion in the supplier's record.

The search for new suppliers to add to the approved list is a continual process. Once a source is added, continual monitoring and evaluation of performance are necessary. The supplier's card in the approved list should indicate his performance in such areas as price, quality, service, and delivery. Since late delivery or poor quality can have serious repercussions on operations, price is only one of the relevant variables in selecting a supplier. Other relevant variables are the supplier's management capability, technical (engineering) ability, production capacity, depth of service, and financial stability. Information can be obtained from personal visits, financial reports, credit reports, and historical performance.

Frequently, foreign supply can result in substantial cost savings. However, there can be problems with communication, language, long lead time, cultural background, and systems of measurement. Small organizations can use the services of importers, trading companies, or agents representing foreign manufacturers to ameliorate foreign entanglements.

Supplier selection is a major purchasing responsibility. The shortages of many basic raw materials in recent years have had serious effects on organizations ignoring the development of good vendor relations. Good sources of supply should be cherished and protected.

Price Determination

Depending on the item, the market may vary from almost pure competition to oligopoly to monopoly. Obviously, price will vary accordingly. Suppliers tend to set their prices on either a cost or a market basis. With the cost approach, a supplier sets his price by covering his costs plus a certain margin for profit. With the market approach, the price is set by the marketplace and may not be directly related to cost. A fair price should be paid to suppliers. A fair price is the lowest price that ensures a continuous supply of the proper quantity and quality. A continuous supply is not possible in the long run unless a supplier is making a reasonable profit.

A basic objective of purchasing is to obtain low prices. Published price lists, competitive bidding, and negotiation are the typical approaches to price determination. For many industrial products, prices are predetermined and not questioned. This is particularly true for low value items that are purchased infrequently in small quantities. Suppliers provide published *price lists* to prospective customers. The published list prices are asking prices, and they may or may not be the actual selling prices.

With *competitive bidding*, requests for bids are sent to several vendors. A request for a bid asks the seller to quote a price at which he will perform in accordance with the terms and conditions of the order or contract should he be the successful bidder. Usually, the lowest bidder receives the order. Normal industrial practice requires at least three competitive quotes wherever possible. Obviously, the number will vary. Generally, competitive bidding is most applicable to standardized products and services that are widely used and produced to stock. Bids are normally secured when the size of an order exceeds some minimum dollar amount. Governmental purchases are commonly on a bid basis, with the award made to the lowest responsible bidder. Some of the reasons why the lowest bidder may not get the order are as follows:

1. The low bidder may be unresponsive to purchase requirements.
2. The higher bid may provide more after-the-sale service.
3. The closest geographical supplier may receive preferential treatment (lead time may be critical or transportation costs lower).
4. Reciprocity may be a factor.
5. Local suppliers are preferred for community goodwill.

In competitive bidding, the mode of purchase results in the selection of the vendor and price determination. *Negotiation* is another important approach to price determination. When time is too short, the number of bidders is small, the dollar value of the order is high, willingness to compete is lacking, or the specifications are vague, the buyer is driven to negotiate. The purchasing agent begins by analyzing cost, profit, and price and then negotiating with the source for a fair price. In the short run, nothing can be done to avoid paying a sole source's price, but in the long run, alternative sources can usually be developed. The mere fact that a buyer is searching for another source often makes the sole source willing to negotiate a better price.

There are a number of erroneous beliefs associated with negotiation. Among these, the most common are:

1. Negotiation is a win-lose confrontation game.

2. The idea is to overcome the other party.

3. Each negotiation is an independent, isolated transaction.

There are three phases to a negotiation. In the initial phase, issues are presented. The factors where agreement exists are defined, and those that require further negotiation are clarified. The second phase involves discussions or arguments and the movement by the parties toward some area of compromise. During the final phase, agreement is reached. Successful negotiations in which everybody wins are to a great degree dependent on advance planning and analysis. During the prenegotiation stage, the following questions must be addressed:

1. What do we hope to achieve?

2. What does the other party require?

3. What are we prepared to concede?

A thorough understanding of the other party's position as well as its strengths and weaknesses can improve a negotiator's position. The other party should always be allowed to "save face" or to have an "avenue of retreat" rather than being forced into a take-it-or-leave-it situation. Small concessions can be presented when the other party must concede a great deal. To maximize a position while yielding nothing can seriously jeopardize current as well as future negotiations.

Quality Control

A supplier who has the lowest price but furnishes materials of substandard quality may actually be a high price source. Interruptions of production and customer service caused by the failure of material to meet quality standards can be very expensive. The type of inspection and quality techniques will depend on the circumstances and quality costs. If considerable variations of quality are acceptable, inspection will be less important than otherwise.

When quality is concerned, purchasing becomes an information source. Questions of quality on maintenance items should be decided by the maintenance department, on operating supplies by the production department, and on office supplies by the office manager. Materials for manufacturing are the responsibility of the engineering and production departments. Although purchasing will not make the final quality decision, it can be helpful.

The purpose of inspection is to verify that the supplier is delivering items per contractual requirements. There is little point in developing specifications without provisions to assure compliance. When an organization has any reason whatsoever to question an incoming shipment, inspection is necessary. Frequently, inspection and testing are included in specifications provided to the supplier. By specifying quality procedures, future difficulties with suppliers on acceptable quality can be averted.

Occasionally, inspection may be performed by an organizational representative in the vendor's plant. On-site inspection can save time and money while minimizing operational delays from inferior quality. When inspection is complicated, the services of testing laboratories may be solicited. Commercial testing laboratories usually employ capable staffs and the most modern X-ray, photometric, electrical, chemical, and physical testing equipment.

Procedures should be established for dealing with inferior quality. Should the shipment be returned to the supplier and the contract canceled? Should the buyer rework the item to an acceptable quality and bill the supplier? Should only rejected items be returned for replacement and acceptable items retained? Who absorbs transportation charges for returned items? Prior stipulation of the treatment of substandard quality can do much to maintain an amicable long term relationship with the supplier.

Discounts

An important aspect of price determination involves discounts that are offered or can be secured by the purchasing agent. Buyers should be familiar with these potential price reductions. Trade, quantity, seasonal, and cash discounts are the types most frequently encountered.

Trade discounts are given to a purchaser on the basis of his classification. A product may be discounted in different amounts depending on whether the buyer is a manufacturer, wholesaler, or retailer. Ordinarily, the list price is considerably higher than the actual selling price. A trade discount represents the compensation of the buyer who assumes certain distribution functions for the seller. The discount is granted to protect a certain channel of distribution. This is achieved by making it more economical for certain classes of customers to buy from the distributor than from the manufacturer.

Quantity discounts are given to a buyer for purchasing larger quantities of an item, or purchasing a specified dollar total on any number of different items. The price is lowered as the quantity of dollar expenditure increases. The discount is justified because of the savings resulting from reduced selling, shipping, handling, and accounting cost per unit when larger amounts are purchased. Quantity discounts are offered to obtain marketing and production economies.

Quantity discounts may be based on a single order or on purchases made over a period. Period quantity discounts are granted as an incentive for continued patronage. Although single source procurement can be dangerous, it is unwise to scatter orders over too large a number of sources. Period quantity discounts are offered by suppliers with the aim of becoming a primary source.

Seasonal discounts exist because of the seasonal variation in the demand for some items. Suppliers offer discounts for purchases made in the off season. Consumer products in this category are bathing suits, snow tires, greeting cards, air conditioners, and so forth.

Cash discounts are given by suppliers for prompt and full payment of bills. When such discounts are given, they are offered as a percentage of the net invoice price. Although the terms vary, a typical cash discount policy is 2/10, net 30. This means that the buyer can deduct 2% of the bill if he pays the bill within ten days after the date of invoice. After ten days, the discount is rescinded and full payment is required before thirty days. Although the 2% may not seem like much at a first glance, it should be noted that it is based on a short period of time. If the discount is not taken, the 2% is equivalent to a loss of 36% per year. Cash discounts are commonly granted by suppliers; the actual terms are largely a matter of trade custom and vary considerably among industries.

Local Buying

The geographical location of suppliers can be very important to an organization. Many large organizations tend to buy directly from the manufacturer instead of going through a local middleman. Even with direct purchases, a substantial number of items can be bought from local suppliers. Operating supplies can be readily procured on a local basis. A local source can frequently offer more dependable service than a more distant source.

There are advantages in buying from local sources. Frequently, the local source can render better service because of personal knowledge of the buyer's needs. Freight cost savings can result from small quantity deliveries over a shorter distance. Prompt deliveries are possible because of the short distances involved and the use of truck transportation. Buying locally generates good public relations because the organization contributes to the welfare of its community.

To improve their public image, some organizations adopt a policy of local buying and play an active role in community affairs, particularly in small towns with sparse industrialization and low economic activity. While local buying has definite social merit, it seriously restricts the buyer in obtaining the best purchase. On the other hand, local sources do shorten the lead time for items, which lowers reorder points and safety stock requirements. It is necessary to weigh the effects of local buying in each case.

Reciprocal Buying

Reciprocal buying, or reciprocity, is the practice of giving preference in buying to those suppliers who are customers of the buying organization. When an organization makes a point of buying from its customers, it is practicing reciprocity. The mere fact that two organizations buy from each other does not constitute reciprocity unless each entity's buying is due to the other's buying. It can be argued that if all other factors are equal, it is good business to purchase from suppliers who are also customers because it strengthens both companies. Reciprocity is perfectly legal as long as it does not become an unreasonable restraint of trade. If a large organization uses reciprocity in a coercive manner by forcing its suppliers to purchase its products or be dropped as vendors, it can be violating the antitrust laws. In the absence of threats or other types of coercion, the use of reciprocity is not regarded as illegal.

On a national level, reciprocity is a vicious, inefficient practice. When firms can sell on some other basis than price, quality, and service, there is bound to be waste. Reciprocal buying practices are more pronounced in producer goods industries (industries selling to other industries) than in consumer goods industries. In producer goods industries, there are more opportunities for large-scale buying and selling.

Many purchasing agents are opposed to reciprocal buying because of the inflexibility of such agreements. It can be argued that freedom of supplier selection is mandatory if the agent is to purchase materials on the most favorable terms. Top management should carefully weigh the pros and cons of all reciprocal buying agreements before entering into them. In the final analysis, the specifics of the case will determine the advisability of such agreements.

Shipping Terms

The cost of materials is not determined solely by the unit price of the material and the quantity. Someone, usually the buyer, must pay for transporting the material to the buyer's location. Careless purchasing practice with respect to delivery terms is a constant source of legal and practical difficulties. It costs money to load, transport, unload, and insure goods. If goods are lost or damaged in transit, someone must bear the loss. Furthermore, if goods arrive before or after the buyer needs them, storage costs or costly delays will result. If possible, purchase orders should specify the shipping terms and routing desired in transporting the material. The choice between equal suppliers is often determined by delivery costs.

The shipping terms in a contract determine who will specify the carrier and the routing. A contract that does not include shipping terms requires the buyer to arrange and bear all the delivery costs. The shipping terms establish the following:

1. When the buyer takes legal title to the goods
2. Who will pay the freight charges
3. Who will prosecute loss and damage claims against carriers

An authorization or requirement for the supplier to ship goods does not mean he must pay the cost of shipment or that he is responsible for shipment loss or damage. There are numerous terms of shipment, but the most common are:

1. F.O.B. buyer's plant
2. F.O.B. seller's plant
3. F.O.B. seller's plant—freight allowed
4. C.I.F. contracts
5. F.A.S.

The F.O.B. (free on board) indicates who pays freight and handling charges as well as when title is passed on the goods. With F.O.B. buyer's plant, the buyer takes title to the goods when they are delivered to the loading dock at his plant; the supplier pays all transportation charges and processes all claims against the carrier for damage or loss of goods. With F.O.B. seller's plant, the buyer takes title when the supplier loads the goods onto a common carrier, and he pays all transportation charges as well as negotiating all freight damage claims with the carrier. With F.O.B. seller's plant—freight allowed, the legal liability is the same as for F.O.B. seller's plant, but the supplier reimburses the buyer for freight charges.

The C.I.F. (cost-insurance-freight) contracts and F.A.S. (free alongside ship) are commonly used in international trade. The C.I.F. contract price includes cost of the material, insurance, and freight. An export shipment from Paris might be listed as C.I.F. New York. In this case, the foreign supplier is responsible for the goods and all charges until the goods arrive at the New York destination. The buyer is responsible for seeing that the goods are unloaded and delivered to their final destination in the United States. With F.A.S. terms, the buyer designates port, berth, and vessel. The supplier is responsible for getting the goods to the ship and the buyer takes title as well as all responsibility thereafter.

TIMING OF PURCHASES

The time at which some purchases are made determines the price paid and influences the total purchasing operation. In reference to the timing of purchases, a buyer is primarily interested in an adequate supply of material at the best price consistent with quality requirements. Timing is not a critical concern when the purchases are made in a stable price market; it is critical when prices are unstable. Although the purchasing agent usually cannot influence the market, he can control to some extent the price he pays.

Purchasing agents can purchase according to current requirements or purchase according to market conditions. If the first policy is adopted, the purchasing schedule adheres to the volume of current needs and disregards the action of the market in which the purchase is made. With the second policy, in addition to current needs, purchasing timing decisions are based on market conditions. Organizations that time their purchases in response to market conditions may adopt any of four purchasing approaches:

1. Hand-to-mouth buying
2. Averaging down
3. Forward buying
4. Speculative buying

The *hand-to-mouth* buying policy procures items only to meet immediate short-term requirements, and purchases not immediately needed are deferred. The quantities obtained are much smaller than those normally considered economical. Hand-to-mouth buying is appropriate when prices are expected to drop, engineering design changes may render materials obsolete, or financial liquidity dictates the release of cash for more pressing organizational needs. The disadvantages of this policy include the excessive ordering costs for numerous small purchases, inability to obtain quantity discounts, higher freight costs for small shipments, excessive stockout costs, and the risk of prices rising instead of falling. Hand-to-mouth buying is not a recommended policy for normal operations.

With hand-to-mouth buying the orders are small and must be placed frequently. Unit prices on small orders tend to be higher than on large orders. Frequently, small order shipments result in higher transportation charges. Handling costs increase because of the additional time spent in packing and unpacking in the shipping and receiving departments. Lead times can lengthen with small orders if suppliers give lower priority to them. Of course, any unanticipated delays with hand-to-mouth buying can stop scheduled organizational activities and increase costs. These are inherent risks with hand-to-mouth buying.

Averaging down on the market means procuring goods at a moment when the market dips sharply in the course of a gradual price change. Prices rarely rise or decline evenly, but tend to follow a saw-tooth pattern of ups and downs. The buyer waits until the price is below the market average for the period before placing his order. For example, assume a buyer expects the price of an item to average $.50 a pound during a time period. If the price is $.50 or higher, he will buy only the absolute minimum of items required. If the price is below $.50, he purchases in much larger quantities. This approach encourages stock accumulation when prices are low and discourages them when they are high.

Forward buying is the procurement of materials in economical quantities exceeding current requirements, but not beyond actual foreseeable requirements. The approach is often used when prices are relatively stable over time. It can also be used when prices are about to increase and bulk buying offers substantial savings. Forward buying is adopted to obtain a favorable price, to get quantity discounts, to purchase in economical transportation units, to secure items when they are available, and to protect against prospective shortages. The forward buyer assumes the risk of a dip in price, and he increases inventory levels, thus tying up working capital.

With *speculative buying*, items are purchased in excess of foreseeable requirements in order to make a profit from rising prices. Opportunities for purchases of this kind occur just before a price increase or when the market price drops temporarily and the buyer has sufficient working capital to finance the speculation. Here the objective is not only to have the needed items available, but also to earn profits from buying low and selling high. Speculative buying seeks profit by purchasing in anticipation of price rises; the other three approaches are more defensive and seek to prevent or minimize losses due to unfavorable price movements.

Hand-to-mouth buying, averaging down, forward buying, and speculative buying require a choice in the timing of purchases. There are inherent risks in all of the approaches, and the purchasing agent cannot be on the "right" side of the market at all times. A buyer may not choose to attempt to capitalize on the fluctuations of an unstable market. To negate the significance of the timing of purchases on commodities, he can engage in *hedging* in futures markets. Hedging takes away the risk of profit or loss on inventories and permits the organization to perform its specialty without regard to market fluctuations.

Hedging means entering simultaneously into two transactions of a like amount—a *cash* transaction and a *futures* transaction. The cash transaction involves the current exchange of the buyer's cash for the physical commodity; the futures transaction involves the buyer's sale of a futures contract on the item with promised delivery at a specified date in the future. With the passage of time, the cash price and the futures price should fluctuate together, approximately paralleling one another. If prices go up, the buyer realizes an inventory profit on the commodity he bought, but since prices move together, he will suffer a loss of like amount on the futures contract. If prices go down, the buyer will lose on his cash purchase, but he will gain a like amount on the futures contract. A hedger simply takes one position (purchase or sale) in the cash market and the opposite position (purchase or sale) in the futures market. Hedging provides reasonable assurance that gains or losses in one market will be offset by losses or gains in the other market. It can be viewed as a form of insurance against unforeseen major movements in price.

The significance of purchase timing depends upon the type of market in which the purchase is made. Timing is usually more critical in less stable markets. In stable markets, purchasing according to current requirements is prevalent. In less stable markets, purchasing is based upon market conditions. In attempting to reduce market risk in less stable markets, a buyer can hedge his purchase if a futures market exists for the item. This stabilizing influence is helpful to many organizations.

CONTRACTS AND LEGAL CONSIDERATIONS

Once a purchase order is accepted by a vendor, it constitutes a contract for delivery of the items in accordance with the terms of the purchase agreement. This legal document contains many other terms in addition to quantity, quality, delivery, and price. Both federal and state laws influence purchase contracts. Most organizations have printed purchase order forms that comply with the laws under which they operate. To promote fair trade, free from restraint and undue favoritism, statutes such as the Sherman Act, Clayton Act, and Robinson-Patman Act must be known and heeded by purchasing agents.

Purchasing enters into contracts and binding agreements on a daily basis. These written and oral actions commit the organization to approximately half of each year's expenditures. The results can be costly unless the organization is legally protected in its transactions. Contracts and legal documents should be drafted by lawyers, and routine commitments approved by legal services.

Few purchasing managers become involved in legal actions, since contractual disputes can normally be resolved without litigation. However, a basic knowledge of relevant legal principles is essential. Without an understanding of the legal implications of the job, legal entanglements become much more likely. Litigation is very expensive, and most organizations utilize it only as a last resort. The purchasing agent should use knowledge of the basic principles of law in such a way as to avoid litigation.

The functions of procurement involve many legal facets which can only be explained and interpreted by a lawyer. The buyer must know enough about the law to know when to consult an attorney. Whenever potential legal problems arise, legal counsel should be consulted. Lawyers should draft all clauses used for routine purchase orders and approve all non-routine agreements. The written purchase contract should take precedence over the oral agreement.

While lawsuits involving buyers and sellers are common in commercial transactions, they are surprisingly rare in industrial purchasing. In most cases, industrial buyers and sellers can resolve their disputes amicably through negotiation. A purchasing agent can minimize litigation by investigating new suppliers' ability to perform their responsibilities and their record of performance with other concerns. The terms and conditions of each purchase contract must be precisely defined to prevent misunderstandings and to avoid potential liabilities. Each purchase contract should be satisfactorily drawn and legally binding on the supplier.

Despite numerous modifications and subcategories, there are just two basic types of purchase contracts: *fixed-price* contracts and *cost-type* contracts. In selecting the best contract to use, the buyer must consider all available contract types and the factors influencing the use of each. The fixed-price contract is preferred by buyers, but rapid change can render it costly and wasteful on some purchases.

When a fair and reasonable price can be established by competition or cost analysis, the fixed-price contract should be used. The financial risks are borne almost entirely by the supplier, and he has the maximum incentive to produce efficiently. Fixed-price contracts do not always have a firm fixed price. They can include an escalation clause for either an upward or a downward change in price as a result of changes in material and labor costs. They can also include a redetermination clause when the amounts of labor and material are not known precisely. Other fixed-price contracts may have a ceiling price (maximum price) with a variable profit formula whereby every dollar by which the vendor reduces his cost will be shared equally between him and the buyer.

Sometimes a purchase contract is for something that is so novel that neither the buyer or seller knows what the cost should be. Cost-type contracts are used in such cases. The buyer assumes most of the financial risk with this type of contract, which is also known as a cost-plus contract. The supplier is guaranteed all his costs up to a predetermined figure as well as a fee in addition to his costs. The fee may be a percentage of cost, a fixed amount, or an incentive. With a percentage of cost fee, the supplier has the least incentive to control costs. With a fixed amount, the supplier receives his defined and itemized costs plus a definite sum of money (fixed fee). With an incentive clause, cost reductions below target costs are shared by the buyer and seller.

Because of the variety of contracts, the purchasing agent must exercise care in selecting one. Business practices in specific industries provide clues as to the best contract instrument. The nature of the goods or services to be procured can often point up advantages of one contract type over another. The type of contract adopted for a purchase can substantially affect pricing. Although it is not always possible, a firm fixed-price contract should be used when conditions permit.

PURCHASE RECORDS

Purchase records provide a history of what has been done in the past, what costs were involved, and who the major suppliers were, as well as the costs, discounts, quality levels, and delivery on specific items. Since purchasing is a repetitive process, accurate records are a necessity for efficient operations. Past experiences in the form of records can provide a wealth of information upon which to base future decisions. A good record system will increase operating costs, but usually by less than the savings due to improved buying efficiency. The special needs of each purchasing department will dictate the structure of its records system. Most purchasing departments maintain the following basic records:

1. Purchase order log
2. Open order file
3. Closed order file
4. Vendor record
5. Commodity record
6. Contract file

The *purchase order* log contains a numerical record of all purchase orders issued. The record is usually not elaborate, but it should contain the purchase order number, supplier's name, description of the purchase, and total value of the order. The log is a convenient record from which to summarize administrative data such as the numbers of small orders, rush orders, purchases from various suppliers, total orders issued, and so forth.

The *open order file* contains the status of all outstanding orders. Each open folder contains the purchase requisition, the purchase order, and any contracts, follow-up data, and correspondence pertaining to the order. The *closed order file* contains a historical record of all completed purchases. It is a useful reference when data are needed to guide future purchases.

The *vendor record* provides quick access to information about suppliers. A separate file is maintained for each supplier. In it are recorded the supplier's name, address, telephone numbers, and other specific data. Many organizations summarize the vendor's delivery and quality performance.

A *commodity record* is maintained on each major material or service that is purchased repetitively. It can be combined into a single file with perpetual inventory records (traveling purchase requisitions). A separate card is kept for each item, showing orders placed, receipts, and disbursements. The part name, part number, specification, vendor, order quantity, last price, and so forth may also be included.

A *contract file* contains the purchase records of items under a term contract. This file is important if the contract is an open one against which orders may be placed. The contract file contains special items that are not normally procured by a regular purchase order.

Purchasing work or activities can be analyzed, simplified, and improved by work simplification techniques. Flow charts can be used to analyze purchasing procedures and documentation flow. Improvement of forms and reduction in the number used will increase efficiency while reducing the cost of the purchasing function. Current trends are toward the mechanization of purchasing records and transactions via computerization.

SURPLUS DISPOSAL

The disposal of surplus materials and equipment is usually assigned to the purchasing department because of its knowledge of markets. Surplus can result from overprocurement, wasteful production processes, and inefficiencies in general. However, surpluses do not necessarily indicate inefficiency; all organizations have surplus decisions to make. It is not uncommon for the sale of surplus materials to make a significant contribution to income. Surplus materials may come from many sources, such as:

1. Scrap
2. Waste
3. Obsolescences
4. Damage or deterioration
5. Forward or speculative buying

Scrap is the residue of process materials left after efficient production operations have been completed (there are few production processes that utilize 100% of materials). *Waste* is the result of inefficient, careless production; it consists of items rejected because of poor quality. *Obsolescences* result in good material that is no longer needed because of design or model changes. *Damaged* or deteriorated items occur because of limited shelf life or improper handling. Surplus materials also result from overexuberant purchasing practices (forward and speculative buying) that prove to be in error.

Surplus materials and equipment should be sold when there is no longer any need for them. Periodic checks can be made to determine inactivity for each item carried in inventory. Usually, an arbitrary rule on surplus material is adopted, such as that any material not active for a year or two is automatically subject to disposal. With computerized inventory control, it is a simple matter to determine inactive items. These items are investigated, and anything that is surplus is sold for the best possible price. Without computerized inventory control, the process is more awkward and slow, but still very necessary.

Regardless of how efficiently an organization is managed, surplus materials will accumulate, and they must be disposed of periodically. The holding costs of inactive materials can be excessive. Therefore all surplus items should be sold at their best price or discarded. Some of the possible disposal routes are as follows:

1. Circulation within the organization
2. Return to supplier
3. Direct sale to another firm
4. Sale to dealer or broker
5. Sale to employees
6. Discard

Not only does the salvage of such items result in additional income; it prevents pollution and serves to conserve raw material resources and energy. Often the excess or scrap items of one organization are valuable operating items to another.

VALUE ANALYSIS

Value analysis is the organized, systematic study of the function of a material, part, component, or system to identify areas of unnecessary cost that can be eliminated without impairing the usefulness of the item. Value analysis is concerned with function, cost, and value; it attempts to identify savings that can be made in any way. It identifies unnecessary costs that do not add value, and it develops acceptable performance at a lower cost.

Value analysis has tremendous income potential. If an organization's after tax income is 10% of sales, then obviously every $100 saved is equivalent to $1000 sold. It can be far easier to save $100 than to sell $1000 more. Thus, slight changes in material costs can exert a great influence (leverage) on an organization's income.

Value analysis measures the functional usefulness of items, processes, or procedures so the greatest value is obtained for the money spent. Better value is obtained by improving the function without increasing the cost, or by reducing the cost without impairing the function. The emphasis is not only on cost (paying the least for what you get), but on value (getting the most for what you pay). A better way of doing things is the ultimate aim. A typical value analysis of an item would ask a series of questions: What is it? What is its function? What does it cost? What is it worth? What else could perform the function? Can it be simplified? Is it necessary? The questioning usually uncovers areas for improvement through substitution, elimination, standardization, combination, or simplification.

Value analysis is a systematic study which can be applied to any item. The value analyst seeks to improve performance by quality-price analysis, market-supplier analysis, and design-process analysis. *Quality-price analysis* seeks the minimum price for an item which meets the minimum quality standards. Extra quality in an item beyond performance requirements usually involves an extra cost, so a quality reduction may result in cost savings. *Market-supplier analysis* focuses on finding the lowest cost supplier consistent with quality and service requirements. *Design-process analysis* determines if an item is adequately designed for the function it performs, or if the item lends itself to more economical manufacture by standard production techniques.

The design-process analysis and quality-price analysis entail a methodical step-by-step study of all facets of the design of a given item in relation to its function. The use of standardized parts, methods, and procedures is a goal. The value analyst determines which functions are necessary and how they might be fulfilled if different materials, tools, supplies, and processes were used. Competitive or substitute products are examined to see how they perform the same or similar functions.

Value analysis is used to detect items whose prices appear excessive or whose costs are disproportionate to the function served. A design-process analysis may result in a new design, substitute materials, or improved production techniques. A market-supplier analysis may result in a substitute product or a revised product design. All of the analyses will be used in the make or buy decision. Although purchasing will probably not make the final decision by itself, it does have a role in the decision and will accumulate the facts for it.

Value analysis can be very effective in dealing with shortages of materials. The emphasis is placed on the availability of alternatives or substitutes. The following checklist can be helpful when dealing with shortages:

1. Have suppliers been consulted for alternatives or modifications?
2. Have unusual forms of material (common and available) been considered?
3. Have technological developments rendered parts or processes unnecessary?
4. Is every item absolutely necessary?
5. Can a different item do the job?
6. Are wider tolerance ranges feasible?
7. Can items or subassemblies be combined?
8. Can a single item provide multiple functions?
9. Can processes be combined?
10. Is the item overdesigned?
11. Are specifications and standards too tight?

Value analysis concentrates on cost reduction associated with product and materials redesign, revision of specifications, more effective purchase or conversion of materials, make-or-buy reanalysis, and related material cost savings activities. It pertains primarily to existing products, but it can be expanded to new or proposed products. It searches for alternative products, procedures, sources, techniques, and processes for improving performance.

Value analysis may reside in purchasing or production. In smaller organizations it can be the responsibility of a committee or team with representatives from the various organizational areas. Both large and small institutions are adopting it as a method for improving performance.

CONCLUSION

The role of purchasing and procurement in modern organizations has increased substantially in the last few decades. Material costs are frequently the largest proportion of a product's total cost. Inflation, shortages, and unstable markets make purchasing decisions important for the overall performance of an organization. No longer can purchasing be considered a routine service function where money is spent and not made. Purchasing is a cost-saving or profit-making organizational function.

The typical steps involved in the purchasing process include (1) obtaining information on products and their specifications, (2) finding suitable suppliers, (3) obtaining competitive bids or negotiating with suppliers, (4) analyzing bids and proposals, (5) preparing purchase orders, (6) expediting and following up orders, (7) verifying proper receipt of material and invoice validation, (8) processing claims, and (9) disposing of surplus materials and equipment.

The purchasing department must be staffed by qualified, well-trained personnel. Professional training beyond that obtained on the job is important. The goal should not be to operate the purchasing department at the lowest cost. It should be to attain organizational objectives at the lowest cost. The buying clerk should be replaced by the value-conscious purchasing agent skilled in the latest techniques of materials management.

QUESTIONS

1. Why is it more beneficial to view purchasing in terms of the purchasing function than in terms of the purchasing cycle?
2. What are the three most common forms used to authorize a purchase?
3. Name four common types of product specifications.
4. What are the three main purposes of product specifications?
5. What is the most important resource limitation on purchasing activities? Why?
6. What is usually the major factor involved in the make or buy decision?
7. Name four criteria commonly used for the evaluation of supplier performance.
8. What are the three approaches to price determination?
9. What are the different types of discounts offered by suppliers?
10. What is the purpose of a trade discount?
11. What is reciprocal buying (reciprocity)?
12. Name the three criteria that are established when shipping terms are specified.
13. When is hand-to-mouth buying advantageous?

14. What are the two basic types of purchase contracts? When should each be used.

15. What is value analysis? Name three analysis methods available to the value analyst.

PROBLEMS

1. A manufacturing firm is adding an optional accessory to its product line and is faced with a make or buy decision. The cost accounting section has provided the following data:

Unit Cost Item	Existing Plant Capacity Available	Expanded Plant Capacity
Variable mfg.	$3.40	$3.40
Additional plant & equipment	.00	.60
Additional factory overhead	.00	.10

A local manufacturer will supply the item at a delivered price of $3.80. Should the item be purchased if idle plant capacity is available? Should the item be purchased if the plant must be expanded?

2. An instrument manufacturer has decided to add a carrying case to its list of optional equipment. A local supplier has offered to supply a satisfactory case for $7.20 each. The sales projections and cost accounting data are shown below. If the existing plant capacity for the case is 6,000 units, should the firm make or buy the case?

Sales (Units)	Probability
3,000	.15
5,000	.40
8,000	.30
10,000	.15

Unit Cost Item	Existing Plant Capacity	Expanded Plant Capacity
Variable mfg.	$5.80	$4.80
Additional plant & equipment	.00	1.50
Additional overhead	.20	1.20

3. One method of comparing suppliers is by a weight-point plan. A total of 100 points are allocated among those factors considered important by an organization. The supplier with the largest number of weight points is the most desirable. An organization uses the following weights to compare suppliers: quality 40 points, price 35 points, and service 25 points. Based on the data listed below, rank the three suppliers by the weight-point plan.

SUPPLIER	SHIPMENTS RECEIVED	SHIPMENTS ACCEPTED	UNIT PRICE	FRACTION OF COMMITMENTS FULFILLED
A	500	480	$1.00	.94
B	600	560	.96	.90
C	80	78	1.20	1.00

4. From the information below compare the four suppliers by the weight-point plan. The quality weight is 40, the price weight is 35, and the service weight is 25.

SUPPLIER	SHIPMENTS RECEIVED	SHIPMENTS ACCEPTED	UNIT PRICE	FRACTION OF COMMITMENTS FULFILLED
A	200	192	$.89	.98
B	240	220	.86	.90
C	60	48	.93	.95
D	10	9	.90	1.00

5. What is the equivalent annual interest rate that would be lost if a firm failed to take the cash discount under the following terms?
   a. 1/15, net 30
   b. 2/10, net 60
   c. 3/10, net 60
   d. 2/10, net 40
   e. 1/10, net 30
   f. 1/10, net 40

Case 1: Make or Buy

The Alphabet Valve Company is a small plumbing supply firm which produces several small items for a local market. The firm manufactures some of its sub-assemblies and relies on contractors for others. Final assembly operations take place on the premises of Alphabet. One of the products, a common exterior water valve, is presently under study by the company officials.

The company has an agreement with one of its contractors to produce the handles for the valve under consideration. The handle is milled from stainless steel to the company's specifications and shipped to a supply point at Alphabet. The handle is attached to the valve body. The entire assembly is then given a coat of corrosion-resistant paint and packaged for shipment. The other major components of the valve are made in Alphabet's own casting plant (presently operating at 80% of capacity).

The reason the valve has come under study is a price increase announced by the handle company. The contractor has a new price of $2.25 per handle. Alphabet's president does not believe that the market will support a price increase for the valve, and he wishes to evaluate alternate sources.

The purchasing agent has researched the problem and has located a used milling machine (price $7,000, life 5 years, no salvage value). He estimates that the machine will cost $1,000 per year to operate and that they can produce the same valve handle for $1.50 (variable cost per unit) with a volume of 4,000 valves per year. The purchasing agent has placed the problem before the other officers of the firm and is soliciting their recommendations.

1. What recommendation would you make to the president?
2. If the handle is manufactured in house, should it be the same handle as was purchased?
3. Could value analysis help resolve the issue?

Case 2: Mr. Older versus Mr. Younger

Mr. Thomas, president of Thomas Manufacturing Company, and Mr. McDonnell, the vice president, were discussing how future economic conditions would affect their product, which was vacuum cleaners. They were particularly concerned about inflation, which was causing their costs to increase at an alarming rate. They had increased the prices of their products last year, and felt another price increase would have an adverse affect on sales. They wondered if there was some way to reduce costs in order to maintain the existing price structure.

Mr. McDonnell had attended a meeting the previous night and heard a presentation by the president of a hand tool company on how they were solving the inflation problem. Apparently, they had just hired a purchasing agent with a business degree who was reducing costs by 15%. Mr. McDonnell thought some new ideas might be applicable to Thomas Manufacturing. The present purchasing agent, Mr. Older, had been with the company for 25 years and they had no complaints. Production never was stopped for lack of material. Yet a 15% cost reduction in the present economy was something which could not be ignored. Mr. Thomas suggested that Mr. McDonnell look into this area and come up with a recommendation in 3 weeks.

Mr. McDonnell contacted several business schools in the area. He said he would be interested in hiring a new graduate, majoring in purchasing. One of the requirements for applicants was a paper on how they felt they could improve the company's purchasing function. Several applicants visited the plant and analyzed the purchasing department before they wrote their papers. The most dynamic paper was submitted by Tim Younger. He recommended:

1. Lower the stock reorder levels from 60 days to 45 days for many items, thus reducing inventory.

2. Analyze the product specifications on many parts of a vacuum cleaner with a view toward using plastics instead of metals.

3. Standardize many of the parts of the vacuum cleaners to reduce the number of items kept in stock.

4. Analyze items to see if more products can be purchased by blanket purchase orders, with the ultimate goal of reducing the purchasing staff.

5. Look for new and lower cost sources of supply.

6. Increase the number of requests for bids, in order to get still lower prices.

7. Be more aggressive in negotiations. Make fewer concessions.

8. Make sure all trade, quantity, and cash discounts are taken.

9. Buy from the lowest price source, disregarding local public relations.

10. Stop showing favoritism to customers who also buy from the company. Reciprocity comes second to price.

11. Purchase as current requirements demand, instead of according to market conditions. Too much money is tied up in inventory.

After reading all the papers Mr. McDonnell was debating with himself what he should recommend to Mr. Thomas. Just last week at the department meeting Mr. Older was recommending many of the opposite actions. In particular, he recommended an increase in inventory levels anticipating future rising prices. Mr. Older also stressed the good relations the company had with all their suppliers and how they can be relied upon for good service and a possible extension of credit, if the situation warrants it. Most of their suppliers bought their vacuum cleaners from Thomas Manufacturing. Yet Mr. Younger said the practice of favoring them was wrong and should be eliminated. Mr. McDonnell was hesitant as to what action he should recommend. He had only one day to make his decision.

1. What recommendation would you make if you were Mr. McDonnell? Why?

2. Analyze Mr. Younger's recommendations. Do you agree or disagree with them?

Case 3: Bypassed and Short Circuited

"If things don't change, I'm going to quit." Bob Riley, the purchasing agent for Jersey Electronics, was complaining about his new job to his wife. He was recently hired by Jersey when the previous purchasing agent was promoted to the position of materials manager. Bob had thought long and hard before leaving his former job to join Jersey Electronics. It was the first time that Jersey Electronics had not promoted from within ranks. They had gone outside looking for a candidate with high management potential. Bob Riley was that man as far as Jersey Electronics was concerned. Bob had not been actively seeking a new position, but the offer made by Jersey Electronics was one he felt he could not refuse. The salary and opportunity for advancement were just too good.

The first month of Bob's new job was very routine. He became oriented to the procedures of Jersey's suppliers. He had very little actual work to do. Bob hoped that as he became more familiar with his six buyers, the scope of his work would increase.

As Bob became more familiar with his job he was upset by the fact that his buyers continually bypassed him with problems and decisions. The buyers were going to John Lynch, the previous purchasing agent, for advice. Lynch maintained what he called his open door policy. He always had time for the buyers' problems and seemed to encourage their visits. Bob was never invited in to discuss these problems.

Six months after Bob had been on the job he asked one of his buyers, Jack Faulkner, for his file on pending requisitions. Bob wanted to do some work on source availability for the specialized equipment needed for the Southland contract.

"Mr. Riley, that file was closed two days ago. John told me to place an order with Beta Tektronics for all that specialized Southland equipment."

"Beta Tektronics! Why them? They don't produce top quality equipment," screamed Bob.

"It was John's decision. We went over all the potential suppliers last Monday and Beta was the choice."

1. What actions should be taken by Bob Riley? Should he resign?
2. What steps could have been taken to avoid the situation?
3. To what extent is Bob Riley responsible for the situation?

Chapter 5

Physical Supply

To some degree all organizations rely on the availability of material to satisfy their performance objectives, whether in manufacturing, commerce, or government. Manufacturing operations are dependent on the availability of raw materials or components, commerce needs finished goods to meet consumer demand, and government needs various material resources to satisfy social needs. Material availability is essential to the performance of even the most routine administrative tasks (even correspondence requires access to common office supply items). Management of those requirements is the subject of physical supply.

Physical supply performs two vital organizational tasks. It provides a service to production and/or distribution; and it performs an important custodial and controlling service for the organization as a whole. In the first instance, physical supply organizes and controls the flow of raw materials into production and the flow of finished products into the distribution system. In the second instance, it is responsible for the internal control of a substantial portion of an organization's assets.

The term physical supply should be distinguished from other popular descriptive names such as warehousing, storage, receiving and shipping, order processing, and logistics. Conceptually, physical supply subsumes and integrates these activities. It recognizes the pervasiveness of supply activities and overcomes the restrictions involved in treating individual activities in isolation. The physical supply function is not confined specifically to the stock of raw material, in-process material, or finished goods. It has significance in relation to the entire flow of material.

Physical supply is concerned with the management of material availability through space. The temporal and spatial features of the material flow cycle are emphasized. The flow of material in the physical supply cycle, as depicted in Figure 5.1, serves other functions by making material available

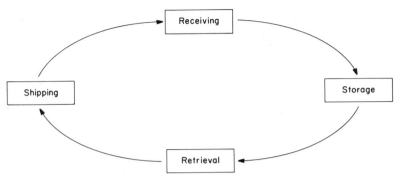

FIGURE 5.1

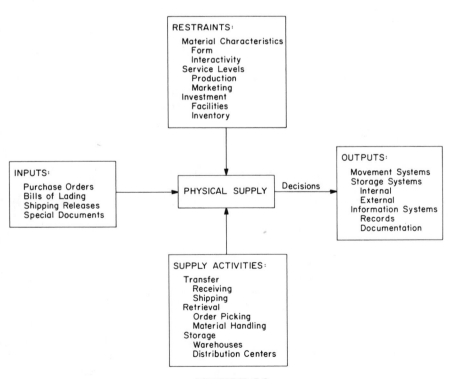

FIGURE 5.2

when and where it is required. Thus, it is a time and place utility producing function which supplies the material to satisfy the needs of other organizational functions.

The physical supply function is conceptually illustrated in Figure 5.2. The parameters of the physical supply function can be defined in terms of inputs, restraints, supply activities, and outputs. Primary *inputs* are purchase orders, shipping orders, bills of lading, and various special purpose documents. An important point to notice is that inputs may enter the material flow cycle on either "side" of production. Material characteristics, service levels, and investment are common *restraints* which modify the decision environment. Of course, the degree to which they do so depends on the individual organization. *Supply activities* which must be accomplished throughout the material flow cycle are transfer, retrieval, and storage. Finally, treatment of the inputs, restraints, and supply activities supports a decision process which generates *outputs*. The major outputs of the function are movement systems, storage systems, and information systems. The remainder of this chapter will further delineate the physical supply function as shown in Figure 5.2.

PHYSICAL SUPPLY INPUTS

Inputs to the physical supply function epitomize the important interrelationships among various organizational functions. Because the realm of physical supply covers the entire material flow cycle, inputs may concern inflow or outflow. Material acquisition necessitates receiving, handling, and storage. Production operations must be supplied with raw materials or components, and finished goods must be handled and stored. Disposition of finished goods for marketing through sale or relocation requires retrieval, additional handling, and shipping. All of these transactions in the physical supply function must be accurately documented to support the inventory control structure.

Thus, inputs are sponsored by or originate from several other organizational functions, such as purchasing, production, transportation (inbound and outbound), materials handling, and sales. Equally important, physical supply acts as an input or restraint to other functions.

While the impetus for physical supply inputs may originate from several sources, the inputs themselves are usually limited to a few transaction types. The most important physical supply inputs are purchase orders, bills of lading, shipping orders, and special purpose documents. A cardinal principle of materials management is that no material is accepted, issued, or moved without an accompanying authorization.

PURCHASE ORDERS

Material requirements of the organization which must be satisfied by acquisition from external sources are reflected in purchase orders. Purchase orders usually originate from purchasing, but they are normally sponsored by requirements in another function such as production. The purchase order stipulates the kind and quantity of material being secured and the terms or conditions of purchase. It authorizes a transaction which initiates and defines the flow of material to the organization.

Prior knowledge of material flow is important to the physical supply function. Receiving activities must be planned to ensure that capabilities exist to accept the incoming flow. Further, storage space must be available, and advance knowledge of the flow is necessary to effect order-receipt accountability.

One facet of prepurchase planning is the evaluation of physical supply capabilities. Purchase orders, either hard copies or summary listings, become a planning tool for the physical supply function. Planning and staffing of receiving activities depend on due-in schedules constructed from purchase transactions. Storage space allocations are based on the inflow and outflow of material. Receipt records are checked and verified against due-in records.

The purchase of numerous components for complex products, long lead-time items, or phased delivery items gives additional significance to the physical supply function. This importance is manifested in the complexity of item identification. A purchase results in possession, but possession is of little value without accessibility. Item identification during the receiving process provides a method of access. Identifiers are usually in a code such as a stock number or part number. To make proper identification possible, material which is stored or used as it is received should bear the identifier on the exterior container. Identifiers are usually found on acquisition documents. Purchase contracts normally stipulate in marking instructions that identifiers, including the purchase order number, appear on the exterior container.

BILLS OF LADING

The bill of lading serves both the transportation and physical supply functions. It is the focal point of interface between the two functions. As a contract for the purchase of common carriage transportation service, the bill of lading specifies the type of service being provided, indicates origin and destination locations, and describes the material being moved. In the physical supply function, the bill of lading is important in receiving and shipping activities.

Upon shipment arrival, the carrier provides the receiver with a copy of the bill of lading. It is used as a delivery receipt and exception record. Since the bill of lading contains information relevant to the material identification and quantity, it can be used to simplify initial steps in the identification and checking procedure. Often the bill of lading contains item identification numbers on the purchase contract, numbers which are helpful in ensuring order-receipt accountability. Exceptions such as overages, shortages, and damages are usually annotated on the bill of lading. These notes may become substantiation for a claims action. The bill of lading becomes even more important when a shipment is received on a collect freight basis. Then, after receiving activities verify the transaction, the carrier representative may request payment.

It is common practice for the shipper of material to prepare the bill of lading. This is usually done by personnel in the transportation function or in the transfer activity (shipping) of the physical supply function. In either case, it is a responsibility of the shipping activity to provide source documentation for bill of lading preparation.

SHIPPING RELEASES

Sales usually result in a requirement to relocate material. The relocation is effected by preparation for movement and transfer to another function. Authority for relocation is documented on a shipping release, or shipping order. The shipping release details the customer location, desired delivery date, item identification, and quantity. By including the price and item identification number, it may be used as an invoice, accounting document, and inventory adjustment record. In the physical supply function, the shipping release is used to actuate the retrieval and transfer activities. It originates an information flow in the physical supply function which causes the generation of other documents to be discussed later.

SPECIAL DOCUMENTS

Not all inputs to the physical supply function are directly related to purchase and sales. Internal demands for material rely on physical supply too, although they are handled in a slightly different manner. For instance, production demands may require relocation of raw materials from storage to manufacturing facilities. Or additional equipment such as tools may be needed for a work crew. These demands may be authorized verbally or on a special purpose document. In either case physical supply is responsible for retrieval from storage, transfer, and the maintenance of accurate records.

Requests for consumable material (raw materials or supplies) are usually made in an internal material request document, usually called a material requisition. The document is similar to a purchase order except that it contains an identifier, such as an account number, which designates the accountable responsibility center within the organization. Relocation is normally made directly to the materials handling function for delivery to the requisitioner.

Material other than consumables stored for internal use is generally retained in a central stores area. Consumable supplies are charged to the accountable responsibility center. Reusable material (such as tools) is similarly charged on checkout, but the charge is liquidated upon check-in or return. Central stores transactions are accomplished with special purpose internal requisitions. Documentation procedures vary, but the requisition usually contains the item identification, quantity, responsibility center identification, signature of the requesting official, and name of the person responsible for pickup.

In multiplant or multi-distribution center organizations, it may be necessary to transfer material among facilities. Here, the principles of documentation can vary; the organization has to design a documentation system suitable to its needs. A major decision point is how the facilities will be treated in terms of physical supply accountability and responsibility. The main question is one of centralized or decentralized control.

RESTRAINTS

Organizational functions are subject to conditions which serve as parameters in the decision making process. These conditions limit the latitude available to a manager in evaluating alternative methods of satisfying objectives. Such limiting conditions are called restraints. The most significant restraints applicable to the physical supply function are material characteristics, service levels, and investment.

This set of restraints is by no means exhaustive, but it does encompass elements common to most decision processes. Additionally, it should be noted that the relative influence of an individual restraint varies with the industry, the organization, and the application.

MATERIAL CHARACTERISTICS

Physical supply is concerned with the flow of material through space. In large part, effective flow and space utilization are dependent on material characteristics. The transfer, retrieval, and storage alternatives are restrained by the physical nature of material, both as to the techniques used and as to the facilities.

Information should be obtained about each inventory item to be stored or moved. It should include the following:

1. Size, weight, and nature of each item
2. Any special handling or security requirements
3. If packaged, the quantity per container
4. Maximum and minimum inventory levels
5. Frequency and quantity of demand
6. Number of movements and their destination
7. Required environmental controls for protection or safety

Material characteristics can be divided into two major categories. *Form* characteristics have to do with the size, shape, and weight of material. *Interactive* characteristics describe the relationship between material and its surroundings. Examples of interactive characteristics include hazard qualities (explosive, poison, or caustic), fragility, and shelf life. Each category represents an important influence on the physical supply function.

Form

The size, shape, and weight of material affect both flow and space capabilities. From raw materials to finished products, goods must be moved among and stored in various locations with differing physical features.

Form characteristics of material are considerations in determining the volume capabilities of flow and space facilities. Specifications for equipment used to transfer material among functions are based on material form. Facility design and layout are dependent to some extent on space requirements dictated by the form of the material or its packaging. While this may appear to be an elementary principle of physical supply, its application is often complicated. If the form of the material remained constant, then the achievement of flow and space compatibility would be relatively easy. But often, particularly in production, material undergoes processing which changes its form. Thus, bulk raw materials may undergo processing to produce individual units of finished goods. Because size, shape, and weight may change, the complexity of their influence on flow and space requirements is compounded.

Interactivity

Similarly, the manner in which material interacts with its environment influences flow and space requirements. Movement and storage of hazardous commodities necessitates the use of specialized equipment and facilities. For instance, spark retardant machinery and environmental control measures may be needed to process explosives. Fragile products may require limitations on the mix of commodities moved together and restrictions on stacking in storage facilities. Products with a short shelf life usually are moved more often (for fast turnover), and the storage environment must be modified to accommodate frequent movement.

Interactive charactistics may also represent influences external to the organization. Because of danger to humans or the ecology, government statutes often set standards for the movement, storage, and processing of materials.

SERVICE LEVELS

The physical supply function exists to satisfy material requirements of other organizational functions. How the needs of other functions are met depends on the volume and frequency of movement and storage activities necessary for operations. The operational interfaces among physical supply and other functions can be described in terms of service levels. Thus, the operating characteristics of the physical supply function are sensitive to demands, or service level requirements, imposed by other functions within the organization.

While functional sensitivity is apparent throughout the organization, the interdependence of physical supply activities is best exemplified in two other functions. Generally, the services provided by physical supply vary according to restraints originating in the service demands of production and marketing.

Production

Physical supply acts as the link between purchasing, transportation, and production. Material entering the production process always flows through physical supply, although the flow characteristics vary with the type of production.

Regardless of the type of production system (continuous or intermittent), incoming material is processed through the receiving cycle of physical supply. However, the type of production system does influence the speed of the flow. The speed of the physical supply flow is *inversely* related to the speed of the production process. Material requirements of a job-shop production process are not subject to stringent critical lead time restrictions. Raw materials and components are purchased only when they are needed to fill a firm order. Thus, they quickly flow through the receiving activity directly to the shop floor.

The faster production processes (continuous) are subject to lead time restrictions and rely on a readily accessible source of input material. Physical supply provides such access by altering the flow speed. This is accomplished by storing material. Storage, then, is the flow of material at a zero rate.

Storage requirements may be for space adjacent to or near the production activity, as with in-process storage (or point of use) for an intermittent process. An example is the storage space required to support a small bakery. Sophisticated facilities and equipment may be needed to store quantities of material demanded by a continuous production process, as with a textile manufacturer using vast amounts of bulk cotton. Obviously, a large or complex organization may need several levels of service to support its operations.

Another influence of production on physical supply occurs during the production process. Processing material in production generates three material outputs—finished goods, by-products, and waste. Here again, physical supply links production to other functions by effecting flow, usually through a storage medium, until further use. Waste and by-products may be stored until they can be recycled to production or disposed of. Of course, waste disposal represents another type of storage. Finished goods and sometimes by-products are returned to the physical supply function until demanded by sales or another use point.

Marketing

Finished goods are stored, retrieved from storage, and shipped upon the generation of sales or relocation orders. Consumption patterns, usually identified by the demand (consumer) distribution, influence the flow of material from production through physical supply. Physical supply makes material available to satisfy consumption demands. The degree of satisfaction provided is referred to as the service level. If material is not available when demand originates, it may cause a loss of customer satisfaction or sales. To prevent these losses, quantities in excess of demand may be retained. However, holding material for this purpose adds to the cost of operations.

Thus, market demand can be followed or anticipated. Following demand requires the physical supply function to supply material directly to a customer with only incidental storage, because production is geared to known orders. Obviously, demand can be followed only if the customer is patient or if the seller is the only source of supply. In most cases, demand is anticipated, which means it must be forecasted. All organizational functions are sensitive to the sales forecast. Storage activities in the physical supply function serve to satisfy the projected demand and provide a buffer against forecasting and production imperfections.

INVESTMENT

Like other functions, physical supply must compete for investment resources available to the organization. The scope of physical supply tends to decentralize the thrust of investment requirements; that is, resources are spread throughout the organization. To illustrate, physical supply activities are apparent in the entire flow of material. Transfer, retrieval, and storage activities represent significant facility, equipment, and personnel requirements. Some facilities and equipment may be shared with other functions such as transportation and materials handling, while others are dedicated solely to physical supply.

Devices to facilitate physical supply are only one area of investment. Funds are also consumed in the value of material within the function, called inventory, and the cost of holding that inventory. Thus, investment requirements in the physical supply function are centered in two general areas, facilities and inventory.

Facilities

Physical supply facilities, including buildings and equipment, typically represent 15% of annual sales in an organization, more or less. Administrative offices will have little capital invested in physical supply facilities; manufacturing concerns will have a substantial investment; and commercial distribution organizations will have a large proportion of their total investment in such facilities.

The cost of facilities can vary widely, depending on material characteristics, flow, and locations. Material with limited restraining characteristics can be transferred, retrieved, and stored with rather unsophisticated (and inexpensive) facilities. As the restraints grow, requiring specialized facilities, so do costs. Material flow determines the requirement for transfer and retrieval equipment, which can involve expensive automated systems. The equipment used depends to a large degree on the quantity and types of material carried in inventory. Of course, physical supply activities may be necessary at several locations, which means investment in multiple facilities.

Inventory

Investment in inventory is the financial commitment of an organization to material held for later use or sale. Raw materials, in-process goods, and finished goods are the generally accepted categories of goods held in inventory. The utility (cost) associated with material in the flow increases with the movement from raw materials to finished goods. Finished goods are in the highest value state, since they are in a form that can be sold (profit propensity).

Investment in inventory is intended as a buffer to absorb uncertainties such as possible price and use fluctuations. Raw materials may be purchased at a quantity discount, in advance of price increases, or in anticipation of commodity shortages. Finished goods may be stocked in quantities sufficient to prevent customer losses due to stockouts or to allow value appreciation during demand acceleration. However, such motives are characterized by several important assumptions:

1. The net benefit of quantity discounts will not be negated by added physical supply costs.
2. Quantity purchases will be productively used.
3. Safety stock costs will be offset by customer satisfaction and related benefits.
4. Value appreciation will not be equaled or surpassed by storage and deterioration costs.
5. Demand will remain constant or increase.

Seldom are these assumptions absolutely reliable. Thus, investment in inventory is made in a state of uncertainty under conditions of risk. Solvency or market position will determine the amount of investment risk an organization is willing or able to assume.

SUPPLY ACTIVITIES

During its flow through space, material is subject to three major activities. The supply activities of transfer, retrieval, and storage define the operating characteristics of physical supply in an organization. While operational procedures may vary from organization to organization, supply activities have universal application in the flow of material.

Transfer is the movement of material among other functions or activities. The movement involved in transfer can be measured in terms of some rate or speed. *Retrieval* is concerned with access to material from a storage location; its speed can be measured in terms of a cycle time. *Storage* represents the flow of material at a zero velocity—the retention of goods for later use or sale.

TRANSFER

The flow of material between the transportation and physical supply usually involves movement to or from a storage location. Storage locations to and from which material moves are referred to as nodal points, and each movement represents a transaction which must be physically accomplished and administratively controlled. Movements to and from nodal points are called transfer activities. Inbound transactions are accomplished through receiving; outbound ones, through shipping.

Receiving

Material is introduced to physical supply by passing through the receiving element of the transfer activity. Receiving interfaces directly with transportation, and organizationally it may even be treated as a part of that function. Receiving is responsible for the physical handling of incoming shipments, identification of material, verification of quantities, routing of the material to places of use or storage, and preparation of reports. Upon completion of the receiving process, material is dispatched to a customer or a storage location. All material accountability and control begins with the proper receipt of goods. Regardless of the organizational setting, receiving procedures commonly involve *in-checking*, *identification*, and *staging*.

In-checking Receiving should have a complete file of all "open" purchase orders. The purchase orders are authorization to accept shipments. When a shipment arrives, the delivery documents are checked against the appropriate purchase order for type, model, condition, and quantity.

Arriving material is unloaded, inspected, and reported as received. Depending on the type of carriage used to deliver, either the carrier or the receiver is responsible for unloading. Before physical movement from the vehicle, the loaded condition of material is observed and delivery documentation (usually a bill of lading) is checked for completeness. After this cursory review, the receiving document is forwarded to the administrative office for additional processing.

Inspection is accomplished during or after unloading. Each piece of the shipment is inspected for discrepencies such as damage, missing parts, or erroneous addressing. Inspection formally establishes the condition of the delivered material. Results of in-checking are documented on a receiving report, which is used to itemize each unit of received material and its condition. The receiving report also contains information such as arrival time, in-checking time, conveyance number, and name of checker.

The receiving report is then passed to the administrative office holding the delivery document. Since the delivery document contains a list of delivered material and the receiving report itemizes received material, they can be compared for a final accountability check. It is here that overages and shortages are noted and discrepancy reports are initiated. Discrepant items are usually described on the delivery document and on the receiving report. Claims actions are supported by both documents.

Identification Incoming material is identified in two ways. First, the material itself must be identified. This usually means the use of some coded number, part number, or component number. Identifiers serve as the standard reference to an item along with the narrative nomenclature. Information about an item is retained under the control of the code rather than its nomenclature. Often the coded identifier is cross referenced with the appropriate purchase or invoice number, and with the narrative nomenclature. Material identification is an important part of the information flow which parallels material flow, particularly in inventory control systems.

Brief mention should be made of one of the more recent developments in material identification. Material can be identified by marks on the exterior container which are read by an optical character recognition (OCR) device. Sensing the identification from special graphics on the material or packaging allows direct input to an automated information system, obviating normal man-machine operations involved in conventional techniques. OCR applications are limited to material without severe form restraints and to material having the necessary graphic identifiers.

The second identification required designates the intended or actual storage location. Space is often defined by identifiers constructed in a grid fashion. For example, buildings (or outside storage areas), levels, rows, and aisles are usually assigned codes. A combination of these codes can completely define a location. Thus, location identifier 83A7 may designate building 8, level 3, row A, and aisle 7. Coding systems for location definition are designed to fit the space requirements of the individual organization, and they vary greatly.

Staging Staging is the marshaling of material in preparation for dispatch to another point of use or to a storage location. After checking and identification, the material is ready to be transferred by material handling equipment to its designated storage site. Staging is accomplished in an effort to consolidate movement in one direction or to a particular location. Goods may be loaded on pallets, spotted at transfer points, or placed on conveyors. In the last case, it is possible to employ mechanized systems which use coded instructions to convey material to predesignated locations.

Shipping

Conceptually, shipping is the reverse of receiving in that it represents the transfer of material *from* a nodal point. In the shipping process, material retrieved from storage is prepared for onward movement, usually by transportation, to another use point. Material is again inspected, identified, and reported. The shipping release is used to substantiate deletions from inventory and to assign packing responsibilities, particularly when many small items are consolidated into a number of larger units. Finally, shipping involves loading shipments aboard carriage equipment, and frequently blocking and bracing material inside the equipment. It should be noted that when shipments are consolidated, individual packing slips must be used as sources for developing a more representative document, called the consolidated packing slip. The packing slip identifies all material inside a container or bound in a single unit. It is placed inside or on the container.

Receiving and shipping have an interface with the transportation function, specifically in the unloading and loading of carriage equipment. Common carriage equipment must be unloaded or loaded within stipulated time periods after vehicle arrival. When the free time expires, there is a charge for holding carriage equipment, called demurrage for rail cars and detention for motor vehicles. *Demurrage and detention* charges are factors bearing on the establishment of receiving and shipping schedules. While overtime or schedule adjustments may be used to avoid demurrage and detention charges, it is advisable to compare the total costs of the two alternatives. Often delay charges are less than the costs associated with overtime and schedule adjustments.

Packaging and Packing Packages can be classified into three general types. A *carton* contains a single product, and protects the contents during shipment and display on store shelves. A *box* is used for packing several cartons. A *shipping container* is a large box used for packing several boxes. Not all items fall into the above package classifications. Several products may require specialized or custom packaging.

Proper packing is important for protection during transportation and preservation during storage. Protection is required against breakage, dirt, dust, theft, and weathering. Some items may require inner packing support, or molding to fit the shape of the product. Fragile items (glass, pottery) are usually packed in boxes divided by partitions. Before a shipping container is closed, usually a packing slip and/or invoice is enclosed. The containerization of finished products is usually much more sophisticated than that of raw materials.

Marking and Identification Prior to actual shipment each container must be marked, weighted, and routed. The weight of the shipment is needed to figure the cost of transportation and to decide the best mode of transportation. The reason for marking shipments is to ensure prompt and safe delivery. Marking places on the outside of the container the written or printed information necessary to transport the shipment to its destination. Specific marking requirements are developed by governments, transportation modes, and internal organizational groups. The identification must be securely applied and must remain clear all the way to the destination.

RETRIEVAL

Availability of material within the physical supply flow is maintained by activities which insure access. Access is accomplished through retrieval procedures, which provide means for locating and removing material retained in storage. While the sophistication of retrieval systems varies, all systems rely on order picking and material handling procedures.

Order Picking

Material is retrieved from storage to satisfy a demand for use at another point. Items are picked from storage to fill an order, which may involve only one or numerous items. Thus, a filled order is the primary output unit from the storage location. Material making up an order must be identified by item and location. This identification is routinely effected by using a *picking ticket* which describes the items and their location. The picking ticket may simply be an order document used to initiate a manual search routine, or it may be a special purpose form supporting an automated or semi-automated order picking system.

Generally, there are two categories of order picking systems. *Sequential* or serial systems involve the use of a single picking ticket, usually the order document, to provide identification information. An employee known as a picker uses the order as he moves up and down each aisle and selects items that appear on the order as they are encountered, much as a shopper uses a grocery list at a supermarket. Essentially, each order is treated individually, and each order (or group of orders) is subject to the same manual search routine. Obviously, the sequential system is characterized by extensive travel and a long order cycle time. These characteristics are not necessarily detrimental to an operation. For example, they may be completely satisfactory for a small automotive parts dealer. Usually, if an organization processes less than 400 orders a day and if the number of items stocked is less than 10,000, a sequential order picking system is adequate.

More demanding order cycle time and volume requirements may overburden a sequential system. The *bulk order picking system* is designed to satisfy more demanding requirements. With this system, storage space is segregated and available labor is divided according to the space segments. One order may require several picking tickets, depending on the dispersal of storage locations. Pickers select items only in their responsible areas (zones). Since several similar items may be selected for an order, each item must be identified with the order it belongs to. One method of assigning selected items to an order is to affix a copy of the picking ticket to the container. All picked items are then moved to a work area for order consolidation.

During order consolidation, items may have to be packed and containers may require identification marking. Unless material is stored ready for shipping, it must be packed for protection against movement hazards. Completed shipment units are marked with appropriate identification nomenclature and addresses.

Frequently, the highest physical supply costs are in the order picking process. It follows that streamlining this process can yield substantial cost savings. An efficient stock layout system can facilitate order picking.

In recent years, significant progress has been made in automating order picking procedures, particularly in the bulk order picking system. Automated applications are termed order processing systems, and they employ computer technology to integrate supply activities. Item and location identifications are stored by a computer, allowing fast information access. Systems vary in complexity from those that generate picking tickets for further manual processing to those that control mechanical picking devices and complete all documentation, weighing, and marking. Large systems are also able to perform work scheduling which prevents bottlenecks in the flow of material.

Material Handling

Material handling equipment facilitates the actual movement of items in the retrieval cycle. Equipment used ranges from a simple hand cart to a computer controlled picking device. Although material handling equipment is used throughout the flow of material, it is mentioned here because of the important relationship to retrieval systems.

Retrieval systems can be labor intensive. Material handling equipment is used to reduce the cost and time required by manual labor. Of course, the benefit of labor saving equipment must be compared with the cost. Thus, material handling decisions should be made in the context of other functional requirements. Common material handling equipment employed in retrieval includes carts, dollies, pallets, trucks, lifts, cranes, and conveyors. The variety of special purpose machinery is almost unlimited.

Sorting systems are of special interest to the retrieval activity. An organization processing a wide variety of material and an extensive product mix must control the flow of many items. In retrieval (and at times in receiving) this means that picked items must be directed to different locations for order consolidation and shipment. Sorting is the process of directing the flow of material to the destinations of specific items. Sorting systems usually involve gravity or powered conveyors. At designated points along the conveyor an item is diverted to another conveyor or chute which transports it to a desired location. Such systems are often controlled by computers and require coded instructions pertinent to storage or destination. Automated sorting systems have important applications in organizations with high volume and an extensive product mix.

STORAGE

Storage takes place in a stockroom, store, crib, warehouse, yard, distribution center, or the like. Storage areas hold materials from the time they are received until they are required by production, marketing, or the customer. The storage area is designed to economically receive, retain, and issue material. Storage is necessary at transit centers, at aggregation points, at distribution points, where modes of transportation change, and where seasonal production occurs. Storage is closely related to transportation. Organizations frequently can reduce storage and inventory costs by employing a faster (usually higher priced) form of material transportation.

Storage is the medium through which material availability is ensured. The net value of that availability depends on the storage incentives of an organization and the costs associated with material retention. Important incentives include the following:

1. Increased customer service
2. Quantity purchase discounts
3. Transportation cost savings
4. Demand/production smoothing

5. Hedge against shortages

6. Hedge against price increases

The advantages of storage are not without risk. Retention of material for later use involves implicit assumptions about the future, which is uncertain. Some of the major costs of holding material are as follows:

1. Capital costs

2. Operating costs

3. Insurance costs

4. Taxes

5. Shrinkage and damage costs

6. Obsolescence costs

Thus the time and place utility provided by availability also represents a cost, and the dynamics of risk have a great deal to do with the relationship between benefits and costs.

Often material can be stored more efficiently in unit containers or packages than in bulk. Unit packaging consists of receiving, storing, and issuing items in standardized containers containing a number of small parts or items, or a standard amount of bulk materials as in drums of oil or bags of fertilizer. When materials can be delivered to users in containers in which they were received, handling costs can be reduced significantly. There is no need to unpack, measure, repack, and issue, so shrinkage is minimized.

Material in storage can generally be divided into three categories: raw materials, in-process goods, and finished goods. Raw materials and finished goods require a facility offering space for retention, unless outside storage is feasible. In-process storage can be at a location convenient to the production process (point of use storage) or it may actually be part of production. Interesting examples of the latter case include chemicals stored in hopper feeders in fertilizer production, and spirits stored in aging tanks during the making of alcholic beverages. Other than simple bins and work racks, there are no standard methods for in-process storage. Warehouse and distribution centers are common methods of storage for raw materials and finished goods.

Warehouses

Warehouses are facilities which confine and specify space so as to create an environment suitable for the storage of material. As nodal points of movement, warehouses represent locations in the flow of material where the movement velocity is zero. Just as material characteristics restrain storage, so do the physical characteristics of a warehouse. Some of the important physical characteristics of a warehouse which influence the specifications of space are:

1. Maximum floor bearing weight
2. Placement and dimensions of doors, aisles, and columns
3. Ceiling height
4. Location of loading docks, rail sidings, and elevators
5. Building codes, fire laws, insurance regulations, and health and safety regulations

Warehouse specifications are important when planning for a new facility and selecting from existing facilities.

Increasing the speed of movement of material through an organization is a key to reducing cost. Speed of movement is enhanced by efficient layout of storage facilities in relation to the rate of turnover of stock items. Store faster moving items at waist to eye level; slower moving items at lower and upper levels.

In determining storage locations, movement must be measured in terms of both frequency and volume. Table 5.1 describes the relationship between location and movement rates. Thus, material with a high movement frequency and a high volume is stored nearest to shipping work stations; material with a low frequency and low volume is farther away.

Table 5.1
Proximity and flow

	FLOW	
PROXIMITY	FREQUENCY	VOLUME
1	Fast	High
2	Slow	High
3	Fast	Low
4	Slow	Low

It is desirable to store similar items in the same vicinity. Order picking time can then be reduced when an order is filled for items which correspond to a particular function. For example, plumbing or electrical items may share a common storage location. Also, separate areas of the warehouse should be designated for special purposes such as temporary storage, minor repair work, and salvage sites.

Distribution Centers

Distribution centers are similar to warehouses in that they serve as nodal points for the flow of material. They are normally used exclusively for the storage of finished goods. Thus, they assume a marketing rather than a production orientation. Their geographic locations are close to large market centers, and it is common for several organizations to share the same facilities.

Since distribution centers are primarily concerned with fast moving items, they seldom have space dedicated to long term storage. Being marketing oriented, they serve many customers and house an extensive product line. The interface with transportation is important to the turnover rate and customer service. The rapid flow of material necessitates use of sophisticated transfer and retrieval systems.

To determine distribution center space requirements, the following factors must be considered:

1. Estimation of material volumes to be stored
2. Conversion of volume to cubic requirements
3. Establishment of height to which goods can be stacked
4. Determination of floor area required for storage
5. Allowances for aisles, staging, shipping, and receiving docks
6. Space requirements for administrative and human services

Recently there has been an interesting development in the design of distribution centers. Historically, storage facilities have been single level buildings, because horizontal movement is less expensive than vertical movement. Today many distribution centers are housed in multilevel facilities, perhaps because of the cost and scarcity of real estate.

The two main strategies for the resupply of regional distribution centers are drop shipment and cascading. With *drop shipment*, the supplier delivers goods directly to the regional center. With *cascading*, the supplier ships goods to the central distribution center and the goods are disseminated to the regional centers. Rather than hold all items in all locations, regional distribution centers may only hold fast moving items (stratified stock holding). The result is slower service for items not stocked regionally. However, it may be less expensive to stock slow-moving items centrally and air freight them to the branches or regions on request. In general, it is more economical to air freight the lighter, more expensive slow-moving items.

PHYSICAL SUPPLY DECISIONS

Because of the diversity of physical supply influence on the management of material, responsibility for functional decisions may be shared by several managers. Certainly decision makers in the areas of purchasing, production, marketing, transportation, and material handling have direct interest in physical supply operations. Indeed, effective management requires that they recognize the interrelationships among the various organizational functions. Evaluation of the characteristics of the physical supply function (the inputs, restraints, and supply activities) is necessary if decisions are to generate desired outputs.

PHYSICAL SUPPLY OUTPUTS

Physical supply decisions produce outputs which affect the long term performance of an organization, by establishing parameters which control the effectiveness of material flow and all functions sensitive to that flow. The major outputs can be classified according to *movement systems, storage systems,* and *information systems.*

MOVEMENT SYSTEMS

Part of the flow of material in physical supply involves movement between use locations. When considered as elements of the entire flow movement, requirements can be approached as a system. Physical supply decisions integrate movement demands and provide policy for the establishment of movement systems. Outputs relevant to movement systems result in several important criteria for implementation, such as:

1. *Requirements definition.* The entire flow of material through all organizational functions is conceptualized and described. Requirements placed on physical supply to support the flow are defined.

2. *Activity positioning.* Activities applicable to material flow (transfer, retrieval, and storage) are positionally related within the function. Flow characteristics will determine whether receiving and shipping will be inputs to the production process, or if they will be consolidated with production. Retrieval positioning will be influenced by the operational orientation of the organization (upflow from production in manufacturing concerns, and downflow in distribution concerns). Of course, positioning at several locations may be necessary.

3. *Activity scheduling.* Throughput capabilities are synchronized with

schedules of related functions. Such coordination establishes manpower and equipment requirements.

4. *Procedure standardization.* Routines for accomplishing necessary activities are formalized into a set of standard procedures. All man and machine tasks are described, and responsibilities are assigned. Administrative procedures are developed, and control forms are designed.

The operating scope and size of an organization will set the level of complexity in establishing or changing a movement system. Generally, complex organizations have complex movement systems, and the decision process for generating desired outputs is more complicated and diverse.

STORAGE SYSTEMS

Ideally, the most economic storage policy would be not to store material. Unfortunately, consumption patterns rarely correspond to the flow of material in an organization. Storage is used to modify the flow for the benefit of performance and the minimization of cost. Deciding on the storage system to employ demands a careful analysis of flow requirements, material characteristics, and investment capabilities. Flow requirements influence facility location and throughput capabilities. Material characteristics can affect design. Investment capability determines the number of alternatives open for consideration.

There are two categories of storage systems available: internal and external. *Internal systems* are under the exclusive control of the sponsoring organization, while *external systems* are controlled by outside interests. Organizations frequently rely on a combination of the two.

Internal

Internal storage systems are often referred to as *private or company systems*. Such storage is frequently referred to as warehousing—that being the most common form of it. Internal storage systems provide the sponsoring organizations with total control and responsibility. Use of such a system implies that an organization has a need for maximum flexibility and also has the financial strength to support the investment.

With private warehousing the organization owns and operates the buildings and/or open (outside) storage facilities. Some advantages are:

1. Complete control over flexibility
2. Better control over cost

3. Easy access to the information flow
4. Fewer restraints on other functions

A special type of private storage capability is called the *field warehouse*. In this case an organization leases a portion of its private warehouse to a commercial (public) warehousing firm. Thus, the public firm has custody of material in the leased space. The public firm issues a receipt for the material to the owning organization. In turn, the organization can use the receipt as security for obtaining a loan. Material remains in the confines of the organization, but is under custody, representing collateral for borrowed funds. Such an arrangement usually terminates when the loan is liquidated. It is useful for securing loans, and has the added advantages limiting material movement and avoiding the cost of external storage.

A stock locator system must be established to indicate where items are stored. There are two basic kinds. The *fixed locator system* stipulates a fixed storage location for each item. The location of an item never changes as long as it is carried in inventory. A detailed drawing of stock locations serves as a map for personnel. To improve efficiency, the stock location can be entered on receiving and shipping documents so warehousemen need not bother with locator maps. The fixed locator system is used when space is not critical and the same products are handled for long periods.

The *random locator system* stipulates the location of an item based on available space, and records must be kept to identify the location. A location code must identify every place of storage, and a central record must indicate where every item is stored, and consulted when an item is to be withdrawn. While the random locator system utilizes storage space more efficiently, it does require more documentation than the fixed locator system. It is used when space is critical.

Employment of internal storage is accompanied by reliance on fixed locations and a large long term investment. The facilities must also be supported by personnel and equipment. Accurate forecasting and planning are essential ingredients of a successful internal storage system.

External

For organizations not willing or able to invest in internal storage systems, the alternative is external storage. External or public storage capability is available from businesses which sell such services (public warehouses). Charges are usually based on storage weight, but various fee arrangements are possible. Some reasons an organization might select external storage are:

1. Lower long term investment
2. Less reliance on fixed facilities
3. Economic storage of small quantities
4. Ability to experiment with storage systems—a hedge against time
5. Storage of internal system overflow

External storage is beneficial to organizations with extensive market areas or those with an erratic material flow. It is usually appropriate for small quantities of material at any one location, since charges are for the space and services used.

External storage systems do have disadvantages. Since they serve a number of customers, their capabilities and procedures are not tailored to the individual needs of a specific organization. Thus, the user may have to modify his procedures to be compatible with those used by the vendor. The organization must depend on its vendor for information feedback. The vendor is usually subject to only limited liability for loss and damage.

The public warehousing market is highly specialized to meet the needs of a variety of customers. A few of the most important types of public warehouses are:

1. *Refrigerated*. For storing material requiring temperature control, such as perishable food items, chemicals, and biologicals
2. *Commodity*. To hold a specific type of material
3. *Household goods*. For personal household belongings
4. *General merchandise*. To store common materials not requiring special services or controls
5. *Bonded*. Authorized to store material upon which taxes or duty has not been paid

The last category, bonded warehouses, is of special interest. Such facilities allow organizations to store material while deferring payment of taxes or duties until after a sale is consummated and the material is withdrawn from storage. Tobacco and liquor products are often stored in bonded warehouses. A hybrid form of the bonded warehouse is a *free trade zone*. It is a controlled area, usually located in or near major port (surface or air) facilities. Material can enter a free trade zone without payment of import taxes and duties. Payment is made when material leaves the zone. Aside from the advantage of deferring an expenditure, it is possible to use the free trade zone for consolidations, incidental fabricating, or processing, and to anticipate local price or demand increases.

At additional cost, public warehousing organizations frequently offer a variety of services complementary to the physical supply function. A few examples of such services are packaging, consolidation, repair, assembly, mixing, shipping, distribution, and order processing.

While internal and external storage systems generally exhaust the major options available to an organization, it should be mentioned that slight modifications to those two classifications can provide alternatives. Obviously, organizations can use a combination of private and public facilities to satisfy their storage requirements. This frequently occurs with geographically dispersed organizations and those with extensive market coverage. Also, it is possible to lease warehouse facilities through a formal contract, thus striking a balance between internal and external storage systems.

INFORMATION SYSTEMS

It has been stressed that physical supply is concerned with the flow of material. However, flow does not exist in isolation. Every movement of material is complemented by an information transaction. These transactions, which may precede, accompany, or follow material movement, constitute the information flow. Of course, information requirements are not peculiar to the physical supply function; effective management in general is only accomplished with the aid of an efficient organizational information system. (The term system should not be taken to imply the use of computers, although they are prevalent in information systems today.)

An important output of the physical supply function is its influence on the information needs of an organization. Like supply items, information must be transferred, retrieved, and stored. Information must be available and accessible to permit flow description, determine item location, dispatch items, adjust accounts, and collect payments. While an exhaustive evaluation of information system design is beyond our scope, two important information conventions deserve comment. These are *records* and *documentation*.

Records

From receiving to shipping, material is described by information elements which define the various movements made. The elements are generally organized in chronological order according to the flow of an individual item. Organized in this manner, the elements of information make up a *record* which provides the current status and history of each item.

It is physical supply's responsibility to verify record accuracy. Periodic physical counts of inventory are necessary to audit and verify the records for financial reporting. Many organizations conduct an annual physical inventory on all items in stock; others use cycle count procedures to verify inventory record accuracy.

Records are used in both manual and automated information systems. They are identified by a unique control code, for instance the part number, which is used to establish filing procedures. Access to records is through the control or file code. Manual systems require clerical filing and access procedures. Automated systems feature faster file maintenance and access. An important advantage of automated systems is that information can be made available at various locations simultaneously through remote terminals. Automated systems also allow greater latitude in cross referencing file information.

Documentation

Purchase orders, receiving reports, packing slips, picking tickets, and shipping releases are among the documents which support the flow of information. They are a part of a standardized internal documentation procedure used throughout the organization. Documents represent the data source for records; they are therefore important components of the information system.

In manual systems, documents become physical parts of the record file. As each transaction occurs, a copy of the supporting document is filed, which creates and maintains a record. With automated systems, documented information must be converted to a machine format (involving keypunching, keyboard entry, or optical scanning) before records are updated. As the size and number of records grow, document storage can become a problem in manual systems. Computer technology obviates this problem in automated systems which offer compact mass storage.

A special advantage to documentation procedures is available in some automated systems. After sufficient information is entered to create an initial record, capability then exists to generate succeeding documentation automatically. To illustrate, stored information concerning material identification and location can be used to produce picking tickets, and purchase order information can be used to prepare shipping releases. Computer technology can provide sophisticated performance analysis without the need for extensive research and clerical support.

CONCLUSION

Physical supply is probably the least efficient function in the production and distribution cycle. Even when production operations are automated or controlled by high standards of efficiency, physical supply does not usually undergo the same degree of scrutiny. The two major areas in physical supply that should be controlled are order handling (cycle) time and space utilization.

This chapter has developed a conceptualized approach to these activities that facilitate the flow of material. Whether or not the activities are organized under the title physical supply is irrelevant. But it is important, even essential, that the collection of physical supply activities be treated as an organizational function. It is also important that the physical supply function be recognized as an interrelated component of the organization, sensitive to and influencing changes in other functions. Without effective material flow an organization cannot be effective. Physical supply forms the "linking pin" between purchasing, production, and marketing. The establishment and management of effective material flow require an appreciation of the physical supply function.

QUESTIONS

1. What are the two vital organizational tasks which the physical supply function performs?
2. Trace physical supply inputs to other important organizational functions.
3. Describe the material characteristics which can restrain physical supply decisions.
4. Explain the relationship between production process and physical supply speed.
5. What is meant by material flow at zero velocity?
6. Explain the assumptions implied in holding inventory in excess of demand.
7. Define and give an example of a nodal point.
8. Distinguish between sequential and bulk order picking.
9. Compare distribution centers with warehouses.
10. Discuss the advantages of private and public warehousing.
11. Explain the characteristics and uses of bonded warehouses.
12. Why are records and documents important to the physical supply function?

Case 1: Lost Customers

John Johnson, foreman of the Shipping Department of the Caldwell Corporation, has been given instructions by Tom Irwin, the plant manager, that all requests for overtime are to be approved by him. Previously the various department foremen had possessed the authority to use their own discretion and schedule overtime (at time and one-half rates) whenever they deemed it necessary. Although several other foremen scheduled overtime regularly, John Johnson had used it sparingly. When the annual report showed a reduction in profits and a large increase in labor costs, the company president issued a statement that all overtime had to be approved by the plant manager.

John Johnson was experiencing an increased work load along with some personnel absences, and his department was behind in shipping important orders. John knew that these orders might be canceled by the customers if not shipped by Friday. John was convinced that overtime would facilitate shipment of the important orders and he attempted to contact the plant manager. Unfortunately Tom Irwin was out of town and could not be reached. John knew that a similar situation had occurred in the Maintenance Department, and Bill Ellison, the foreman of that department, had authorized overtime without the necessary approval of the plant manager. Bill was criticized for his decision.

John Johnson was perplexed. If he approved overtime, he would be overstepping his authority. If he did not, some of the orders would be shipped late and possibly canceled by the customers. John tried to contact the president of the company, but he could not be reached. John decided to be on the safe side; he did not ask his employees to work overtime. As he feared, several orders were canceled by irate customers.

1. Did John make the correct decision? What action would you have taken?
2. What actions should be taken to ensure that the problem does not recur?

Case 2: Contemporary Lighting

Everyone is happy at the Contemporary Lighting Company from the president on down, except Mr. Brasso. Sales of their new line of lights has skyrocketed, and the company is realizing higher profits. Marketing has had a 10% increase in distributors and a 25% increase in sales. Consumer acceptance is high, and the marketing staff predict sales will continue to climb.

The production department is happy, even though it has been busy. It has a 3 month backlog of orders. Production of lights in other lines has been suspended temporarily to catch up with new orders. The production line has been speeded up, and overtime is common. At time and a half, even the lower level personnel like the extra hours. Purchasing has been taking advantage of quantity discounts and has been stocking up on high volume items as a hedge against inflation.

Why is Mr. Brasso unhappy? He is in charge of physical supply, and the warehouse looks like a jungle. The normal storage areas are full, and material keeps on arriving at the plant. Even with all the material on board, the production line had to stop twice last week for lack of material.

The perpetual records indicated that 725 units of a certain electrical switch were in stock location 61A2. Only 500 switches were found in that location. A week later the missing 225 switches were found in stock location 89A3. Apparently the order was split because the location could not accommodate the entire 725 units. The problem with the switches is typical of the last several months of operation.

The president has requested that Mr. Brasso investigate additional storage capabilities. A foreman has told Mr. Brasso of a warehouse for lease outside the city limits. The shelves in this facility average 10 feet high, while the ceilings are 15 feet high. The bin spaces are very large, and several different items can be stored in one bin space. Mr. Brasso is not sure what action he should recommend.

1. Should Mr. Brasso recommend that an additional facility be acquired?

2. What are the internal problems in the physical supply department? How can they be solved?

3. What problems in physical supply result from the actions of other departments? What changes do you recommend?

Case 3: Muser Valve and Pump Company

A lively conversation was taking place in the office of the executive vice president. Present were the vice presidents for production, marketing, and physical supply. The discussion was centered around a long standing problem at Muser: unresponsive in-house supply support to production and marketing.

Production. The production head explained that he received complaints almost daily from his subordinates, from the first-line foremen on up, that holdups were occurring in all three production lines as well as the job-shop oriented repair group. Parts were frequently not available when required on the line, and even when parts were available, far too many parts were being placed in the wrong work bin or assembly line. His foremen stated that when they personally went to the warehouse to check on needed raw materials, the response was generally that the material was somewhere in the warehouse system (either in inspection, storage, staging, or transit), and it would take several hours to track it down. The foremen usually left totally frustrated.

Marketing. The marketing head's comments echoed those of production, with the accent on finished products. He stated that because of inaccurate records of finished goods on hand, his salesmen had become wary of promising delivery dates to customers. He cited a recent example where one of their largest customers required three special pumps which inventory records showed to be on hand. The customer was promised prompt delivery, but once the order was processed, only one pump was actually found available. A special production run had to be set up for the other two pumps, with several thousand dollars in additional costs.

Physical Supply. The physical supply department at Muser was responsible for all inventories and inventory control, warehousing, purchasing, transportation, and associated record keeping. The physical supply head stated that his group was doing the best it could, but could not obtain up-to-date information from production on what lines were running and what was scheduled for the next several months. Without schedules, he stated, there was no way he could project stock levels and keep the bins full. He also stated that his budget was not large enough to allow him to run the department as he wanted. He didn't have sufficient qualified warehouse help, and there was little automation either in the materials handling equipment or record keeping areas. He dismissed the marketing head's comments rather curtly by stating that salesmen often made wild promises to customers just to exceed their quotas without checking on actual inventories.

1. As executive vice president, what would be your initial remarks to your three managers?

2. How do you resolve the sensitivities among the different interests?

3. What could production and marketing do to alleviate some of the problems?

Case 4: Not My Job

The National Supply Corporation is a major supply house specializing in automotive parts and accessories. Headquartered in Indianapolis, Indiana, it markets through four regional distribution centers located in Boston, Atlanta, Kansas City, and San Diego. The company is departmentalized as shown in Figure 5.3.

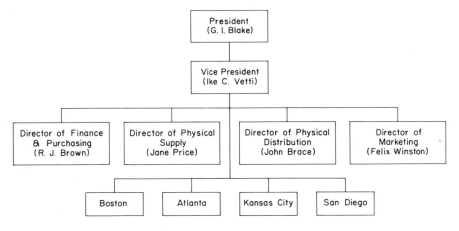

FIGURE 5.3 Table of organization for Case 4.

Recently, the manager of the Kansas City region forwarded a recommendation made by his transportation manager, Joe Hillard, to headquarters. The recommendation proposed a procedure for consolidating shipments of fast-fill orders (those requiring delivery within one week) to reduce the cost of many small movements. Joe suggested a ninety day test for the program so results could be fully evaluated. He noted that the test would require minor modifications to computer programs supporting order processing, which is a functional responsibility of Jane Price, the director of physical supply.

A relatively new member of John Brace's staff, Lou Bragg, was assigned to review the proposal. After extensive analysis he determined that the test would be justified if data processing changes could be quickly and economically accomplished. In his briefing to the director of physical distribution, he was surprised at Mr. Brace's comments, which were:

"You did not stick to the subject. Our only concern is with physical distribution. The matter of data processing changes should have been taken up with Jane Price's shop. If Kansas City wants to talk to them about it, it's their business."

1. How would you respond to John Brace if you were Lou Bragg?
2. Who should be responsible for coordination of programs or recommendations?
3. Should the company be reorganized or restructed? If so, what are your recommendations?

Chapter 6

Inventory Control Systems

A good control system provides for self-control and only requires attention on an exception basis. The starting point in developing a control system is an analysis of the objectives of the intended systems. This analysis discloses the critical activities in the operation where control can be most effective. Inventory control systems have advanced beyond the rudimentary concepts of control. They are well established and developed, but they still experience the usual control problems.

In this chapter the emphasis is on control procedures for the totality of inventory. An organization may have one or more control systems for managing its inventory. Since there are usually thousands of distinct items in inventory, it is imperative that the control mechanism satisfy the service objectives of the institution at lowest possible cost. The selection of the control system (or systems) is a top management responsibility. The type of inventory control system selected will have an impact on almost all other organizational activities.

An inventory control system is a coordinated set of rules for routinely answering the questions of when to order and how much to order. The system should indicate how routine and nonroutine situations are to be treated via predetermined rules and procedures. An effective system will accomplish the following:

1. Ensure that sufficient goods and materials are available
2. Identify excess, fast, and slow moving items
3. Provide accurate, concise, and timely reports to management
4. Expend the least amount of resources in accomplishing the first three tasks.

A comprehensive inventory system involves much more than quantitative inventory models. All aspects of the system must be considered. There are six vital areas:

1. The development of demand forecasts and the treatment of forecast errors
2. The selection of inventory models (EOQ, EOI, EPQ, MRP, and SOQ)
3. The measurement of inventory costs (order, holding, stockout)
4. The methods used to record and account for items
5. The methods for receipt, handling, storage, and issue of items
6. The information procedures used to report exceptions.

The use of sophisticated mathematical techniques *per se* does not necessarily result in an effective system. Precise, highly mathematical techniques are of little use unless the information to feed into the models is available at a realistic cost. Systems that select approximate, reasonable inventory levels with low data processing costs are often preferable. In many cases, the lack of accurate and timely data nullifies the advantages of complex control systems. It should be remembered that a breakdown in any one of the above six vital areas (not just the inventory model) can undermine the efficiency of the entire system.

TYPES OF CONTROL SYSTEMS

It is difficult to classify the various inventory control systems in an orderly fashion. There are several types of inventory control systems in use today. Nevertheless, it is possible to distinguish among the systems most frequently used. Common types of inventory systems are the perpetual, two-bin, periodic, optional replenishment, and material requirements planning systems. The perpetual, two-bin, periodic, and optional replenishment systems usually apply to end items while the material requirements planning system applies to materials and components used to produce an end item.

The perpetual and two-bin systems have a fixed order quantity and a variable review period; the periodic and optional replenishment systems have a fixed review period and a variable order quantity; and the material requirements planning system is geared to planned production requirements (the order quantity is variable and the review period can be fixed or variable). The two-bin system is a special type of perpetual system while the optional replenishment system is a special type of periodic system.

The perpetual and two-bin systems are referred to as fixed order size systems (quantity-based). The periodic and optional replenishment systems are referred to as fixed order interval systems (time-based). The material requirements planning system is termed a derived order quantity system (production-based). Quantity-based systems are checked continually with each demand to determine if an order should be placed (thus, the name perpetual). With time-based systems, a count of stock is only made on designated review dates (thus, the name periodic). Production-based systems order stock only to preplanned manufacturing schedules.

There are two major variables in establishing an inventory system. They are the order quantity and the frequency of the ordering process. If one of the variables is held constant, the other tends to fluctuate. The perpetual inventory system holds the order size constant and lets the frequency of ordering fluctuate according to demand requirements. The periodic inventory system holds the frequency of ordering constant by establishing a fixed order period and lets the order size fluctuate according to demand requirements. In the optional replenishment system, the review period is held constant and the order size is variable but no orders are placed until the stock level is less than or equal to a reorder point. The optional replenishment system is really a subset of the periodic inventory system while the two-bin system is a subset of the perpetual inventory system.

PERPETUAL INVENTORY SYSTEM

A perpetual system keeps records of the amount in storage and it replenishes when the stock drops to a certain level. This system is based on the concepts of economic order quantity (EOQ) and reorder point. Under this system the reorder point and order quantity are fixed, the review period and demand rate are variable, and the lead time can be fixed or variable. Figure 6.1 describes the behavior of the perpetual inventory

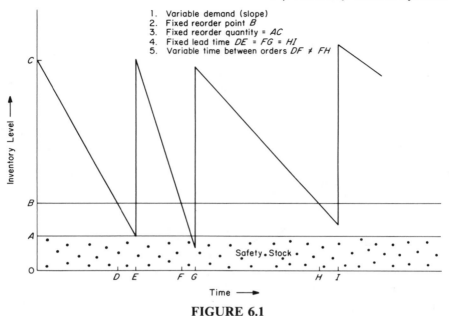

1. Variable demand (slope)
2. Fixed reorder point B
3. Fixed reorder quantity = AC
4. Fixed lead time $DE = FG = HI$
5. Variable time between orders $DF \neq FH$

FIGURE 6.1

system for a single item. The average inventory is the safety stock plus one-half the order quantity (average inventory = $S + Q/2$).

With the perpetual system, each time a unit (or units) is issued from stock the withdrawal is logged and the stock position is compared with the reorder point. If the stock position is at or lower than the reorder point, an order is prepared for a fixed number of units. If the stock position is higher than the reorder point, no action is taken. Thus, with the perpetual system there is constant or perpetual accountability on all items.

The perpetual system is completely defined by knowing the order size and the minimal stock level which signals the placing of an order. The major disadvantage of the perpetual system is that it requires perpetual auditing of the inventory in stock. Since an order can occur at any time, this prevents the economies which result from the amalgamation of several items from one supplier into one order. These potential amalgamation savings can be of considerable magnitude.

Fixed order size systems require a continuing review or observation of inventory levels. The object is to know as quickly as possible when the reorder point is reached. The review may consist of analyzing perpetual inventory records (manual or computerized) as they are posted or visually noticing the physical stock when it reaches the reorder point (the two-bin system is based on physical identification without all the additional records). The fixed order size system with perpetual inventory records is excellent for high cost items needing close control.

The advantages of a perpetual system are as follows:

1. An efficient meaningful order size
2. Safety stock needed only for the lead time period
3. Relative insensitivity to forecast and parameter changes
4. Less attention for slow moving items

A perpetual system can have the following weaknesses:

1. If managers do not take the time to study inventory levels of individual items, order quantities tend to be established by clerks.
2. Reorder points, order quantities, and safety stocks may not be restudied or changed for years.
3. Delays in posting transactions can render the system useless for control.
4. Clerical errors or mistakes in posting transactions can make the system impotent.
5. Numerous independent orders can result in high transportation and freight costs.
6. Large combined orders, which can frequently result in supplier discounts based on dollar value, must be foregone.

The cost of operating a perpetual record system may far outweight its advantages. The cost of record keeping as well as the clerical staffs ability are important considerations in the selection of a system. It is advantageous to use systems which are not quite optimal when the cost of attaining the optimum is prohibitive.

Perpetual control means there is continuous control over the physical units of inventory. Inventory records are kept up to date, an entry being made each time an item is issued or is received from a supplier. Daily records are recorded manually or on punch cards, or are processed by a computer for disk or tape storage. The perpetual system requires (1) an inventory clerk, (2) daily records, (3) material issue and receiving slips, and (4) a guarded or locked storeroom. The two-bin system functions without the daily records, and therefore is a simplified version of the perpetual system.

TWO-BIN INVENTORY SYSTEM

The two-bin system is a fixed order size system. Its distinguishing feature is the absence of a perpetual inventory record. It represents an obvious reduction in clerical work. Records are not maintained of each withdrawal.

The reorder point is determined by visual observation. When stock in one bin is depleted, an order is initiated, and demands are then filled from the second bin.

The system can even be used with only one bin. An order can be triggered when the inventory level reaches a physical mark such as a painted line or a given volume level (for gasoline or other liquids). The reorder point quantity can also be placed in a bag or container, so that when the stock is drawn down to the sealed quantity an order is placed.

The two-bin system is best suited for items of low value, fairly consistent usage, and short lead time, such as office supplies, nuts, bolts, and so forth.

PERIODIC INVENTORY SYSTEM

In a periodic inventory system the number of items in storage is reviewed at a fixed time interval. A count must be taken of the goods on hand at the start of each period.[1] In the perpetual system an actual count is not required, since the inventory records contain receipts, issues, and balance on hand. With the periodic system the quantity to be ordered is not fixed; the decision maker changes it to reflect changes in the demand rate. Under this system, the review period is fixed; the order quantity, demand rate, and reorder point are variable; and the lead time can be fixed or variable. Figure 6.2 describes the behavior of the periodic inventory system for a single item. A maximum inventory level E is established for each item. The order quantity is the maximum inventory level minus the inventory position on the review date.

With the periodic system, the number of units remaining is not reviewed each time a unit (or units) is issued from stock. The periodic system usually accounts for the number of units in stock on the review date by an actual count. The size of the replenishment order is variable and depends on the number of units in stock. The order quantity varies from period to period and depends upon demand.

In the perpetual (continuous review) system, a replenishment order is initiated as soon as the inventory level drops to the reorder point. In the periodic (discrete review) system, the inventory position is checked only at specified time intervals. The perpetual system treats inventory items continuously and independently. The periodic system treats them discretely and dependently. Frequently, it is worth while to treat items in a dependent manner and order them in groups. The advantages of joint orders are

[1]The count may be from an information system relying on a perpetual inventory record, or during an inspection. New point of sale registers and business machines maintain inventory records as well as registering sales. The new machines serve multiple functions and are part of a management information system.

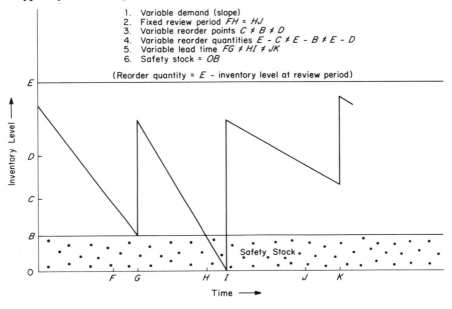

1. Variable demand (slope)
2. Fixed review period $FH = HJ$
3. Variable reorder points $C \neq B \neq D$
4. Variable reorder quantities $E - C \neq E - B \neq E - D$
5. Variable lead time $FG \neq HI \neq JK$
6. Safety stock $= OB$

(Reorder quantity = E - inventory level at review period)

FIGURE 6.2

as follows:

1. A reduction in ordering cost may be possible because items are processed under a single order.

2. Suppliers may offer discounts for purchases exceeding a given dollar volume. The lumping of several items into a single order may attain the discount.

3. Shipping costs may be significantly decreased if an order is of a convenient size, such as a boxcar. The simultaneous ordering of several items can result in convenient sizes.

The presumption in the periodic system is that some sort of physical count is made at the time of review. In many instances records of transactions (sales slips) are available, but the accuracy of the information system may require an actual count for verification (lost or stolen items are not apparent from transaction records). Automatic data processing equipment can provide perpetual inventory records, order decisions still being made on a prescribed basis without the need for an actual physical count of items. Some accommodation must be made in these systems for the return of sale items, errors in transaction accounting, lost items, and stock shrinkage.

The periodic system is completely defined by the order period and the maximum inventory levels. In the perpetual system the safety stock represents protection against demand fluctuations during the lead time period.[2] With a fixed order period, the periodic system requires safety stock for protection against demand fluctuations during both the review period and the lead time. This means that the periodic system will require a larger safety stock for a given item than the perpetual system. This additional safety stock results in the optimal perpetual system being less expensive than the optimal periodic system, though this may be offset by the economies of single supplier item amalgamation. The periodic system is well suited for inventory control when the supply sources are few or when a central warehouse is used.

OPTIONAL REPLENISHMENT INVENTORY SYSTEM

The optional replenishment inventory system, which is also referred to as a min-max system, is a hybrid of the perpetual and periodic systems. Stock levels are reviewed at regular intervals, but orders are not placed until the inventory position has fallen to a predetermined reorder point. Figure 6.3 describes the behavior of the optional replenishment system for a single item. The maximum inventory level is established for each item. If the inventory position is above the reorder point on the review date, no order is placed. If the inventory position is at or below the reorder point on the review date, an order is placed. The order quantity is the maximum inventory level minus the inventory level at the review period.

The optional replenishment system is commonly referred to in the literature as the (s, S) system, where s is the reorder point (B in our notation) and S is the maximum inventory level (E in our notation). The system is defined by three parameters:

1. The length of the review period, T
2. The maximum inventory level E
3. The reorder point B

Note that the perpetual and periodic systems are both defined by only two parameters, while the optional replenishment system requires three parameters.

---

[2]It can be shown that the average inventory will be lower if orders are placed when needed rather than only at set times. However, the cost of operating the continuous record system may far exceed the advantages to be gained from it.

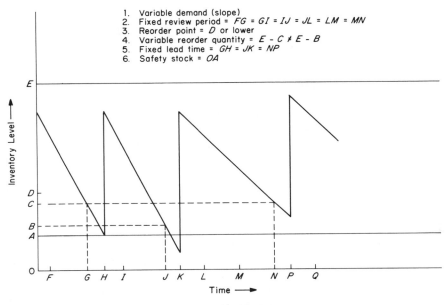

1. Variable demand (slope)
2. Fixed review period = $FG = GI = IJ = JL = LM = MN$
3. Reorder point = D or lower
4. Variable reorder quantity = $E - C \neq E - B$
5. Fixed lead time = $GH = JK = NP$
6. Safety stock = OA

FIGURE 6.3

The system permits orders to be placed in efficient quantities. Fewer but larger orders than the periodic system are placed, so order costs are lower. When the review period is so long that an order is triggered at almost every review, the optional replenishment system is indistinguishable from the periodic inventory system.

The optional replenishment system can require substantial safety stocks. If the inventory level at the time of review is slightly above the reorder point, coverage is required for two order intervals plus the lead time. The review period length is established by procedures appropriate for periodic systems. The reorder point will consist of safety stock plus the expected demand over the lead time and the review period. The safety stock S is determined by analyzing the demand variation occurring for the period covered by the lead time L and the review period T.

MATERIAL REQUIREMENTS PLANNING INVENTORY SYSTEM

The material requirements planning (MRP) inventory system is used extensively with planned production. It is suitable for items which have a derived demand. For items that are materials or components used for end items, stock levels are derived from the requirements dictated by the end item. The material requirements planning system is a derived order quantity system.

This system (also referred to in the literature as a requirements planning system) functions by working backward from the scheduled completion dates of end products or major assemblies to determine the dates and quantities of the various component parts and materials that are to be ordered. The system works well when (1) a specific demand for an end product is known in advance and (2) the demand for an item is tied in a predictable fashion to the demand for other items.

OVERVIEW OF INVENTORY SYSTEMS

Some features of the common types of systems are displayed in Table 6.1. All the inventory systems have advantages and disadvantages as well as different areas of application.[3] The perpetual system is well suited to high cost items where constant review is desirable. The two-bin system has application where constant review is not necessary because of low activity and /or low unit cost. The two-bin system defers action until a reasonable size order can be placed, but it can result in relatively high freight costs.

The periodic system finds applications where (1) there are many small issues of items from inventory, so that posting records for each issue is impractical, as in retail stores, supermarkets, automobile parts supply houses, and similar establishments; (2) purchase orders are placed for many different items from one source or a central warehouse; (3) transportation and ordering costs can be reduced significantly by combining orders. The cost of maintaining the periodic system may be higher because of larger safety stock and the review cost.

The optional replenishment system has the advantages of close control associated with the periodic system and fewer item orders associated with the perpetual system. The optional replenishment system requires the largest safety stock, and the material requirements planning system requires the smallest safety stock. When demand exhibits an upward trend, the perpetual is more desirable than the periodic system. With an upward trend the perpetual system orders more frequently and the safety stock must be increased, but in the periodic system the orders get larger and larger, and more safety stock is required.

Whereas the periodic system involves higher holding costs, the perpetual system tends to cause higher clerical processing costs due to its close control over every transaction (inflow and outflow). The perpetual system

---

[3]For a more detailed quantitative analysis of inventory systems see Richard J. Tersine, *Materials Management and Inventory Systems*, New York: Elsevier North-Holland, 1976.

Table 6.1
Inventory System Features

INVENTORY SYSTEMS: FACTOR	PERPETUAL[a]	TWO-BIN[a]	PERIODIC[b]	OPTIONAL REPLENISHMENT[c]	MATERIAL REQUIREMENTS PLANNING[d]
Order quantity	Fixed	Fixed	Variable	Variable	Variable
Reorder point	Fixed	Fixed	Variable	Fixed	Variable
Review period	Variable	Variable	Fixed	Fixed	Fixed/variable
Demand rate	Fixed/variable	Fixed/variable	Fixed/variable	Fixed/variable	Fixed
Lead time	Fixed/variable	Fixed/variable	Fixed/variable	Fixed/variable	Fixed/variable
Safety stock	Medium	Medium	Large	Very large	Small/none

[a]Perpetual and two-bin systems (Q, B): Review inventory status with each transaction. If inventory $I \leqslant B$, order Q_0. If inventory $I > B$, do not order.
[b]Periodic system (E, T): Review inventory status at intervals of T. Order $E - I$ on each occasion.
[c]Optional replenishment system (E, T, B): Review inventory status at intervals of T. If inventory $I \leqslant B$, order $E - I$. If inventory $I > B$, do not order.
[d]Material requirements planning (MRP) system: Order items to meet production schedules.

with fixed order sizes will be more appropriate if:

1. The number of transactions is low compared to annual demand.
2. Transaction paperwork costs are low compared to ordering costs.
3. The unit cost of the item is high.
4. The stockout cost is high.
5. Demand fluctuations are great and difficult to predict.
6. Holding costs are high.

If the above conditions are reversed, the periodic system will be preferred.

The periodic system has been used extensively in the past. It is probably the most widely used system because of its application at the retail level. With the advent of computers and other less costly business machines, perpetual posting of inventory is becoming more prevalent. At the retail level, the cash register is being replaced by a device that electronically updates inventory levels from the point of the cash or credit transaction. These developments permit the manager to determine inventory levels and investment almost instantaneously. They also make available a substantial amount of information (that was previously unavailable or too costly to obtain) with which to control inventory levels and to make decisions.

SELECTIVE INVENTORY CONTROL

Materials management involves thousands or even millions of individual transactions each year. To do their job effectively, materials managers must avoid the distraction of unimportant details and concentrate on significant matters. Inventory control procedures should isolate those items that require precise control from those that do not. Selective inventory control can indicate where the manager should concentrate his efforts.

It is usually uneconomical to apply detailed inventory control analysis to all items carried in an inventory. Frequently, a small percentage of inventory items account for most of the total inventory value. It is usually economical to purchase a large supply of low cost items and maintain little control over them. Conversely, small quantities of expensive items are purchased and tight control is exercised over them. It is frequently advantageous to divide inventories into three classes according to dollar usage defined as the product of annual usage and the unit purchase cost or production cost. This approach is called ABC analysis. The A class are high value items whose dollar volume typically accounts for 75–80% of the value of the total inventory, while representing only 15–20% of the inventory items. The B class are lesser value items whose dollar volume accounts for 10–15% of the value of the inventory, while representing 20–25% of the inventory items. The C class are low value items whose volume accounts for 5–10% of the inventory value but 60–65% of the inventory items. Figure 6.4 shows a typical ABC inventory classification. The breakdown into A, B, and C items is arbitrary, and further groups or divisions may be established.

The inventory value for each item is obtained by multiplying the annual demand by the unit cost. Annual demand is used to avoid any distortions due to seasonal usage. The entire inventory is listed in descending order from the largest value to the smallest. The items are then designated by the ABC classification system.

The same degree of control is not justified for all items. The class A items require the greatest attention, and the class C items the least attention. Class C items need no special calculations, since they represent a low inventory investment. The order quantity might be a one-year supply with a periodic review once a year. Class B items could have EOQs developed with a semiannual review of its variables. Class A items could have EOQs developed with a review of the variables each time an order is placed. The major concern of an ABC classification is to direct attention to those inventory items that represent the largest annual expenditures. If

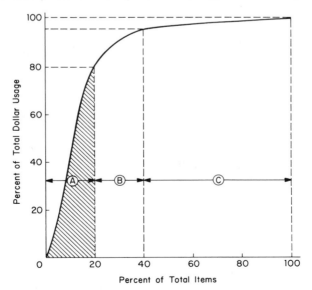

FIGURE 6.4

inventory levels can be reduced for class A items, a significant reduction in inventory investment will result.

The purpose of classifying items into groups is to establish an appropriate level of control over each item. The ABC analysis is useful for any type of system (perpetual, periodic, optional replenishment, and so forth). With the periodic system, the ABC analysis can be subdivided so high usage items receive a short review and low usage items receive a much longer review. On a periodic basis, class A items might be ordered weekly, B items biweekly, and C items quarterly or semiannually. Note that the unit cost of an item does not determine the classification. An A item may have a high dollar volume through high usage despite low cost (or through high cost despite low usage). Likewise, C items may have a low dollar volume because of low demand or low cost.

The ABC classification emphasizes which items should receive the greatest control, on the basis of dollar usage or sales volume. It indicates nothing about their profitability or criticality. Frequently the absence of a C item can seriously disrupt production. The item can then be forced into the A or B classification even though its dollar usage alone does not warrant its inclusion.   Management judgment must be exercised in the control of critical items.

Class A items deserve close control, because each item represents a significant amount of inventory value. For this reason, the perpetual system is often used. Class B items are of less value than A items, and the optional replenishment system is frequently employed. It is usually more economical to combine orders for several items. Class C items may have a loose policy with six month to one year purchase quantities. A two-bin inventory system can be used effectively for these items, since it requires very little paperwork. The service levels for Class C items can be set very high because of their limited investment. Class A and B items usually have a lower service level determined by an economic cost analysis.

The advantage of an ABC analysis lies in a relaxing rather than in a tightening of inventory control (separate the "vital few" from the "trivial many"). Control is relaxed in that less emphasis is put on C items, which represent the bulk of the inventory items. The ABC analysis gives a measure of inventory importance to each item.

The A, B, and C classes are artificially produced strata. Organizations may choose to group their inventory into more than three classifications, but the principle is the same. High value items receive the most attention and low value items the least. Each organization should tailor its inventory system to its own peculiarities.

Before items can be classified, other factors than financial ones must be evaluated. Additional considerations can drastically change an item's classification as well as its control procedure. Some important factors might be:

1. Difficult procurement problem (long and erratic lead time)
2. Likelihood of theft
3. Difficult forecasting problem (large changes in demand)
4. Short shelf life (due to deterioration and obsolescence)
5. Too large a storage space requirement (very bulky)
6. Operational criticality

The ABC system does not apply to dependent demand items controlled under an MRP system. Its primary application is to end items, which are characterized by demand independent of other end items. Dependent demand items tend to be of equal operational importance for the continuation of production. Even the lowest cost item can totally disrupt dependent organizational activities. Therefore, operational criticality overrides the item's financial influence.

INVENTORY SYSTEM DEVELOPMENT

The development and implementation of an inventory control system to meet the needs of a specific organization is a customizing operation. Since inventory management is not an island unto itself, the system must serve the goals of the organization as well as the service objectives of other departments. It is usually easier to develop an inventory system for a new company which has just been created. If a revised system is planned for an existing company, the period of change can be traumatic. When a new system is introduced, operational procedures must be revised, forms and reporting techniques are changed, employee work patterns are modified, and operating efficiency is usually diminished.

The decision to implement or subsequently redesign an inventory system rests with top management. However, the ultimate fate of an inventory control system usually lies in the hands of operations personnel lower down. To avoid resistance to change and implementation difficulties, the affected departments should be included in the design of the inventory system. Their inclusion usually results in a better system with fewer behavioral problems when it is installed. Departments which help create the inventory system tend to nurture it during the implementation phase and correct unanticipated design flaws. Without employee support, any inventory system is subject to demise or at least a turbulent future.

Should the system be manual or computerized? Just as with any prospective investment, a cost-benefit analysis should be conducted. The decision will be influenced by many factors, the most important probably being the volume of work to be handled. Mini-computers and similar business machines are making electronic control a viable alternative for more and more organizations. Since electronic systems are providing additional benefits (accounting, control, and administration) beyond stock control, it is no surprise that they are popular.

A popular retail and wholesale device is called a point-of-sale terminal. There are two types: keyboard and wand reader. The wand reader automatically inserts information in a terminal by reading magnetic strips on specifically designed tapes when the product is passed over a sensing device. The keyboard is similar to a cash register, but it updates records of inventory status with each sale or withdrawal.

The use of computers in materials management is growing rapidly. Manual methods in many cases have reached their limit. The computer can perform and develop forecasts, reorder points, order quantities, order intervals, product explosions, record maintenance, customer billing, inventory status, and supplier payments. Manual systems with clerical control are viable for small organizations with fewer material needs.

When initiating an inventory system, the following hints can be helpful:

1. Inventory will invariably increase very quickly. Items whose order quantity is increased will be ordered at once, and the stock will increase. Items whose order quantity is decreased will take time until their level is worked off.

2. Forecasting should be based on daily or weekly data, since lead times are frequently shorter than a month. Monthly forecasting data can conceal patterns of demand occurring during the month and complicate estimates of shorter lead times.

3. Try the system on a limited number of items initially to solve any unforeseen problems with it before it is totally implemented.

4. Run the pilot study manually (with a calculator) on a small number of items, so personnel can understand it thoroughly. If the final system will be computer-based, the pilot study can be manual as well as automated.

5. Before the total system is to be implemented, verify that all personnel involved understand it and are committed to its success.

There are many approaches to designing an inventory system; this section will cover a single approach that can provide a general framework. The generalized procedure is outlined in Figure 6.5.

A necessary precondition for developing the inventory system is forecasts of all end items produced or used by the organization. Item forecasts

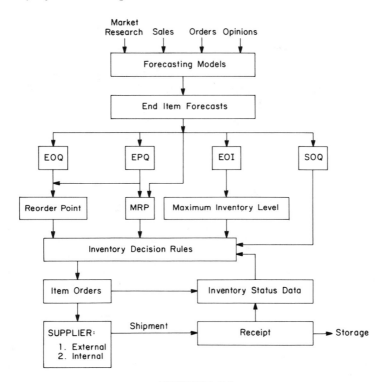

FIGURE 6.5

are developed from forecasting models such as were covered in Chapter 3. After item forecasts are obtained, an ABC analysis of the inventory will indicate what system or systems would be preferable. If a perpetual or two-bin inventory system is indicated, the EOQ and EPQ models can be employed. If conglomerate orders are necessary, the EOI model can be utilized for the periodic or optional replenishment inventory systems. If items fall into the single order category, the SOQ model can be incorporated. If items are needed to support scheduled production operations, the MRP model can be applied.

From the various models and an understanding of the peculiarities of the organization, inventory decision rules can be established for all items. When inventory decision rules indicate items should be ordered, purchase requisitions are transmitted for the appropriate supplier. For external suppliers, purchase requisitions are transmitted to the purchasing departments which then contracts for the items. With internal suppliers, production requisitions are transmitted to the production control department, which then schedules the production of items.

When ordered items are received from the suppliers, they are quality accepted and put into inventory. Needless to say, all of the transactions involve the generation of paper for accountability and control. Inventory systems are best maintained from a central control location that can indicate the status of any item. These records become the data base for forecasting models. Because of the quantity of items and the proliferation of paperwork, inventory systems are good candidates for computer control.

The ultimate success of an inventory system is in the transformation of inventory theory into workable detailed procedures. The design of forms and procedures can be more important than precise quantitative accuracy. Any inventory system requires the collection and processing of vast quantities of data.

The foundations of any inventory control system are input data and control records, which must be current and accurate. Inventory control is based on the accuracy of records of inflows and outflows. Poor records and data can destroy a perfectly designed control system. Inadequate records result in operating personnel finding informal methods (usually to the subversion of the formal procedures) for satisfying inventory needs: hoarding, stockpiling, overordering, early ordering, and so forth. Accurate and up-to-date records permit an inventory system to function efficiently and effectively.

Modern analytical techniques have taken much, though not all, of the guesswork out of inventory management. No longer need stock levels be determined solely by habit, hunch, or accident. Formulas are available to establish order quantities and order intervals, while statistical probability theory can be applied to safety stock determination. Intelligent and informed management judgment has not been replaced, however, but only supplemented. Both qualitative and quantitative evaluations involving considerable study, collaboration, and teamwork are usually required before intelligent decisions can be made and effective systems implemented.

The design of inventory systems must include sufficient flexibility to permit growth, expansion, and internal change without upsetting the operational system. The system must be able to cope with the exceptional item or event. It should also be capable of being integrated into the other organizational systems with little difficulty.

SURPLUS MATERIALS

Of all the problems facing the materials manager, three tend to be particularly troublesome:

1. Disposition of scrap, obsolete, and surplus materials
2. Ever increasing storage space requirements
3. Slow moving materials

Scrap is defective material that cannot be used in its present condition. It may be reworked, or discarded if no salvage value is evident. *Obsolete material* is good material for which a need no longer exists because of design or model changes. *Surplus material* is good material of which the available quantity is excessive. If management discards or salvages scrap, obsolete, or surplus material, the inventory turnover will increase, but profit for the period will be reduced. The decision to retain or salvage can be based on a cost-benefit ratio. If the following inequality holds, the material should be retained in inventory; otherwise it should be subjected to salvage:

$$\frac{p(M)P}{FV} > 1,$$

where

$p(M)$ = probability of sale or use within a year,

P = cost or market value of the material,

F = annual inventory holding cost fraction,

V = salvage value.

Surplus material, or inventory for which there is no exhibited demand, should be searched out and disposed of. Usually some arbitrary rule is applied, such as that material that has not been active for a period of one year is classified as surplus. All surplus items should be sold at their best price or discarded. Surplus inventory can be expensive because of the resulting perpetual holding costs. Any losses on surplus inventory are charged off against income, and income taxes are reduced.

Some of the possible disposal routes are as follows:

1. Circulation within organization
2. Return to supplier
3. Direct sales to another firm
4. Sale to a dealer or broker
5. Sale to employees

Mistakes are inevitable. Items are procured for needs which do not materialize, requirements are overestimated, plans change, and excessive stock tends to mount. Regardless of how efficiently an inventory is managed, surplus materials will accumulate and must be periodically dispositioned.

INVENTORY SYSTEM IMPROVEMENT

Each purchase or production situation must be preceded by a decision making process. The number of items involved can range from scores to millions, and the number of transactions is far in excess of the number of items. The decision making process may be simple or complex, programmed or nonprogrammed, intuitive or mathematical, hasty or deliberate. There are many ways an inventory manager can reduce his costs. Some of the more apparent methods are as follows:

1. *Reduce lead times.* By selecting local suppliers (close to the organization's geographical location), substantial reductions in cost can be achieved. Local supply can reduce lead times, which lowers the reorder point and safety stock. Frequently, it is worth paying a higher unit cost for a local supply, since inventory can be maintained at a lower level. Local supply can eliminate purchase order preparation, since one can phone in orders.

2. *Inform suppliers of expected annual demand.* If suppliers are aware of your annual needs they can plan their production to have sufficient inventory available to meet the expected demand. This action can reduce lead time and permit the supplier to better plan and schedule production operations.

3. *Contract with suppliers for minimum annual purchases.* Contract to purchase a fixed annual quantity from suppliers, with payment on receipt of materials. Quantity discounts can be obtained in this manner, while materials are ordered and received in economic quantities. This approach can also be a hedge against future price increases.

4. *Offer customers a discount on preordered items.* If customers order items before they need them, inventory reductions can be achieved by specially ordering items. However, if customers received too great a discount on such items the price reduction may outweigh the increased holding costs associated with high inventory levels.

5. *Maintain multiple suppliers.* Multiple suppliers can increase costs by reducing bulk purchases. However, multiple suppliers provide an alternate source if one supplier fails to deliver the goods. It is not uncommon in production systems for reliability of supply to be more important than minor price differences. Multiple suppliers also permit cost comparisons which help to maintain a competitive price structure. With supplier competition, unit costs tend to be lower.

6. *Buy on consignment.* Arrange with suppliers to pay for their items as

they are sold or used. This will transfer a large portion of the holding costs to the supplier.

7. *Consider transportation costs.* Failing to consider transportation costs and the most economical mode of transportation can increase the unit cost considerably.

8. *Order economical quantities.* Overbuying in relation to needs results in excessive holding costs.

9. *Control access to storage areas.* Protect against losses from theft, spoilage, unauthorized withdrawals by employees, and the ravages of the elements.

10. *Obtain better forecasts.* More reliable and precise forecasts can substantially reduce safety stocks.

11. *Standardize stock items.* Inventories can be reduced by reducing the quantities of each item or the number of different items used in stock. Inventory investment can be lowered by carrying one standard item instead of five different items that are used for essentially the same purpose.

12. *Dispose of inactive stock.* On a regular basis all stock should be reviewed to identify obsolete, poor quality, surplus, and slow-moving items. Disposal alternatives include return to the vendor, scrapping, reworking, salvage, and reduced-price sales.

Frequently the quickest, most effective way to reduce inventory is better priority planning and control of operations. A poorly devised operating system may appear efficient with the aid of excessive inventory. Improved planning and scheduling of operations can reduce the investment in inventory.

Organizationally, the inventory control function is usually assigned to the purchasing or the production control department. Purchasing feeds the inventory reservoir, while production control draws from it. Because department managers tend to neglect the significance of costs outside their own departments, the materials management concept has developed. The materials manager consolidates purchasing, inventory control, and production control into a single operating unit. The materials management concept grew out of the frustration of many companies at not being able to control inventory effectively. It is not uncommon for departments to continually find fault with each other, when the true culprit is an inadequate organizational structure.

The number of items in inventory has been growing because of the increasingly technical nature of the items, a demand for greater variety by customers, and requirements for better service. The number of dollars invested in inventory is growing at a faster rate than the number of items. Computerization may hold the key to the solution of these problems. The computer aspect of materials management has been intentionally downplayed so as not to divert the reader from the really important subject matter. The computer's contribution lies in its power to execute a multitude of straightforward procedures in a very short time. While it is an essential tool of materials management, it is not essential to·the understanding of the fundamentals.

Decisions to add new products, purchase foreign components, and add distribution points can have a dramatic effect on inventory investment. Likewise, uncontrolled product proliferation, errors in transaction documentation, and outdated bills of material create serious problems. Computer routines and analytical techniques do not obviate the need for good management.

AGGREGATE INVENTORY MEASUREMENT

Aggregate inventory measurement relates to the overall level of inventory and the techniques for its measurement. Since aggregate inventory management plans and controls for the totality of inventory, it in essence "looks at the forest and not each tree". Four common ways to measure aggregate inventory are as follows:

1. Aggregate inventory value
2. Ratio of aggregate inventory value to annual sales
3. Days of supply
4. Inventory turnover

An organization may use one or more of the above for aggregate inventory measurement.

Aggregate inventory value is simply the total value of inventory at cost. It is very simple and easy to use, but it neglects the dynamic nature of inventory and its other financial interactions. The *inventory to sales ratio* is the total value of inventory at cost divided by annual sales. This ratio recognizes the dynamic relation between inventory and sales, but it can vary substantially due to cost and/or selling price changes.

The *days of supply* is the total value of inventory at cost divided by the sales per day at cost. The days of supply recognizes the dynamic nature of inventory, but it can become distorted if the cost of sales is not maintained and controlled. The *inventory turnover* is the total value of inventory at cost divided into the annual sales at cost. Inventory turnover recognizes the dynamic nature of inventory, but like all ratios it too can easily become distorted.

Aggregate inventory measurement techniques reduce inventory items to a common financial measure (dollars). The techniques measure results in absolute terms or ratios. The desirable range of performance is established historically, by industry data, or by management judgment. While measurement in financial terms is desirable, inventory should also be viewed in its other dimensions (composition, flexibility, contribution to organizational objectives).

CONCLUSION

An effective inventory system should be relative, dynamic, and truthful. *Relative* refers to meeting the needs of other organizational functions or departments. The system is dependent on the needs of others. *Dynamic* refers to the time varying nature of inventory needs. Any system must react to expected and unexpected changes. *Truthful* refers to the ability to report accurately the stock or position of inventory when required.

It is not uncommon to have different types of inventory systems in use in the same organization at the same time. Management's responsibility is to manage the organization's assets, both human and nonhuman, in the light of preconceived goals. Inventory tends to have an impact upon all the functional areas. It should not be surprising that inventories are troublesome and controversial in view of their manifold influence. The inventory function is outlined in Figure 6.6.

Control can be a two-edged sword. Intense overcontrol is just as undesirable and costly as undercontrol. A *carte blanche* attitude towards new sophisticated control systems can be very costly. New systems that save hundreds and cost thousands of dollars are unhealthy investments. A control system (or systems) should be installed on the basis of its cost-benefit relationship and not to achieve control as an end in itself.

The design of aggregate materials management systems can be approached from different angles. Often emphasis is put on specific control models rather than the relevant systems. A broad based aggregate program should include at least the following elements:

1. Determination or delineation of organizational goals
2. Assessment of the significance of materials management to organizational goals
3. Determination of aggregate material needs

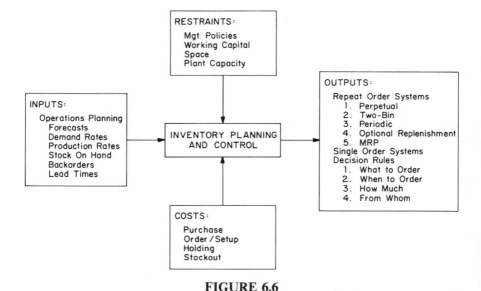

FIGURE 6.6

4. Design of appropriate material control models
5. Design of forecasting models
6. Measurement and collection of model parameter inputs
7. Model testing and implementation
8. Variable reporting and model redesign
9. Operationalization of the materials management system

The decision to institute a materials management system can be just as important as the choice of the particular models for the system. Too frequently an organization is adapted to a mathematical model rather than vice versa. The system designers must tread a strait and narrow path between the pitfalls of oversimplification and the morass of overcomplication.

The problems of inventory and materials management are ubiquitous and complex. No simple formula takes into account all of the variables encountered in real situations. The value of good approximations in permitting a practical and understandable solution to a problem is often far greater than any loss caused by a lack of accuracy or precision. Aggregate inventory analysis is not a precise science.

QUESTIONS

1. What is an inventory control system?
2. What should an effective inventory control system accomplish? What typical areas should be considered in developing a comprehensive inventory control system?
3. What are the two major variables in establishing an inventory control system?
4. Name five of the most frequently used types of inventory control systems.
5. What are the advantages of the perpetual inventory control system?
6. What is the major advantage of the two-bin inventory control system when compared with the perpetual inventory control system?
7. For what types of items are the perpetual and two-bin inventory control systems best suited?
8. What two values completely define the periodic inventory control system?
9. Compare the safety stock requirements of the periodic inventory control system with those of the perpetual inventory control system.
10. What are the advantages of the optional replenishment inventory control system?
11. What is a derived demand?
12. What considerations can drastically affect an item's classification as well as its control procedure in an ABC inventory analysis?
13. What are the differences between scrap, obsolete, and surplus materials?
14. How can inventory costs be reduced by offering customers a discount on preordered items?
15. How can inventory costs be reduced by maintaining multiple suppliers?

PROBLEMS

1. Given the following group of inventory items in the table, develop an ABC inventory system where A items constitute 80% of the total dollar value, B items 15%, and C items 5%.

Table for Problem 1

ITEM	UNIT COST	ANNUAL UNIT DEMAND
1	.15	2,600
2	.05	6,500
3	.10	22,000
4	.22	75,000
5	.08	110,000
6	.16	175,000
7	.03	8,500
8	.12	2,500
9	.18	42,000
10	.05	2,000

Case 1: Higher Service Levels

Hopson Steel is a distributor of steel and metal products. It has sales territories in twelve states which are served from six warehouses. Each warehouse is autonomous and carries enough inventory to cover sales in two states.

Profits and sales at Hopson Steel have not changed appreciably over the last five years. To the dismay of the major stockholders, the profits of competitors have increased. In an effort to institute change, Mr. Benton, the President, has replaced the company's general manager with Mr. Arnold Cohen. With considerable effort and a substantial salary offer, Mr. Cohen was persuaded to leave his position with a sporting goods firm.

Upon arrival with the firm, Mr. Cohen examined sales records and market forecasts for the steel industry. He predicted a substantial increase in demand for several products. After commenting several times that increased sales would be the salvation of Hopson Steel, he issued the following directives to each of his six material managers.

1. Purchase and stock at each warehouse *all* items listed in the general supply catalogue.

2. Purchase large quantities of products for inventory so quantity discounts can be recognized.

3. If economically possible, purchase economic order quantities (EOQs).

4. Inventory levels will rise, but the larger holding cost will be offset by increased sales due to the higher service level.

5. All managers who exceed last year's performance will receive bonuses.

Within a few months, sales increases were reported along with predictions of even greater increases by year end. The warehouses reported the largest stock of steel products in the company's history. Labor negotiations between the steel industry and labor unions were at an impasse, and it appeared that a strike was imminent. Fearing that a strike would deplete inventory levels when sales were increasing, Mr. Cohen urged the procurement of even larger quantities of steel products from any source available.

Although a strike did occur, it lasted for only a week. At the end of the year, Mr. Benton reported a sales increase for the company but a loss on operations. He attributed the poor performance to high inventory levels and other unexpected costs. Although with some reservation, Mr. Benton predicted a brighter year ahead, with increased sales and a return to profitability. He reaffirmed his complete trust in Mr. Cohen's ability.

1. Discuss the merits of each of Mr. Cohen's directives to his material managers. Do you agree with them?

2. Do you share Mr. Benton's trust in Mr. Cohen?

3. As a stockholder, what would be your opinions about the president's comments on the future of the company? Do you foresee any major problems?

Case 2: Material Shortages and Delayed Production

Zoom Equipment, Inc. produces a full line of earth moving equipment including tractors, dirtmovers, and shovels. It manufactures almost all component parts for the machines, with a few exceptions. Sam Irwin, the new production manager, realized quickly that a major problem existed in the production department. A shortage of parts on the assembly lines was costing Zoom thousands of dollars.

Sam's first step in attempting to alleviate the problem was to investigate the company's make or buy decision procedures. He started his investigation in the accounting department. After some searching, he realized he'd have to get actual out-of-pocket costs from the manufacturing department itself. There he was told that actual costs of parts varied considerably from one run to another for several reasons, the main one being that when it came time to assemble a piece of equipment there was seldom a sufficient quantity of all parts needed. The result was usually a schedule-upsetting rush order through the machine shop to make the needed parts.

Sam decided to track down the reasons for the parts shortage on the assembly lines. He spent the next several days talking to the workmen and supervisors. Sam learned that the marketing department forecasted sales of all equipment and parts about nine months in advance. The production control supervisor then prepared a list of all parts required and added a manufacturing spoilage allowance to the quantities needed. This allowance was as follows:

a. Large items, 1%

b. Costly or intricate parts, 2%

c. Other parts, 3%

The quantities of parts in inventory were compared with this list. If requirements exceeded inventory, a purchase order or manufacturing order was placed to bring inventory up to the required level.

Sam got the impression that the shortage problem had existed for some time: the cost accounting department actually budgeted for excess labor costs resulting from shortages on the assembly lines. After completing his investigation Sam made a list of reasons for the shortages, and they included:

a.   Inadequate spoilage allowances

b.   Errors in annual physical inventory count

c.   Incorrect count of parts put into production

d.   Poor machine loading

e.   Insufficient raw materials purchased

f.   Foremen performing clerical tasks

1.   Are any of Sam's reasons for shortages on the assembly line valid?

2.   How would you correct the shortages?

3.   What type of inventory control system should be adopted by Zoom?

Case 3: Control and Operating Methods

Automobile dealerships have a large and continuing need for supplies and materials in their function of selling and servicing automobiles. Facilities usually include buildings spread over several acres of land. The departments that have special needs for supplies are:

a.   *Office*—office supplies and special forms

b.   *New car predelivery service*—cleanup material and lubricants

c.   *Used car reconditioning*—cleanup material and lubricants

d.   *Body shop*—paint and materials, including thinner, sandpaper, files, tape, etc.

e.   *Mechanical shop*—supplies and materials.

At Tidewater Motors, salesmen from various suppliers make regular calls, check inventory levels, and recommend purchases. Normally the dealership parts manager acts as purchasing agent. However, salesmen go directly to the foremen of the different departments, since in most cases the supplies are stored at the department location. Thus, the foreman is the real purchasing authority and instructs the parts manager to issue the necessary purchase orders.

The advantages of the existing system are that the salesman can solve any problems with his products, salesmen can check inventory levels, and very little of the parts manager's time is required. Disadvantages are that the salesman tries to sell the foreman and workers on his products (this often creates problems when brands are changed), the salesman tends to oversell actual needs, and price increases frequently go unnoticed.

Recently, Dick Terry took over as owner of the Tidewater Motors dealership. Upon reviewing his investment in inventory, he concluded that his inventory turnover was too low. He decided to investigate new control and operating procedures that might reduce his inventory investment.

1. Should all material and supplies be kept in one central location instead of being stored in close proximity to where they are used?

2. Should the parts manager make all decisions concerning the purchase of supplies?

3. Should salesmen be able to deal directly with foremen and workers, or should they deal only with the parts manager?

Inventory Valuation

Inventory, in an accounting sense, represents value assigned to goods either acquired or produced for subsequent sale or for use in production. Inventories are normally valued at cost or some modification of cost, such as the lower of cost or market value. Inventory accounts at a particular point in time are a snapshot view of the total value of inventory items either on hand or in process. As a corollary, the amounts deducted from inventory accounts during any particular period of time are the basic data for determining the cost of goods sold during the period. Obviously, consistent policies and methods of inventory valuation are imperative for the useful measurement of performance between time periods and for interpretation of financial position at any given time.

Inventory poses problems in valuation, control, safeguarding, and cost allocation. They directly affect the income statement and the balance sheet. They usually represent a significant fraction of current assets or even total assets.

Inventory has physical and financial characteristics. The physical characteristics (flow of goods) are factual and objective, whereas the financial characteristics (flow of costs) are more subjective. The physical and financial aspects are usually distinct and independent problem areas for an organization. In this section, emphasis will be placed on the financial problems associated with the flow of costs.

The financial significance of inventory is attributable to the need for measuring operating performance or income over a particular time period (month, quarter, or year). The valuation of items consumed during the period is needed for this purpose. Inventory influences performance additionally in that suboptimal inventory policies will reduce income by incurring unnecessary expenses.

Inventory costs and expenses will depend on the accounting procedures adopted. Accounting procedures determine when and how a change in assets owned will be recognized, and when and how assets are transformed into costs and expenses. Facts are not altered, but accounting procedures govern the recognition of events which affect periodic income determination.

The importance of matching costs with revenue for the income statement is generally acknowledged. In periods of rapid price change (inflation), a part of the increase in earnings is attributable to the rise in prices. During an inflationary period, the goods on hand at the beginning of the period will generally be sold at a higher price than contemplated at the time they were purchased. This increase in revenues will be reflected in the income for the period; however, if inventory is maintained at the same quantity levels, the additional revenues received will have been expended to a substantial extent in purchasing the replacement inventory units. Thus, the increase in income is illusory; it is frequently termed "inventory profits".

The primary basis for inventory accounting is cost. Cost for inventory purposes may be determined under any one of several assumptions as to the flow of costs. Material is ordered, not just once, but on a continuing basis. Therefore, organizations have to plan on the same basis. There is no one prescribed procedure to be used in the determination of inventory cost for accounting purposes. There are a number of standard procedures, together with combinations and variations of them. The major objective in selecting a method is to clearly reflect periodic performance. To determine the dollar amount of inventory at any given point in time, the quantity of inventory items on hand must be known and a value must be assigned to those quantities. The quantity of items on hand is obtained by counting or measurement. The value assigned to individual items is based on one of several accounting methods. The accounting method used is very important, since the total dollar amount of inventory and the related cost of goods sold can be significantly different based on the method adopted.

The inventory accounting problem can be subdivided into the method of valuation and the inventory flow method. There would be no problem if unit costs were constant; but during a period of time, items are frequently purchased or manufactured at different unit costs. Thus one must decide how to cost the items sold for the income statement (cost of goods sold) and how to value unsold items for the balance sheet (inventory).

FLOW OF COSTS

The inventory flow method refers to the way items are taken from inventory. The assumed flow for accounting purposes may not be the same as the actual physical flow of goods. The selection of the assumed inventory flow method by the accountant will determine the flow of costs. There are various inventory flow assumptions in use today. However, four of them account for more than 90% of current usage. In decreasing order of frequency of use, they are:

1. FIFO (first in, first out)
2. LIFO (last in, first out)
3. Average cost
4. Specific cost

The above inventory flow methods are primarily concerned with the flow of costs rather than the flow of physical goods. The selection of a flow method will depend upon several factors, including the type of organization, the projected economy, industry practice, the tax rules, and other regulations. Once a flow method is adopted, it is not easy to change to another method, because of income tax requirements and accountants' concern for consistency in reporting to outsiders.

All of the inventory flow methods are simply schemes to carry costs from the balance sheet to the income statement as expenses. The costs allocated do not have to match the actual physical flow of goods. Goods can be sold by the oldest-first scheme and yet be assigned costs by the last unit produced. The flow of goods does not have to be related in any way to the flow of costs.

FIFO

The most widely used inventory flow method is called FIFO, which stands for "first in, first out". It is assumed that materials are issued from the oldest supply in stock, and units issued are costed at the oldest cost listed on the stock ledger sheets, with materials on hand at all times being the most recent purchases. Under FIFO, inventory cost is computed on the assumption that goods sold or consumed are those which have been longest on hand and that those remaining in stock represent the latest purchases or production.

FIFO tends to coincide with the actual physical movement of goods through many organizations. It is scrupulously followed for goods that are subject to deterioration and obsolescence. The ending inventory from FIFO closely approximates the actual current value, as the costs assigned to these goods are the most recent. While this technique tends to produce inventory assets at current costs, the advantage of an accurate balance sheet presentation can be offset by distortions of the costs of sales for the income statement. When the price of materials and other costs are subject to change, FIFO is not likely to result in matching costs against revenues on a current basis. Thus, cost changes can create income statement distortions from what would be obtained if current costs were applied.

FIFO is fairly simple and compatible with the operations of many organizations. Inventory records are usually kept on a perpetual or periodic basis. With perpetual systems, all changes to stock (additions, subtractions, or deletions) are recorded for each incoming or outgoing transaction. With periodic systems, only additions to stock are entered, and a physical count of stock is made at specific time intervals to determine stock status. FIFO is adaptable to either perpetual or periodic inventory systems. The use of FIFO simplifies record keeping requirements, as the actual flow usually coincides with record keeping activities.

LIFO

LIFO, which stands for "last in, first out", assumes that the most current cost of goods should be charged to the cost of goods sold. Under LIFO, the cost of units remaining in inventory represents the oldest costs available, and the issues are costed at the latest costs available. The stocks sold or consumed in a period are those most recently acquired or produced; the remaining stocks are those earliest acquired or produced. LIFO charges current revenues with amounts approximating current replacement costs.

The underlying purpose of LIFO is to match current revenues against current costs. However, LIFO can result in an unrealistic inventory valuation for balance sheet purposes which distorts the current ratio and other current asset relationships. It decreases income during periods of rising prices and increases income during periods of falling prices. It is often favored because it results in reducing income taxes during a period of rising prices. Just like FIFO, LIFO can be used with either perpetual or periodic inventory systems.

During inflationary periods, LIFO can mean lower profits, lower income tax, and more cash on hand. Inflation can create a ballooning effect on income if goods sold are costed at their purchase cost, which has subsequently increased. Such income ("inventory profits") is unrealistic because it ignores the need of an organization to replenish inventories at higher prices. LIFO protects against "inventory profits". For organizations with a high rate of inventory turnover, LIFO provides no benefit, since their costs are closely matched to revenues anyway.

AVERAGE COST

In an attempt to provide the elusive perfect combination of a realistic ending inventory and cost of goods sold, the average cost method was developed. This method does not attempt to indicate what unit went out first or last, but rather to determine the average cost for each item during a time period. There are three types of averages that can be used:

1. Simple average
2. Weighted average
3. Moving average

All three averages can be used with a periodic inventory system, but only the moving average is well suited to the perpetual inventory system.

The simple average is determined by dividing the sum of production or purchase unit costs by the number of production runs or orders. The simple average neglects the size of the lot (number of units) and gives the unit production or purchase cost of each lot equal weight regardless of the variation in the number of units. The weighted average corrects the distortion of the simple average by considering quantity as well as unit cost. The weighted average divides the cost of goods available for sale or use by the total number of units available during the period. The moving average computes an average unit cost after each purchase or addition to stock. It is well suited for computerized inventory operations.

The simple average and weighted average cannot be calculated until the period is over. Thus, they are not well suited to perpetual inventory systems. The moving average is used for perpetual inventory systems. All of the averages are well suited for periodic inventory systems, in which costs are not allocated until the end of the period.

With the average cost method, the costs of all like items available during the period are averaged to obtain the ending inventory value. During periods of increasing or decreasing cost, the average cost method tends to narrow the range of costs. With a trend upward or downward, the average cost changes more gradually than the other inventory flow methods. The average cost method, while simple to apply, has all the limitations of any average figure. The resulting cost cannot be related to any tangible unit, and it does not reveal price changes as clearly as may be desired.

SPECIFIC COST

Of all the inventory flow assumptions, the specific cost method provides the most realistic valuation of ending inventory and cost of goods sold. The cost of maintaining records under the specific cost method can mount very quickly, however, so its application is usually limited to large, expensive items handled in small quantities. The procedure consists of tagging or numbering each item as it is placed in inventory so its cost is readily discernable.

This inventory valuation method is frequently used in job shops where custom-made products are produced to customer order. Although if a large number of custom orders are in process, its implementation can be costly and difficult. Of course, the cost flow and the physical flow are identical with this method. It has the added flexibility of being suitable for either perpetual or periodic inventory systems. With a large number of items or operations, costs tend to average out, and the extensive record keeping expense is not warranted by the added accuracy of specific cost identification.

There are many methods of inventory costing or valuation. The method chosen should be practical, reliable, and as easy to apply as possible. As long as unit costs remain the same, all the methods are essentially equivalent. When unit costs change dramatically, major differences appear. If the inventory turnover is very high, the differences among the methods are diminished. There is no standard recommended practice for inventory costing. The choice depends upon the organization and its objectives.

INVENTORY RECORDS

Inventory items should be classified and properly identified so they can be located for proper verification. Control over inventory includes the methods of storage and handling. Control is necessary to ensure against errors (inaccurate counts), embezzlement, damage, spoilage, and obsolescence. Control is usually accomplished through a series of inventory records and reports that provide information on usage, balances, and receipts. Appropriate control requires a periodic verification of items and records. It is desirable for record verifications and physical counts to be conducted by an independent agency with no interest of its own in the operations.

Some of the basic data required to keep meaningful and useful inventory records are as follows:

1. Item identification and/or classification
2. Item location
3. Unit cost and net prices
4. Interchangeable and/or substitute items
5. Shelf life
6. End item (what it is used on or with)
7. Dates item entered inventory
8. Dates of withdrawal
9. Supply sources
10. Unit balance

Every inventory system must be concerned with inventory record accuracy. An inventory system is doomed to failure unless data integrity can be maintained. It is not uncommon for more attention to be given to the more interesting technical aspects of a system while overlooking the "mundane" aspects of inventory record accuracy. Whether manual or computerized, record accuracy is critical to operations. Two requirements for accurate inventory records are:

1. A good system for recording all receipts and disbursements
2. A good system for auditing record accuracy which discovers and corrects the causes of errors

The condition of inventory records is influenced by the personnel involved, physical control, and the system. The *personnel involved* are the people who physically receive, issue, and store material, as well as the first line of supervision of those people. The stockroom supervisors must accept responsibility for and take pride in maintaining record accuracy. Without their full support their subordinates cannot be expected to strive fully for record integrity. Operatives must be instructed and trained in stockroom operating procedures so they recognize the importance of accuracy. It is desirable to set accuracy goals, measure accuracy, and post records of performance in comparison with goals.

An important aspect of *physical control* is to limit and control access to the storeroom. Each time a part is added to the stockroom or withdrawn from it, the transaction should be logged in the appropriate record.

Unauthorized and undocumented transactions must be stopped, or control is virtually impossible. An enclosed and locked storeroom with access only to authorized personnel can do much to control undocumented transactions. It is desirable for all parts to be identified by part number and geographical location in the storeroom. A clean and well-ordered storage area will reduce lost and misplaced items.

An efficient way to utilize space in the stockroom is to use a locator system. The stockroom is divided into sections and subsections with an appropriate numbering scheme. Parts are stored in the same location or in an available one, and the location is noted on the receipt card along with the part number. As part issues are required, the warehouseman proceeds to the designated location of the part. A well-devised locator system can contribute much to data integrity.

A physical count of items is necessary to verify the integrity and accuracy of inventory records. Differences between book (record) and physical inventories must be ascertained. Any differences (variances) must be adjusted and the amount of overage or underage properly accounted for. A periodic physical count of inventory can be made of all items, or a cycle count program can be instituted. A physical count of all items usually involves a closing of the facility for a limited time while the quantities of all items are substantiated and records updated. The cycle count method involves the continuous counting of inventory throughout the year.

PERIODIC COUNT METHOD

The periodic count method refers to the periodic auditing of the inventory balances on hand to verify and maintain accurate inventory records. The inventory record may be manually posted, machine posted, or maintained by a computer. The periodic count method requires a complete count of all categories of inventory over a short time period. For most organizations, an annual or semiannual verification is adequate. If only one physical inventory is taken in a year, it is usually timed to coincide with the yearly low point in production and inventory levels.

Taking an annual physical inventory is like selecting a marriage partner: the time spent in preparation can pay off handsomely in the final results. A written standard procedure should be prepared which can also serve as a training document. Preparation for the physical inventory should involve the following:

1. *Housekeeping.* Arrange material in its proper location so it can be inventoried easily.

2. *Identification.* Make sure all items are properly identified with part number and nomenclature.

3. *Instruction.* Review inventory-taking forms and procedures with personnel prior to taking inventory.

4. *Training.* Train appropriate personnel in use of scales, counters, and measurement procedures.

5. *Teams.* Establish inventory teams of two or more members and assign responsibility to count, check, and record the inventory levels.

On the day of the count, operations in the storage areas should be terminated. A holding area should be designated to retain all material received during the period so it is excluded from the count. All internal movements and shipments should be suspended for the duration except for emergencies. If the count will require several days, customers should be advised of the shutdown dates.

The tag method of recording inventory levels is universally used. Tags are appropriate for manual and computer systems. The inventory teams take the count, fill out the tags, and place them on the materials. When an inventory team has completed an area, it is checked to ensure that all items are tagged (spot checked for accuracy) and the tags collected. Items in the shipping dock, export holding area, returned goods area, marketing displays, and so forth should also be included in the count.

The inventory records and the physical inventory should be reconciled from the inventory tags. The inventory data from the tags are transferred to inventory summary sheets. An auditing team should check any significant discrepancies and reconcile them before materials start to move again. Appropriate adjustments should be made to inventory records and general ledgers so the record balance agrees with the quantity actually on hand.

The frequency of taking physical inventory is often determined by the value of the item and the ease of disposing of the item in the open market. Expensive or precious items may be inventoried much more frequently than general inventory items.

CYCLE COUNT METHOD

This method requires continuous counting of stock throughout the year. A limited number of items are checked every day or on some other time interval. Personnel can be assigned to cycle count on a full-time or part-time basis. The stock items to be checked may be selected at random or according to a predetermined plan. Of course, the cycle count method does not require a disruptive termination of operations as the periodic count method does.

The cycle count method is becoming more widely used by organizations. It permits the use of specialists or regularly assigned stores personnel to conduct the physical count. When regularly assigned stores personnel are utilized, they can perform the cycle count during lulls in their assigned duties. When specialists are used, they are full-time personnel who continually count inventory items. In large organizations specialists are desirable, since they become familiar with items, the locator system, the storage system, and "peculiar" things that can occur.

The cycle count tests the condition of inventory records and provides a measure of record accuracy. Record accuracy can be measured by the percentage of items with error and the relative magnitude of the errors. The significance of the error is related to the relative value of the item. An error of one unit for an expensive item is significant, while an error of plus or minus 2% might be acceptable for low cost items.

Cycle counting can prioritize concentration on the integrity of inventory items with high annual dollar usage (ABC principle). The A items (highest annual usage items) should be counted most frequently; C items the least frequently. A items might be counted every one or two months, B items every three or four months, and C items every year. Since C items represent the bulk of the inventory items but a small percentage of investment, less effort is expended on them. Each organization must establish a cycle count based on its own peculiarities.

Several procedures have been developed to vary the cycle count frequency. Some of the more prevalent systems are as follows:

1. *ABC system.* Stratify items on the ABC principle with the highest frequency on A items and the lowest on C items.

2. *Reorder system.* Count items at the time of reorder.

3. *Receiver system.* Count items when replenishment order is received.

4. *Zero balance system.* Count items when balance on hand is zero or negative (backorder).

5. *Transaction system.* Count items after a specific number of transactions have transpired.

Of course, various combinations of the above systems can also be used.

With cycle counting only a small portion of the total stock is being investigated at a given time. This reduces the magnitude of the problem substantially. Each day's count can be reconciled promptly without delay. Cycle counts can be established so all inventory items are counted at least once during a year, or on a statistical sampling basis. With statistical procedures, only a random sample of items in a given category are counted, and the results are generalized to the population of items.

The cycle count method is an excellent method for maintaining record accuracy. Some of the more apparent advantages are as follows:

1. Operations do not have to be terminated during the cycle count, and the annual physical inventory is eliminated.
2. Errors are discovered quickly, inventory records adjusted throughout the year, and the causes of errors eliminated.
3. Records and the statement of assets are improved in accuracy. Inventory counts are not performed under pressure; this usually results in more accurate measurements. Year-end inventory writeoffs can be eliminated; one has a correct statement of assets throughout the year.
4. Specialists become efficient in obtaining good counts, reconciling differences, and finding solutions for systematic errors.
5. Efforts can be concentrated in problem areas.

INVENTORY SECURITY

Security requirements vary widely among organizations and are dependent upon the nature of the material—its value, size, weight, application, utility, and resalability. Generally, the more valuable an item, the greater the need for security. However, some expensive items require relatively little protection because of their size, weight, and limited utility (for example, large castings, or special molds).

Materials can be safeguarded by establishing and enforcing storeroom regulations. A periodic auditing of storeroom operations can reveal existing or potential security problems. The following measures apply to storeroom operations:

1. Limit access to store areas to authorized personnel.
2. Count, weigh, and measure all materials received.
3. Require authorized orders and requisitions for all material transactions.
4. Store valuable items in locked cabinets or in safes if necessary.
5. Keep storerooms locked and enclosed except during working hours.
6. Periodically spot-check stock on hand against inventory records.
7. Investigate unusual consumption for improper use.
8. Periodically check the authenticity of signatures and authorizations.
9. Provide security bonds for storeroom personnel to protect against losses through negligence or theft.

The effort, time, and money spent on the security of inventory should be allocated among the items in proportion to their relative importance. At no time should the cost of security exceed the benefits to accrue from it.

QUESTIONS

1. What is meant by the term "inventory profits"?
2. What are two components of the accounting inventory method?
3. Name the four most commonly used inventory flow methods.
4. Which method is best suited for goods that are subject to deterioration and obsolescence?
5. What is the primary disadvantage of the FIFO inventory flow method?
6. How does the LIFO inventory flow method protect against "inventory profits"?
7. Name three types of averages that can be used in the average cost inventory flow method. To which types of inventory system does each apply?
8. What are the limitations of the average cost inventory flow method?
9. What situation is suitable for application of the specific cost inventory flow method?
10. Under what conditions are the four inventory flow methods essentially equivalent? Different?
11. Differentiate between the periodic count and cycle count methods of taking a physical inventory.

Case 1: Loose Security and Employee Theft

The Westside Automotive Company repairs automobiles and sells related parts and equipment. The owner, Bill Westside, recently read an article in a newspaper about employee theft. He decided to conduct a study to see if Westside had a theft problem. Bill was shocked when he discovered a substantial amount of money was being lost due to theft. He immediately began a program to tighten control.

Part of the new control procedure was to spot check employees' vehicles as they left work for the day. When the contents of one mechanic's pickup truck were examined, ten boxes of spark plugs, ten sets of points, three distributor caps, and two sets of new spark plug wires were discovered. Further investigation revealed that Bob Gavin, the mechanic, was operating a small repair shop out of his garage with parts and equipment stolen from Westside.

Because Gavin had been with the company fifteen years and was one of the best mechanics in the area, the company decided to handle the matter internally, instead of reporting it to local authorities. Gavin was asked to appear before a group of three people: Bill Westside; John Stephens, a union representative; and Alan Jones, the personnel manager. Gavin's only defense was that everybody took parts and supplies from the company quite frequently. A thorough investigation found this to be correct. The company accountant estimated that about $6000 in supplies and equipment had been stolen within the last 12 months.

After considering all the factors and implications of the situation, the personnel manager recommended that Gavin be fired. This, he claimed, would set an example for the other employees. John Stephens argued against firing Gavin. He contended that, through lax control procedures, Westside actually encouraged theft. He also argued that since theft was so widespread, it would be unfair to single out Bob Gavin. Bill Westside was very concerned about losing his best mechanic.

1. What action would you recommend against Gavin? Why?
2. Could the situation have been prevented? How?
3. Is this type of theft common in organizations?
4. What security precautions would you implement for the company?

Case 2: A New Neighbor

Harold Hosiner is the director of material for Conforma Foams Inc., a producer of styrofoam forms used in floral and holiday decorations. Harold's neighbor is Gerry Burns, a junior executive with a local accounting and auditing organization. Gerry recently moved to the area, so, to get acquainted, Harold invited him to his next backyard cookout.

At the cookout Harold and Gerry began to talk shop. Gerry was enthusiastic about his last two assignments, auditing a small plumbing distributor and a producer of eyeglass frames. Gerry's most interesting comments concerned inventory valuations:

"From what I have seen in the past few weeks, I see no reason why all businesses don't switch to LIFO. The profits realized by our clients more than pay for our services. With the economy the way it is today, we are recommending LIFO across the board."

Since Conforma was not using LIFO, Harold had some questions, but the hamburgers had to be turned and Gerry began to mingle with other guests.

The next morning Harold sat in his office pondering the conversation of last evening. He knew Gerry's firm had a good reputation, and he thought Gerry was an intelligent young man. Could a switch in inventory valuation policy improve Conforma's profit picture? Was Gerry's experience applicable to Conforma? Harold began to analyze these questions when he received a call from the director of finance. This would be an excellent opportunity to begin discussions on the feasibility of moving to LIFO.

1. Do you agree with Gerry Burns' comments on LIFO?
2. What advice would you offer to Harold Hosiner?

Case 3: Evaporation or Shrinkage

E. G. Truck Rental is a large national truck leasing and rental company. Although located primarily in the northeast of the United States, it has districts in every state except Alaska and Hawaii. For the last ten years E. G. has maintained an edge over its competition by providing better service to its customers. One key aspect of this better service is always being able to supply its long-term lease customers with fuel. E. G. guarantees lease customers that none of their vehicles will sit idle during any fuel shortage.

Prior to a major fuel crisis E. G. purchased all its diesel and gasoline fuel from one major supplier. Fuel was delivered in drops of either 6500 or 8500 gallons. Deliveries were made on a regular basis (usually three times per week), and underground fuel tanks were checked daily. Dipstick readings were recorded and compared weekly against inventory records kept by the office personnel. Pricing of the fuel inventory was also done by office personnel and was a fairly routine task when the price of diesel and gasoline fuel was stable.

When the fuel shortage hit its peak, E. G.'s major fuel supplier refused to fulfill its commitment and supply all the fuel needed. In an attempt to keep its promise to its long-term lease customers, E. G. purchased fuel from several national and local suppliers. Deliveries were made at all hours of the day and night, including weekends. Although dipstick readings of E. G.'s underground fuel tanks were still taken daily, it became very difficult to match the inventory records maintained by the office personnel to the actual gallons of fuel received. Also, some small local suppliers actually pumped less gallons of fuel into the underground tank than they billed for.

Due to the fuel shortage the price of diesel and gasoline fuel began to fluctuate by as much as twenty cents per gallon. Many suppliers sent duplicate billings to E. G.'s home office in New Jersey requesting payment, even though they had already billed the location to which the fuel was delivered. In a six months period, approximately 15,000 gallons of fuel were unaccounted for or stolen.

1. How could the fuel shrinkage have been prevented?

2. During times of rising prices what inventory flow method is desirable?

3. Will the shrinkage influence the dollar value of inventory?

Chapter 8

Materials Handling

Various departments or locations in an organization are responsible for influencing the flow of material. Responsibilities can be categorized in terms of organizational functions, each subjecting material to activities supporting their organizational objectives. As it is made available to production, physical supply, or distribution, material must be processed, stored, counted, and transported. Availability requirements demand the movement of material within and among organizational functions. Materials handling is concerned with all aspects of the flow of material *within* an organization. Material movements within a plant or warehouse are referred to as materials handling, while movements outside the plant are known as transportation and physical distribution.

The objectives of materials handling are usually:

1. To eliminate handling wherever possible,
2. To reduce travel distance to an absolute minimum,
3. To increase speed of processing by providing uniform flow free of bottlenecks,
4. To reduce goods in process in order to provide a faster turnover of working capital,
5. To minimize losses from waste, breakage, spoilage, and theft.

Handling material is a major portion of the cost of manufacturing, distribution, and marketing. Every time material is handled, costs are incurred. Movement and control generally add no value to a product, so handling operations should be minimized. The importance of materials handling to an organization is related to the proportion of materials handling cost to total product cost. In the production of low unit value, bulky items the handling cost is usually a major cost factor; in the production of high unit value items, it is usually minor. In either case, however, poor materials handling can lead directly to product damage, customer dissatisfaction, production delays, and idle employees.

It is common to consider materials handling as an auxiliary activity hosted by the function representing the most intense material movement, usually production. However, a brief review of a typical flow pattern reveals the presence of movement demands throughout an organization. Depicted in Figure 8.1, materials handling requirements are apparent in each of the following areas:

1. Physical Supply
    a. Receiving
    b. Counting
    c. Storing
    d. Order Picking
    e. Sorting
    f. Shipping
2. Production
    a. Work station transfer
    b. In process storage
3. Transportation and Physical Distribution
    a. Loading
    b. Unloading
    c. Staging
    d. Transporting

Materials handling occurs over the entire range of the flow of material. In order to treat the entire flow of material in an integrative manner, it is necessary to recognize the interdependence among the various organizational functions. The   pronounced influence of materials handling on several organizational functions makes it a significant determinant of

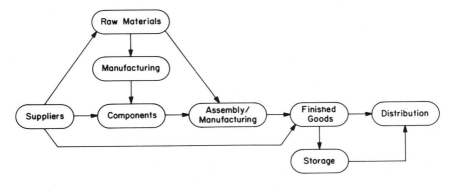

FIGURE 8.1

operational efficiency and effectiveness. As such, it is appropriate to evaluate materials handling as a separate organizational function.

Conceptually, the materials handling function offers a cohesive mental framework for evaluating the functional influences of the flow of material. Because of its bearing on organizational effectiveness, the materials handling function has recently attracted increased managerial interest. Materials handling activities are essential to performance in other functions. Managed as discrete activities within individual functions, they become duplicative, costly, and ineffective. Treated as an integrated function, materials handling offers important opportunities for cost control and operational efficiencies.

As illustrated in Figure 8.2 the materials handling function is characterized by inputs, restraints, flow factors, and outputs. Inputs include supply demands, production demands, distribution demands, and flow analysis. They are complicated by the fact that they may originate from variable sources and the temporal frequency is difficult to predict.

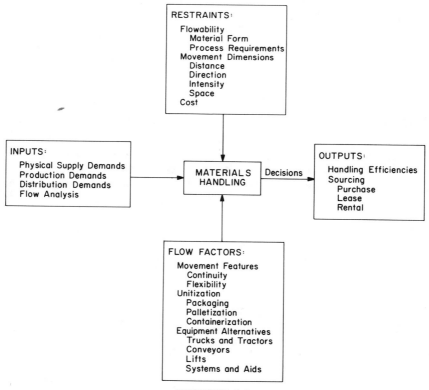

FIGURE 8.2

Restraining the decision process are considerations of flowability, movement dimensions, and cost. Features of the decision environment which require attention are called flow factors and include movement features, unitization, and equipment alternatives. Ultimately materials handling decisions result in the functional outputs of handling efficiencies (related to system's definition) and sourcing (related to equipment selection).

MATERIALS HANDLING INPUTS

A major obstacle to understanding the materials handling function is the absence of a concise set of documents serving as functional inputs. In an effort to establish paper inputs, some documents from other areas might be designated as inputs. Obviously, the bill of lading has a role in materials handling with respect to receiving and shipping. Similarly, picking tickets play a part in order retrieval and transfer, while work orders may dictate handling procedures in production. However, the arbitrary selection of inputs is both fallacious and excessively limiting. The fallacy is apparent in that concentration on inputs closely related to other functions forces a disjointed approach, giving a treatment of materials handling as a set of discrete activities, which is not supportive to a functional view. It is limiting because relevant inputs are not necessarily definable as a convenient collection of common use documents.

While materials handling does exist as a unique and definable organizational function, it has qualities which broaden the scope of potential inputs. Materials handling facilitates flow and serves other functions. To be effective it must be highly integrated with each function served. That requirement tends to cause materials handling to assume characteristics similar to those of the functions served. Thus, in receiving, shipping, and order processing, materials handling may appear as a part of the physical supply function. In manufacturing operations, it takes on characteristics of the production function. In vehicle loading and unloading, it appears as an element of the distribution function. However, materials handling does retain its functional identity. The relationships between materials handling and the functions it serves can be described as being *functionally transparent*. While its visibility is diminished by other more obvious activities, it still exists as an identifiable entity.

Functional transparency can generate an invalid perception of the materials handling role, but it also accents the important functional relationships in the flow of material. The relationships involve a transmission of influence from functions served to materials handling. These influences can be evaluated as inputs to the materials handling function. Major inputs are derived from demands originating from the physical supply, production, and distribution. Additionally, materials handling requirements are often specified in a flow analysis document.

SUPPLY DEMANDS

Since the physical supply function concerns material transfer, retrieval, and storage, it must be able to move products among and within points of use. These requirements are demands on the materials handling function. The most visible means for satisfying movement demands is in the wide variety of handling equipment. Mechanical handling aids are obvious in receiving, shipping, order picking, and storage.

Physical supply activities are interwoven throughout the material flow cycle. It is through materials handling capabilities that physical supply maintains the integrity of the flow. *Frequency* and *volume* parameters determine service loads which must be met by materials handling. Likewise, materials handling offers service flexibility to respond to changes in the physical supply function. Materials handling methods and equipment may vary from activity to activity in the physical supply function; however, it is a normal objective to employ common and interchangeable methods and equipment. The potential for use of multipurpose methods and equipment is apparent in the similarity of demands originating in receiving and shipping or storage and retrieval.

Receiving and shipping demands are usually met with equipment characteristic of the materials handling function. Fork trucks, conveyors, hand trucks, and dollies are common devices used in receiving and shipping. Equipment used in retrieval and storage is often more difficult to classify in such a fashion. Order picking equipment may appear to be a part of an order processing system, and storage devices may be seen only as warehouse facilities. It is important to isolate specific movement demands and then integrate handling techniques to meet functional objectives even though the technique may be a logical part of another function.

PRODUCTION DEMANDS

Production demands for materials handling capabilities are either expressed through the physical supply function or placed directly on the materials handling function. Expressed through the physical supply function, demands usually involve movement of raw material and components from a place of storage to the point of production or from there to a place of storage or use. Common handling equipment such as trucks, conveyors, and dollies is used for these purposes. Job-shop and intermittent production systems usually place simple demands on the materials handling function. It is also normal for additional handling support to be required for in-process storage and production staging. Such support may involve the use of bins, roll-carts, racks, pallets, or tables. Manpower may be employed directly with or without mechanical handling aids.

Sophisticated production processes require closer support from materials handling. In continuous production systems, materials handling is often considered an integral element of the production process. Since material undergoes handling and production simultaneously, the two operations must be in concert. Examples are in the production (and handling) of soft drinks and crushed stone. In the former case, raw materials (syrup and carbonated water) are gathered in hoppers for injection into containers (bottles or cans) as they *move* in the *handling* system. They are then sealed and packaged or crated. In the latter case, raw stone is usually fed by conveyors to the crushing mill, processed, and then packaged or conveyed to a storage location. Notice in each case the dependence on movement in the handling systems. Numerous other examples in the areas of television, glass, fertilizer, automobile, and tire manufacturing illustrate the interdependence between production and materials handling.

It is apparent that production capabilities have been greatly enhanced through technology. Almost without notice, materials handling has become a high technology industry. This phenomenon is relatively easy to appreciate if materials handling is viewed in a context of satisfying production demands. Complex and sophisticated production procedures generate similar handling requirements. Witness the role of materials handling in achieving balance in continuous production processes. In modern production, movement represents inefficiency. The objective of materials handling is to minimize the inefficiencies inherent in the production function. High technology production capability is only as efficient as the materials handling function that serves it.

DISTRIBUTION DEMANDS

The most significant demand originating from distribution is for the handling capability to generate maximum-density load units compatible with vehicles of conveyance. Operational and cost effectiveness of the physical distribution function depends in large part on handling techniques providing optimal load characteristics. Here, handling equipment and handling aids are important. Handling equipment includes common devices such as trucks and conveyors; handling aids include devices to unitize loads. For load unitization, the pallet and the container are primary handling devices. They not only establish characteristics for a load, but they also serve to consolidate items into units which can be easily handled by mechanical devices. These devices receive more extensive attention later in this chapter.

FLOW ANALYSIS

Materials handling derives its inputs from various other functions in the organization. Because it influences the flow of material, which does not recognize functional boundaries, materials handling must be evaluated in terms of all active inputs. Discrete inputs must be synthesized into a statement of demands placed on the handling function. To this end the flow analysis is important. A flow analysis will indicate the path of travel which material will follow as it moves from station to station. The flow may be straight, circular, serpentine, U-shaped, or irregular.

Flow analysis refers to a method for defining the functional demands placed on materials handling. Results are usually embodied in the form of a chart using common symbols to represent features of a procedure. Several of the most prominent chart types are *process charts*, *operation process charts*, and *flow process charts*. Process charts graphically represent events during a series of operations, such as procedural events in the assembly of a product. Operation process charts offer graphic representations of operational sequences and material introduction in a procedure. They may include other information such as operator time requirements, machine requirements, and machine locations. While both process charts and operation process charts are helpful in evaluating an operation,

Subject_____ Date_____

Operation Number	Process Type				Distance (feet)	Time (min)	Description
	O	•	□	▽			
1			□			2	Inspect 3 pieces
2		•			20	1	Move to polisher
3				▽			In process storage
4	O					5	Polish each piece
5		•			50	1	Move to packaging
6			□			1	Inspect
7	O					1	Pack
8		•			500	5	To shipping
9				▽			Await order

Conventions: O - Operation   ▽ - Storage
              □ - Inspection • - Transport

FIGURE 8.3

materials handling requirements are usually more apparent in the flow process chart.

As illustrated in Figure 8.3, flow process charts graphically represent the sequence of all operations, including transportation, inspection, delay, and storage events. Other information may include time requirements and movement distances. Notice the inclusion of important handling demands: material, time, place, and distance. Further, analysis often adds movement *intensity* to the flow process chart, expressed as volume and frequency of movement. With the flow process chart, the inputs to the materials handling function are interpreted and analyzed in an interdependent manner. The aim is to attain maximum movement efficiency while remaining cost effective. Anything less than an integrated systems approach is too costly or inefficient.

RESTRAINTS

Like other materials management functions, materials handling is subject to considerations which limit decisions. These restraints help define the scope of a decision environment by establishing boundaries within which attention is focused. Restraints set the tone of decision making because they exert a continuous influence on other elements of the function. They continue to operate even if management ignores them. Thus, careful evaluation of materials handling restraints is a prerequisite to effective decision making.

The restraining factors vary from organization to organization, depending on the size of the organization, the particular type of enterprise, and economic conditions. However, there are several rather broad categories of restraints which are common to all organizations and are valuable reference points for evaluation. They include flowability, movement dimensions, and cost.

FLOWABILITY

Flowability refers to the affinity of material and process characteristics with flow requirements. Given that material must move within and among points of use, the efficiency of movement is directly related to flowabililty. Therefore, flowability can be adequately explained by evaluating material and process characteristics that influence movement. While each can be analyzed separately, it is important to note that final evaluation must be accomplished by considering the simultaneous and interacting influence of material form and process requirements.

Material Form

The form of the material restricts the number of handling methods available to increase flowability. Material forms can be generally segregated into three categories, each with important relations to flowability. *Bulk* material exists in a loose unpackaged state without constant dimensions. Material in a bulk state such as stone, wheat, sand, and petroleum is easy to move in a fixed flow pattern using conveyors and pipelines, but it is not efficiently moved in a variable flow pattern. *Itemized* material exists as discrete parts, components, or assemblies with definite dimensions. It may be packaged, or maintained in a loose state. Small items are efficiently moved individually in a fixed flow pattern using conveyors, or in a variable flow pattern by hand or using light mechanical aids such as dollies and carts. Large items can be moved in a fixed pattern using specialized equipment (overhead cranes, monorails, and underfloor tows) or in a variable pattern using manually operated trucks. *Unitized* material is a set of consolidated items grouped together to afford form characteristics more conducive to effective handling. Bulk or itemized material may be packaged, containerized, or affixed to a platform (pallet), or a combination of the three, to make it more flowable. Such units can be efficiently moved on either a fixed or a variable path. Containerized and palletized material can be moved with fixed path methods, but they have the added advantage of being efficiently moved by the commonest variable flow device, the fork truck. Regardless of the form of material, there are other physical characteristics which cannot be ignored. Characteristics such as fragility, hazard, and deterioration can affect or even determine flowability.

Complicating the impact of material characteristics on flowability is the probability that material form will not be constant. For example, in most production and fabricating operations, the form of raw material and component parts is appreciably different from that of the finished product. Handling methods for raw material and component parts may not be appropriate for the finished product. Distribution (marketing) oriented organizations have a similar problem in that they must handle many products to satisfy consumer demands. While form does not change, it varies with the product. Thus, form homogeneity plays an important role in determining the degree of difficulty in achieving effective flowability.

It is interesting to note that properties of material are not generally modified for the purposes of flowability. Material may be rearranged, packaged, containerized, or palletized, yet it retains its essential physical properties. The necessity for flow exists regardless of physical properties. The methods and mechanics of flowability are usually designed or modified to accommodate material characteristics.

Process Requirements

Different production and distribution processes have different effects on flowability. In a production organization, the activity level (speed) and number of operations dictate flowability. A continuous production process requires a continuous material flow, usually fed by fixed flow handling systems. High volume, repetitive handling operations result in fixed paths of material flow. On the other hand, intermittent and job shop processes usually require variable flow handling procedures. Very complex processes and those with demanding production tolerances may require a high degree of flexibility.

With numerous product types, distribution organizations depend on accessibility and selectability. It is common for materials handling systems to support both fixed and variable flow capabilities. Because of the similarity in operations, computer technology has enjoyed wide application in achieving access and selection efficiencies in distribution organizations.

MOVEMENT DIMENSIONS

Movement dimensions quantify the flow of material. For any given flow problem, a materials handling solution is restrained by several operational and environmental dimensions. These dimensions are physical and lend themselves to analysis and measurement. The most important dimensions of a material flow are distance, direction, intensity, and space. Since they often cannot be readily altered, they act to restrain decision making. Evaluation of movement dimensions usually begins with the flow analysis and its descriptive charts. Once dimensions are established and measured, further analysis is necessary to determine their impact on handling decisions.

Distance

Material flow connotes movement between points of use over some geographic distance. Obviously, as distance increases, so does dependence on handling capabilities. Directly related to distance are temporal considerations, since timing demands control the speed of movement between points of use. Geographic and temporal characteristics of distance restrain handling in several ways. As the distance between use points increases:

1. Materials handling costs increase.

2. Efficiency decreases.

3. Reliability decreases.

The costs, which will be addressed subsequently, include expenditures for equipment and labor as well as indirect expenses. Efficiency decreases because of additional time involved in the flow of material or because of the technical complexity of accelerating the flow. Efficiency also deteriorates because material being handled is not usually available for production. Finally, reliability is diminished when material is subjected to extensive travel because of influences such as vibration, damage in handling, or handling system failure.

One of the major objectives of the materials handling function is to maximize flow efficiency. Movement between locations is not productive, and materials handling must serve to make movement efficient. One way to accomplish it is simply to eliminate movement. Since that is generally impractical, one optimizes the flow of material by minimizing distance. With this in mind, it is not surprising that most handling equipment and systems are designed for movement over short distances.

An interesting relationship among materials handling and the other functions it serves becomes apparent. As movement distances become very small, materials handling approaches production or physical supply as a function. Conversely, as distance increases, materials handling functionally approaches transportation and distribution. For example, newsprint requires handling during printing, but that is accomplished as an essential part of the production operation; gravity fed picking racks are simple materials handling devices usually associated with physical supply activities. Material flow which entails movement over great distances, as between plant locations, is referred to as distribution rather than materials handling. Between the two extremes lies the realm of materials handling, a realm in which the efficiency of unavoidable movement must be maximized through minimizing distance.

Direction

The direction in which material flows plays a major role in determining the efficiency and cost of a materials handling system. Frequently, direction is predetermined by existing facilities and operational (production, physical supply, or transportation) procedures. In such cases, efficiency depends on the availability of materials handling equipment. In terms of direction of flow in an existing facility, the materials handling function is restrained to the point of being controlled by rather static parameters. The most opportune method available to overcome this restraint is to include directional considerations in the initial planning during the flow process analysis.

Mechanical efficiency in the direction of flow is greatest when the amount of work required to effect movement in minimized. In order of decreasing efficiency, movement may be *downward, horizontal*, or *vertical*. Downward movement allows the flow of material to take advantage of gravity, a power source which is constant, requires no motorized aids, and most important, is free. Excellent use of gravitational forces is made in some conveyor applications, chutes, and gravity fed bins. Unfortunately, gravity provides a flow which is unidirectional, which will not satisfy all movement requirements in the material flow cycle. Where gravity applications are not possible, horizontal movement is most efficient. Horizontal flow requires artificial power (push or pull, man or machine). The amount of work required is usually lessened by the use of wheels or rollers. Carts, dollies, some conveyors, and trucks are examples of equipment frequently used to move material horizontally. With vertical flow both down and up movement is necessary. Here, of course, lifting requires work. Since material generally has to flow in various directions, one should keep in mind the importance of direction relative to flow efficiency and cost.

Intensity

Intensity is the movement dimension which quantifies the amount of material handled. Often referred to as *flow loading*, intensity is specified in measures of volume and frequency. Volume is a measure of the gross amount of material to be moved over some planning period—a single movement, or a week, month, or year. Frequency is the measure of how often a constant volume is moved during a given period of time. Intensity is dictated by functions other than materials handling and acts to limit the selection of handling procedures and equipment. Interaction between production operations and other functions is frequently expressed in terms of volume and frequency of interacting material flow. Preventing bottlenecks by balancing the flow between use points is a major responsibility of the materials handling function.

Space

The physical environment of an organization is an important restraint on the flow of material. Specifically, plant layout represents static confines to material flow, within which materials handling must seek to provide necessary dynamic flow capabilities. Available space in a facility is allocated to the various organizational functions according to priority of need. Thus the functions compete for space. Like other resources, space can be effectively used only if it is efficiently distributed. It has been noted that materials handling activities are apparent in other functions, primarily production, physical supply, and distribution. Thus, materials handling competes for space in two ways, directly for its own unique needs and indirectly through the sponsorship of other functions.

Direct demands for space include obvious needs such as floor space for fixed equipment, operating room for mobile equipment (turn space and aisle width), and clearance for equipment with overhead tolerances. Aisles must be wide enough so personnel and mobile handling equipment can move through the facility. The layout of the facility should permit an efficient flow of men and material.

Space utilization is so important that special management techniques have evolved to ensure acceptable performance. Simply stated, these techniques represent planning criteria with which requirements and capabilities can be projected and performance evaluated. By function, the major planning tools are: shop floor planning for production, stock planning for physical supply, and movement planning for distribution. Each considers the functional impact of materials flow, including requirements for space.

Because of the rising cost of real estate, the spatial environment in many organizations is following a trend away from the single level, land intensive facility. Multilevel structures are often more economical to acquire or construct when land is expensive than sprawling single story buildings. This tendency has a major influence on the materials handling function. Multilevel facilities require vertical material flow, which is less efficient than horizontal flow. Thus, it is probable that the materials handling function will have a greater dependence on expensive mechanically powered equipment.

COST

Investments in personnel and capital equipment are made with the intention of benefiting by some discernible economic return. With outlays for materials handling, it is difficult if not impossible to isolate a measurable return. It is therefore considered a cost center in most organizations. The cost is frequently an indirect accounting charge to production, physical supply, distribution, or operations. Or it may be absorbed in the general overhead of the organization. In general, materials handling costs are included in indirect labor and burden. Whatever its accounting classification, materials handling cost is substantial, representing up to 50% of total production cost in many basic processing industries.

To appreciate the full thrust of materials handling costs, it is useful to classify cost elements under direct and indirect charges. Some of the major cost elements are summarized in Table 8.1. In evaluating expenditures for materials handling it is important to remember that an objective of the

Table 8.1
Materials Handling Costs

Direct	Indirect
1. Equipment	1. Down time
2. Labor	a. Equipment
3. Maintenance	b. Labor
4. Operating	2. Damages
	3. Overhead
	4. Opportunity

materials handling function is to minimize total cost. Thus, increased materials handling expenditures (costs) may result in reduced overall organizational cost. Materials handling costs are not completely avoidable, only controllable. Decision makers face a cost problem in which a comparison should be made of the costs of making or not making an additional expenditure.

Whether materials handling systems are manual, mechanized, or automated is another comparative cost consideration. *Manual systems* are highly labor intensive with little reliance on support equipment. *Mechanized systems* tend to reduce labor intensity and use a combination of labor and handling equipment. *Automated systems* minimize the labor content and are highly equipment intensive. Most automated handling systems are custom designed and constructed for each particular application. The selection of a handling system should be based on an incremental or cost-benefit analysis.

In high-volume, repetitive operations, materials handling systems are automated. With automation, direct supervision of handling activity is eliminated. Automation increases the importance of materials handling to an organization. A major portion of the final cost of a product with an automated system will be the materials handling cost.

FLOW FACTORS

In addition to restraints that temper the decision environment of materials handling by limiting management prerogatives, several other considerations are important because of their influence on decisions. These considerations, called flow factors, serve as a common foundation of rudimentary information upon which intelligent decisions can be based. An understanding of the flow factors reveals that they broaden the scope of decision alternatives rather than act as restraints. Thus, flow factors possess an affinity for modification which offers flexibility to the decision making process.

Three essential categories of flow factors are embodied in the materials handling function. *Movement features* describe the variability of material flow, *unitization* is concerned with methods of enhancing material flowability, and *equipment alternatives* encompass the vast array of hardware available to meet handling requirements.

MOVEMENT FEATURES

While flowability restrains materials handling in facilitating flow, the flow itself exhibits movement features which can be modified to accommodate restraints. Through flow variation, materials handling is subject to management control. Freedom to adjust variables is dependent on the organizational setting and its attendant functional restraints. However, as elements of management control and as instruments capable of overcoming restraints, movement features are important to all organizations.

To address movement features it is convenient to establish two categories universally descriptive of material flow. Continuity and flexibility are ubiquitous characteristics of all materials handling systems. Together they are primary operational considerations in equipment selection. A separate analysis of the role of each as a movement feature is necessary.

Continuity

Handling systems should be tailored for compatibility with the particular flow they service. Since materials handling physically serves production, physical supply, or distribution, the interfacing functions dictate the minimum levels of compatibility necessary. Several different levels of compatibility are frequently required where materials handling serves several functions simultaneously within an organization.

Compatibility is maintained through control over continuity. Continuity can be controlled by the design of handling procedures to affect flow frequency. Variation of frequency can be accomplished for operations that are *continuous, intermittent,* and *discrete.* Each category has unique movement characteristics which describe a flow. They are normally distinguishable by the category of equipment employed.

Continuous movement requirements usually originate from the production function. Materials handling equipment must be capable of facilitating a constant flow of material to and from various operations at specified rates. Such demand normally necessitates the use of mechanically powered conveyor equipment. Equipment supporting a continuous process (with continuous handling requirements) which is controlled by mechanical intelligence (a computer) is referred to as an automated materials handling system. Continuous handling must be subject to standards which allow compatibility with process demands.

Intermittent movement can serve production, physical supply, or distribution. Flow is not constant, but occurs at more or less constant intervals. Equipment used to furnish intermittent handling capabilities may be wheeled or of a conveyor type. Both powered and nonpowered devices are common. Handling systems using wheeled or conveyor type equipment without automated controls are called mechanized.

Discrete movement occurs in a random manner. Although such demands may develop in any function, they are most common in distribution. Equipment is usually limited to unitizing aids, nonpowered conveyors, lifting devices, and powered or nonpowered trucks. Discrete movement procedures are labor intensive; they tend to be manual or mechanized systems.

A summary of the continuity movement feature is provided in Table 8.2. Continuity has an important influence on materials handling decisions. Continuous movement represents long term commitment to rather static capabilities, and decisions entail substantial risk if future demand for such capability is uncertain. Intermittent and discrete movements require more movement flexibility, and they are less sensitive to shifting operational demands.

Flexibility

The finality of a materials handling decision can be mitigated by flexibility in equipment alternatives. Flexibility depends on the nature and constancy of the material flow, which is described by the path of movement. Paths of movement are *fixed*, *semifixed*, and *variable*. As with continuity, each is characterized by equipment types satisfying its movement demands. Also, the several paths with associated handling requirements may appear in any mix within an organization. Finally, paths are established to serve the sponsoring functions in an organization.

Table 8.2
Continuity Characteristics

FLOW	POWER	EQUIPMENT TYPES	CONTROL SYSTEM
Continuous	Mechanical	Conveyors	Automated
Intermittent	Mechanical	Conveyors, Trucks	Mechanized
Discrete	Mechanical, Manpower	Trucks, Handling Aids, Lifting Devices	Mechanized, Manual

Fixed path systems, having stationary equipment and a constant movement pattern, possess the least handling flexibility. In a continuous flow, however, fixed path equipment provides efficiency in return for this inflexibility. Such systems are common in automated or mechanized processes in production and physical supply. Examples of equipment employed are powered conveyors, monorails, underfloor tows, fixed cranes, elevators, and automated sorting devices.

Semifixed path systems have similar characteristics, but they can be modified between jobs. They are useful with fairly constant movement patterns requiring infrequent flow changes. Primary applications are found in intermittent processes that can tolerate the time out for modification between operations. Semifixed equipment is usually mechanized rather than automated and is of greatest benefit in the production and physical supply functions. Movable conveyors and mobile cranes are typical semifixed equipment.

When the flow of material has no stable pattern, greater flexibility is needed. *Variable path* equipment is mobile; it imitates or models the material flow path. It may be mechanized or manual, but not automated. Human operation or monitoring is essential. Variable path systems are found in production and physical supply, but they are most common in physical distribution, where operations are frequently discrete and nonstandardized. Equipment includes handling aids such as pallets, containers, carts, dollies, and powered equipment such as fork lift trucks and tractors.

UNITIZATION

Unitization consolidates material into bodies which offer optimal handling characteristics. Essentially, unitization seeks to adjust the form of material to enable application of effective handling techniques. Having standard sizes, weights, and shapes make it possible to systematize handling procedures and use labor saving devices. Unitization acts as a significant hedge against flowability restraints. Enhanced flowability is the objective. It is approached in three ways—packaging, palletization, and containerization.

Packaging

Packaging can be subdivided into the two categories: commercial and industrial. *Commercial packaging* is geared to marketing objectives such as (1) offering package sizes to meet consumer demands, (2) differentiating products through unique packaging, (3) promoting the product through advertising, (4) identifying and protecting the product, and (5) serving as a utility producing extension of the product. *Industrial packaging* is concerned with achieving maximum flowability through efficient and economic movement. Commercial and industrial packaging are not mutually exclusive, since marketing and flowability objectives are both complementary and interdependent.

Packaging contains and confines material to facilitate use or handling. Industrial packaging facilitates by standardizing physical dimensions so that material may be efficiently handled. It is a useful tool for control over the flow of material because packaging alternatives tend to counteract flowability restraints. For example, small electronic components are often boxed (with or without internal protective packing) to allow more efficient handling in movement and storage. Packages are designed to withstand the hazards of materials handling. Of course, design parameters will vary with the material and its handling environment.

Often packaging appears as part of the production process as finished goods are prepared for distribution. As an example, soft drinks are actually packaged during production. For operations without close production-packaging affinity, the packaging industry offers a wide assortment of mechanized devices which can be employed as a detached subsystem of either production or physical supply.

Two final packaging considerations are important: identification and cost. The package usually permits visual recognition of the material it holds. While visual graphics are useful to identify and even promote package contents in marketing, they may not be sufficient for effective materials handling. Content identifiers are often coded using numeric or mnemonic descriptors. Recently machine scanable graphic indicators have become popular. Called Univeral Product Codes (UPC), they are sensed by a mechanical reading device which interprets the symbols to identify contents.[1] The UPC, illustrated in Figure 8.4, is used on both commercial and industrial packages for item identification requirements in material locations, retrieval, counting (inventory), pricing, and sales.

While packaging is a useful tool, it can be an expensive one. It is common for packaging to represent as much as 20% of the final product cost. This is particularly true of very sensitive high technology material and small consumer items. Because of its cost, packaging must be evaluated in

FIGURE 8.4. Universal product code.

[1]Such identifiers are also known as distribution codes and bar codes.

terms of the benefits it provides to materials handling and other organizational functions. Seldom is it economical to invest in maximum packaging.

Palletization

Of all the techniques of unitization, palletization is the most common and universally accepted. A pallet is simply a platform upon which material is placed to form a movable collection of items. With the desired quantity of material on it, the pallet is called a *load unit*. Such units are desirable because several pieces of material or very heavy single items can be moved with minimum handling frequency and difficulty. The load units are too heavy for manual movement, but the pallet is compatible with handling equipment such as fork trucks and large conveyors. This permits movement of large load units with convenient and efficient *terminal weights*.

Depending on its intended use, a pallet can be constructed of numerous materials and in various sizes. Metal is often required for very heavy material, but wood is used for lighter commodities. Another consideration is the number of times a pallet will be reused. Numerous attempts have been made to standardize the dimensions of pallets, but success has been limited because of the variety of functional areas influencing pallet design. The typical warehouse pallet is four feet by four feet, but nonstandard dimensions may be required for one use or another.

While it is beyond our present scope to describe in detail the various pallet designs, it is important to recognize the basic components of a typical pallet. As depicted in Figure 8.5, the primary parts of a pallet are the face and the stringer. The *face* is made up of deck boards which form the platform. Pallets have either single or double faces, the latter offering two equivalent sides, one used for a platform and the other as a flat ground contact surface. *Stringers* support the platform, normally about six inches off ground level. Being spaced off the ground allows entry of fork lift tines (blades). If the stringers run the entire length of the pallet it can be approached by a fork truck from two sides, and it is called a two-way entry pallet. Four-way entry is possible if stringers do not cover the full pallet length. Here, of course, the platform board must also be supported by edge boards.

Material is secured to a pallet using tie-down straps, metal bands, chains, nets, or shrinkable film. These tie-down devices keep the unit load together. The last mentioned is a recent innovation—plastic film which shrinks when heated. It is placed over a palletized unit load and subjected to uniform heat, sealing the material configuration and pallet into a single unit. While useful, shrinkable film is limited to fairly light commodities which are not extremely heat sensitive.

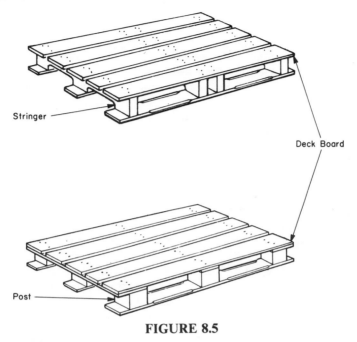

FIGURE 8.5

Containerization

By improving materials handling efficiency, containers offer benefits similar to packaging and palletization. Containerization is a method for confining material in convenient load units. Containers are designed to be easily handled. Two categories of containers are distinguishable, for internal use and for external use (shipping containers).

Internal use containers are used to hold material while it is awaiting use or movement. Common examples are boxes, bags, bins, drums, and carboys. The most frequently used box is constructed of fiberboard. Boxes are also constructed of wood, either as a crate, as a frame for fiberboard, or as sides of a box pallet. Bags are often used for granular or powdered material. Cushioned bags have recently become popular for holding small parts, books, and documents, particularly when they are mailed. Bins are usually stationary containers, although they can be on wheels. Similar to an open box, they are used to hold frequently used material such as parts and tools. Drums and carboys are used to hold liquids or other pourable material. Drums are usually made of metal, wood, or fibrous material, depending on their contents and the number of reuses intended. Carboys are ceramic or glass containers used for materials with special characteristics such as acids.

Shipping containers are unitization devices designed for material consolidation and transfer. They provide handling efficiencies for physical supply, transportation, and distribution. In distribution, they are intermodal (can be transferred between modes of transportation). In other areas, shipping containers are interfunctional (can be used in and moved among several functions).

Shipping containers can hold bulk, packaged, and palletized material. They are constructed of fibrous material, wood, and metal, but metal is most popular. A shipping container is usually shaped as a rectangular solid. It may serve as a large box for consolidation, a mobile truck trailer, or a rail boxcar, all without modification. Other containers are designed for specific purposes, such as to fit passenger airliner cargo compartments (called igloos), or for liquids and gases.

The metal shipping container, called a rigid container, has meant a revolution in the shipping industry. Shipping containers are available in several standard sizes. They provide efficient unit loads, handling, economy, material security, environmental control, and multimodal capabilities. They survive many uses. While not universally applicable, they can be an effective part of a materials handling system.

Specialized equipment is often needed to move shipping containers. Since they rest on rail cars, act as truck trailers, and are stacked in ships, containers require handling equipment capable of lifting heavy weights fairly long distances. Cranes and "container movers" (large fork trucks) are used for these purposes.

EQUIPMENT ALTERNATIVES

Of major importance to the manager considering a materials handling system is an appreciation of the equipment alternatives. The materials handling industry offers an enormous variety of labor saving devices, and just about any handling equipment need can be met with specially designed, unique purpose systems. Because of the sheer number of alternatives available, it is not possible to enumerate all of them. It is possible, however, to put the alternatives in categories and briefly discuss each. There are four basic categories of handling equipment:

1.   Trucks and tractors
2.   Conveyors
3.   Lifts
4.   Special systems and handling aids

Trucks and Tractors

Trucks and tractors are wheeled vehicles useful for moving material along a variable path, usually in an intermittent or discrete fashion. Characteristically, trucks lift and carry, while tractors push and pull. A few examples of trucks and tractors are shown in Plate 1. Trucks may be manual or powered. The most familiar kind is the fork lift, which is available in a number of sizes and styles. Fork lift capabilities depend on such factors as terminal weight of material to be moved, reach (height) requirements, and space available for maneuvering. The fork lift truck is not economically adapted to long distance horizontal movement, because of the large labor cost per unit of transfer. It is most commonly employed in shipping and receiving, or to place material in high cube storage. Industrial trucks of various types are used for transporting nonuniform unit loads intermittently over varying routes.

Tractors are powered equipment used to move other equipment, usually without lifting. Dollies and carts are often pushed or pulled by a tractor. Vehicles not under power (trailers, vessels, and airplanes) are moved with tractors or related equipment. Most earth moving equipment is dependent on a tractor.

Conveyors

Conveyors provide for continuous or intermittent movement over a fixed or semifixed path. Conveyor systems provide efficient flow, but they are relatively inflexible. While many types of conveyors exist, they fall into two categories: those with stationary surfaces and those with moving surfaces. Stationary conveyor surfaces consist of rollers, wheels (casters), or bearings over which material moves. Such arrangements are common in gravity systems or where material is pushed or pulled along the conveyor surface. Conveyors with moving surfaces employ power to provide material flow along with the surface flow. Typical moving surfaces include belts, chains, slats, and buckets. Examples are illustrated in Plate 2.

Conveyor equipment includes tracked and pneumatic devices, which possess similar movement characteristics, benefits, and limitations. Monorails and underfloor tows use fixed tracks to guide the flow of material. Gravity and mechanical power sources are used in monorails, which are employed to move material suspended above ground level. Underfloor tows are also tracked, but they are generally mechanically powered to push or pull wheeled vehicles. Pneumatic material handling equipment is essentially a pipeline through which material is forced. The pneumatic conveyor is a system of tubes or ducts through which material is moved by pressure

216

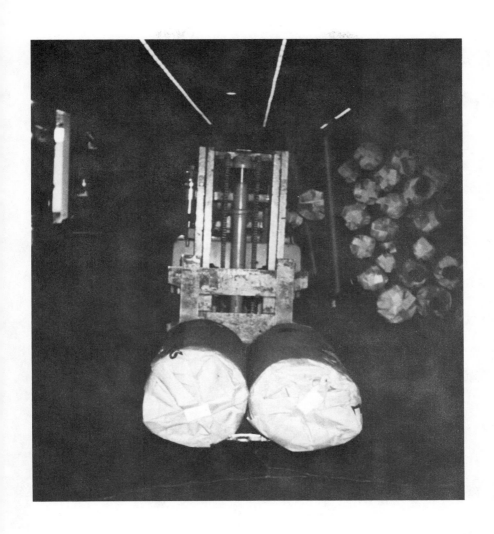

PLATE 1. Trucks and Tractors

Lift truck interfacing with retrieval system (*opposite top*); special dolly for
tote boxes (*opposite bottom-left*); cart for manual order picking (*opposite
bottom-right*); lift truck with roll adapters (*above*). PHOTOGRAPHS
COURTESY OF AMERICAN CHAIN & CABLE COMPANY

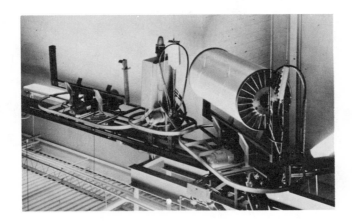

PLATE 2. Conveyors

Opposite, moving clockwise from top-left: Belt conveyor; roller conveyor; extendible conveyor for shipping and receiving; underfloor tow; pallet conveyor; roller conveyor in order picking operation. *Above top*: Overhead hanging garment sorting system; *above bottom*: monorail yarn spool handling line. PHOTOGRAPHS COURTESY OF AMERICAN CHAIN & CABLE COMPANY

PLATE 3. Lifts
Construction cranes (*opposite top*); bridge crane (*opposite middle*); gantry
crane (*opposite bottom*); jib crane and hoist (*above top*); vacuum lift for
sheet products (*above bottom*). PHOTOGRAPHS COURTESY OF AMERICAN
CHAIN & CABLE COMPANY

PLATE 4. Systems and Aids

Drum handling and storage retrieval system (*opposite top-left*); sorting system in a modern warehouse (*opposite top-right*); storage retrieval system for handling barstock (*opposite middle-left*); freight sorting system (*opposite middle-right*); automatic sorting system (*opposite bottom*); palletizing units (*above top*); control console for an automatic sorting system (*above bottom*). PHOTOGRAPHS COURTESY OF AMERICAN CHAIN & CABLE COMPANY or vacuum. Familiar examples are the grain pumps used to load and unload grain elevators, vessels, and other vehicles. Pneumatic tubes are used to move capsules of material among use points in production, warehousing, or retail facilities.

Lifts

Trucks, tractors, and conveyors do possess the capability of vertical movement, either by lifting or by moving on an incline. However, there is a category of equipment uniquely designed for vertical movement. As a category of handling equipment, lifts include hoists, elevators, cranes, and derricks. Shown in Plate 3 lifts are mechanically powered and are frequently used in conjunction with other handling equipment. Elevators may be conventionally designed to provide discrete up and down movement, or they may employ conveyor techniques to allow continuous movement. Cranes and derricks usually lift by means of cables, chains, or pneumatic pumps. Cranes may be fixed or mobile; derricks are normally fixed.

Special Systems and Aids

The final category of equipment includes an almost unlimited variety of custom designed handling systems and unique handling aids, some of which are depicted in Plate 4. Special systems are useful or necessary when materials handling is an integral part of another function. For instance, in beverage bottling, container and ingredient handling effectively are a part of production, and complex sorting systems become part of the order processing activity of physical supply.

Because handling activities are necessary throughout the flow of material, and because not every activity fits into the above categories, handling aids must be available. Several handling aids, such as pallets and containers, have been mentioned. Other aids available are hand trucks, carts, dollies, jacks, equipment racks, ball mats (for turning heavy and bulky material and pallets), and small hand tools. All are labor and time saving devices used to make movements more efficient.

A prerequisite to the design of a materials handling system is a knowledge of the different kinds of handling equipment available. The selection of handling equipment will be based on several factors, some of which are:

1. Functional adequacy of the equipment
2. Capital investment required
3. Equipment reliability and life expectancy
4. Cost savings potential

5. Safety considerations
6. Equipment flexibility
7. Maintenance requirements
8. Spare parts and service availability
9. Fuel and power requirements
10. Complexity of manpower training

Trucks are prevalent in handling material in intermittent production. With intermittent operations, material has a variable path, so variable-path equipment (trucks, forklifts, or tractors) is used. Conveyors are prevalent in handling material in continuous production. With continuous operations, material usually follows a fixed path, so fixed-path equipment (chutes, conveyors, elevators, or pipes) is used. Fixed-path equipment usually costs less to purchase and to operate. Variable-path equipment requires an operator and additional manpower. Usually fixed-position transfer equipment is controlled by manufacturing or maintenance, and mobile transfer equipment without a permanent work location is controlled in a transportation pool.

MATERIALS HANDLING DECISIONS

Inputs, restraints, and flow factors fully define the decision environment of the materials handling function. Handling decisions are made subject to environmental influences and in concert with decisions of other organizational functions. Realization that the materials handling decision environment is shared by and interacts with other functions is a prerequisite to effective management. Also, materials handling is a dynamic area subject to rapid technological innovation. As technology improves, the manager must understand and anticipate changes to ensure that his decisions are responsive to both functional and organizational objectives.

Materials handling methods can be decided only after the following are known:

1. The kinds and amounts of material to be handled
2. Locations to and from which materials are to be transported

In principle, work stations can't be located without considering the space for loading, unloading, and movement of handling equipment. Thus, the location of work stations will influence the choice of handling equipment, and vice versa.

Manpower and equipment requirements can be estimated from flow charts and work analysis information. Work sampling and predetermined time studies (standard data) may be employed. Speeds, loads, distances, and technical data concerning the capability of equipment are usually available from manufacturers. Comparisons can be made between maximum and minimum flow requirements. It is usually desirable to design a system around the maximum possible capability (peak work load requirements). Allowances for growth should be considered, as well as maintenance and down time. Typical quantitative tools that can improve decision making are flow analysis, work measurement, work sampling, predetermined time standards, incremental analysis, linear programming, queuing theory, and simulation.

MATERIALS HANDLING OUTPUTS

Like the inputs, the outputs of materials handling decisions are difficult to identify with convenient descriptors. The ultimate objective, of course, is to facilitate an effective flow of material. Outputs should be designed to accomplish that objective. Appreciation of the environment and principles of materials handling is a necessity. One must also assess the availability of equipment resources and know how they are acquired. Thus, the two primary outputs of the materials handling function can be designated as *handling efficiencies* and *sourcing*.

HANDLING EFFICIENCIES

Handling efficiencies are aspects of materials handling which lead to decision criteria for the entire function. Once assimilated by the manager, they establish a conceptual framework for approaching any materials handling problem. Table 8.3 contains a list of handling efficiencies which should be beneficial to the manager concerned with the materials handling function. They are drawn from considerations of inputs, restraints, and flow factors.

Caution must be exercised in using this or any list of principles or efficiencies. Neither the list nor any of its elements is a universal. Every situation is unique in some way. Principles are useful if they fit situations; situations can seldom be made to fit principles. Nevertheless, appreciation of handling efficiencies as a part of the body of knowledge known as materials handling is invaluable to the manager.

When studying materials handling, safety must be considered. Better methods and personnel training should result in fewer accidents as well as lower costs. Handling equipment can be dangerous if misused or not

Table 8.3
Handling Efficiencies

1. Minimize material movement where possible.
2. Minimize manual handling and man movement.
3. Move material instead of men.
4. Maximize unit load size.
5. Maximize unit load terminal weight.
6. Where possible use gravity to move material.
7. Minimize idle time by reducing terminal time.
8. Use direct path movement schemes.
9. Minimize backtracking and parallel movement.
10. Use mechanized devices to ensure predictable activity rates.
11. Employ line production techniques if appropriate.
12. Ensure optimum use of space, particularly aisle areas.
13. Consolidate handling operations with production, physical supply, and distribution where possible.
14. Move larger weights short distances.
15. Combine operations whenever practical to eliminate handling between them.

properly maintained. Education, safety programs, and preventive maintenance can considerably reduce hazardous situations.

SOURCING

Sourcing is concerned with the methods of obtaining resources for materials handling. Acquisition involves an investment in manpower, equipment, and services. Manpower requirements are directly related to the labor intensity of the materials handling function, which is controlled by the mix of equipment (and type of equipment) and services rendered. Sourcing is equipment oriented when equipment is bought directly; it is service oriented when equipment is leased or rented.

Purchase

Outright purchase of equipment represents a long term commitment of funds and an implicit assumption that handling demands will not decrease. These risks are balanced by the internal control gained over the equipment. Because of the risks and costs, it is necessary to include materials handling in the equipment planning activities of an organization.

Although direct purchase can offer significant advantages, it must be carefully evaluated because of the magnitude of expenditure required.

Absorbing up to 20% of production costs, materials handling is a competitor for substantial portions of available resources, and is under corresponding pressure to economize.

Lease

Risks can be lessened if a lease arrangement is used, where commitment of funds is limited by a contract. With a lease, the responsibility for equipment upkeep and maintenance is usually the vendor's. Control is exercised by the leasee, but subject to contractual terms. The lease payments are treated as expenses and charged to the period, whereas with direct purchase, depreciation methods are employed. It is routine for handling organizations to offer lease-purchase agreements and consultant services, which can be valuable to organizations with limited handling expertise. Leasing methods are appropriate for a wide range of equipment requirements, from handling aids to the design and implementation of complex systems.

Rental

The minimum possible investment is under rental arrangements. Rental is provided as a service by a materials handling equipment organization which features short term commitment requirements. It is beneficial to employ rental services if:

1. Long term investment is limited by availability of funds.
2. Alternative investment is more profitable.
3. Future handling requirements are uncertain.
4. Handling requirements occur cyclically.
5. Extensive operational changes are in progress or anticipated.

Upkeep and maintenance may be a part of the rental agreement or the responsibility of the sourcing organization. Rental equipment normally includes a limited range of equipment and aids such as common use trucks and conveyors.

CONCLUSION

Materials handling is a very subtle function in most organizations. It can be seen both as an active participant in other functions and as a function itself. It must be accomplished, yet its objective is to minimize costs. Thus, the most efficient handling system usually involves the least amount of handling.

It would be a mistake to approach materials handling as a totally independent function. Fraught with numerous variables and sensitive to change throughout the organization, it nevertheless describes a relatively confined body of knowledge. It can be defined by its functional inputs, restraints, flow factors, and outputs. Having defined the materials handling function and its activities, it is possible to establish a framework for its management.

The key to efficient materials handling in the future is the systems approach to evaluating the materials handling function. Careful economic and engineering studies must be made to determine the system, facility, and equipment to use, considering the relevant restraints. A properly designed and implemented handling system will reduce costs, reduce waste, increase productive capacity, improve working conditions, and improve distribution. Cost savings are realized through lower inventory and production control cost, better space utilization, minimum handling, and shorter production cycle time. Waste is reduced because improved handling lowers damage and results in less scrap. Production capacity is increased because of better control of materials, handling system coordination, constant production rates, and decreased machine idle time. Thus, it is through the systems approach that materials handling becomes more controllable.

QUESTIONS

1. What is important about the absence of a concise set of documents serving as materials handling functional inputs?
2. What is functional transparency?
3. Identify three charts used in flow analysis.
4. Define flowability.
5. Name and briefly describe the three categories of material form.
6. How do the geographic and temporal characteristics of distance influence materials handling?
7. Describe the relationships between materials handling and other functions as movement distances become small and large.
8. What is movement intensity?
9. What is the major tradeoff in deciding between a single level and a multilevel facility?

10. Relate the degree of materials handling sophistication to fixed and variable costs.

11. What are the three major categories of movement paths in materials handling?

12. Distinguish between commercial and industrial packaging.

13. What is a pallet?

14. Name the four basic categories of handling equipment.

15. Identify five handling efficiencies.

Case 1: Cadillac or Model T

Ray Hart, general manager of Peterson Farm Products, is uncertain what action he should take on a comprehensive report and recommendation on updating Peterson's materials handling systems.

Peterson Farm Products is a family owned firm which has been in business for over fifty years. It is located in St Louis, Missouri and is a manufacturer and wholesaler of chemical fertilizers. During the last five years the company has experienced tremendous growth which, among other things, has necessitated the upgrading of the management team from four to ten people. Mr. Hart has been with the firm ever since his graduation from college in 1959 and has worked his way through virtually every part of the firm. Mr. Clark has just assumed responsibility for warehousing, transportation, and inventory management. His previous position had been as head of marketing for a major manufacturer of materials handling equipment. As such he has earned a reputation as an expert in materials handling system design.

One of Mr. Clark's initial tasks at Peterson was to conduct a critical review of the materials handling functions with the objective of lowering labor costs in the overhead functions. The result of that review was the cause of Mr. Hart's dilemma. The report recommended a wholesale updating and mechanization of all materials handling functions in the firm. Adoption of the plan would require a substantial investment of capital for which there were already several competing investment opportunities.

Mr. Clark's recommendations were supported by a detailed analysis of the costs and labor savings that would result from the investment. He had conducted a detailed work sampling and time standards study of every materials handling function as presently performed and compared it with actual demonstrated labor costs in similar firms using equipment comparable to that which he had recommended. He made precise calculations of the present values of the cash flows. A thorough and detailed study of the analysis failed to disclosed any inaccuracies. However, Mr. Hart's intimate familiarity with the firm led him to the intuitive feeling that he was being offered a Cadillac when, in fact, a Model T was adequate.

1. What factors not addressed in Mr. Clark's analysis might be relevant to the decision?

2. What recommendations can you suggest to Mr. Hart on evaluating the report?

3. Should the new materials handling system be purchased?

Case 2: City versus Suburbs

Wisconsin Cameo Press is located in downtown Milwaukee in an old five story building. Its primary business is printing telephone directories and magazine supplements. The process used up to now has been intermittent. The management is concerned about many current problems, mainly rising costs. Most of the costs involved are high labor and materials handling costs. The materials arrive at the plant in boxes and rolls. Most are stored on the first floor on pallets until needed. There is one small elevator in the front of the building for personnel use only, and another much larger one at the back used for transporting materials from floor to floor.

Different operations are done on different floors. Printing is done on one; binding and cutting on another. Under ideal conditions a truck moves the books or inserts on pallets from one station to the elevator. The elevator moves the load to the desired floor, and another truck waits to take it off and move it to the next station. Frequently a fork lift truck isn't available when the elevator arrives. As a result the elevator holds up several other movements.

The management has been looking for a solution to the problem of materials movement. The alternatives they came up with ranged from more fork lift trucks on each floor to a new facility in the suburbs.

Management has been divided on the subject, with one group favoring modernization of the existing downtown building and another group favoring a new plant. One of the best modernization plans is to streamline the operations and storage areas. It was suggested that all receiving should be done in the back of the first floor, where it would be checked and coded. From there it would go to the fourth floor for storage until needed. The fifth floor would be used for offices. Printing would be done on the third; binding and cutting on the second. The first floor would be used for finished goods awaiting packaging and shipment. The plan suggested uses gravity chutes to transport items between floors.

Those favoring a new plant don't like the idea of the offices on the fifth floor. The present building is old, and they are worried about fires. They think that there would be less traffic congestion in the suburbs. The plant could be laid out to optimize successive operations, thus reducing the distance between work stations, which would reduce costs. Although they have considered fixed path flow and semifixed path flow for the telephone directories, they feel that either would reduce the plant's flexibility. The orders that came in to the factory require flexibility, since they vary in size and amount. Pallets in conjunction with fork lift trucks are still believed to be the best method for materials handling. The binding operation could be mechanized, which would reduce the number of personnel by six. The cutting station could be made more efficient, which would reduce personnel by one. In the long run, the suburb faction felt that the new building's cost would be offset by savings in materials handling due to reduced distance and time. Labor costs would be reduced along with the workforce.

1. What are the advantages of modernization of the existing facility?

2. What are the advantages of moving the business to the suburbs?
3. What recommendations would you make to the plant manager?
4. What other factors might influence the final decision?

Case 3: Dwindling Profits

Virginia Products, Incorporated is a manufacturer of custom made wood furniture such as chairs, sofas, tables, cabinets, dressers, and chests. Orders are received from furniture dealers, directly from end-use customers, and from other manufacturers to augment their own product lines. Sales for the past five years have increased steadily by 7 to 11% per year, but profit has increased only 2% overall. Since the firm's prices are already higher than other manufacturers', management does not feel it can increase prices at this time.

The company prides itself on its custom operations and its quality in manufacturing. Management is very much against any reduction in labor force or additional mechanization in manufacturing processes. John Weston, the plant manager, estimates that the cost of the average piece of furniture contains about 25–30% handling costs, which includes packing, packaging, and the movement of products between the various work areas throughout the plant.

Since the company has stressed the "hand-made" quality of its furniture, each employee's work area is well equipped and spacious, but little thought has apparently gone into the general arrangement of machines, work benches, receiving areas, and flow through various stages of manufacturing. All movement is of individual pieces on wooden pallets by fork lift trucks. This has caused frequent work stoppages at individual work benches. As each worker finishes his task, he calls the fork lift truck operator and tells him where the material is to go next. Since there are only three fork lift trucks, bottlenecks and delays occur frequently. These delays have always been viewed as unavoidable costs of being a custom manufacturer, and little change has taken place since the firm went into business. The employees feel that since theirs is a highly skilled craft, they deserve the occasional work breaks caused by the slow piece movement.

Much the same is true of the movement of raw material (primarily wood and various fastening devices). The production manager and the work center supervisors call for material as required without a formal schedule for utilizing the handling equipment. The three fork lift trucks used in the manufacturing process are augmented by two additional ones and a portable conveyor for storing smaller pieces of raw material in the second tier of the warehouse.

The packing area has operated on the principle of giving the customer the best quality possible. Each piece of furniture is individually handblocked and braced by experienced employees who pride themselves on the fact that the result is a crate which could withstand virtually any rough handling and remain intact. As a result, a large backlog of pieces to be packaged is normal.

1. What changes in operations would you suggest to John Weston?
2. What improvements could be made in materials handling equipment?
3. What would be the impact of a more efficient work station arrangement?
4. Should changes be made in packing and packaging?

Chapter 9

Transportation and Physical Distribution

233

Practically every product consumed must be transported—usually several times—before it reaches its final destination. Historically, transportation/physical distribution has been a necessary foundation for the economic growth of any nation. Transportation/physical distribution creates both "time" and "place" utility. Large-scale production systems require the transportation of tremendous amounts and types of raw materials to processing and assembly facilities. Likewise, massive distribution systems are necessary to move the final product to the consumer. Physical distribution broadens the product market and provides the means to deliver the outputs of large-scale production. The primary role of transportation/physical distribution is to support the activities associated with production and marketing.

There is substantial confusion in the literature concerning the conceptual foundations of transportation/physical distribution. Traditionally, two schools of thought have been popular. One school, *traffic management*, considers only the techniques of managing physical movement. It is rather specialized and narrow in scope. The traffic manager is usually a specialist in rates and routes serving as a purchasing agent for transportation services. The other school, *physical distribution management*, views the system as including traffic, inventory control, warehousing, materials handling, packaging, and other related activities.[1] Physical distribution man-

---

[1]See Donald J. Bowersox et al., *Physical Distribution Management*, New York: Macmillan, 1968.

agement is marketing oriented and places major emphasis on outputs (final products) rather than inputs (raw materials) to the organization. We reject both of these schools as outdated and ineffectual in meeting total organizational needs in a materials management framework. The traffic management approach is too narrow and the physical distribution management approach is too broad. Physical distribution and traffic management frequently refer to only outbound movements. We shall use transportation/physical distribution to include inbound shipments as well as outbound movements.

Transportation and physical distribution can be differentiated, although the terms mean the same to many people. Physical distribution can be given a broader interpretation than transportation, by defining it as the management of the movement of goods through space (by transport) and through time (by storage, warehousing, production scheduling, and so forth) from their origins as raw materials to their final consumer. With this definition, physical distribution includes aspects of purchasing, inventory control, receiving, storage, warehousing, scheduling, and transportation. Physical distribution will not be given so broad an interpretation herein, but will be used interchangeably with transportation.[2]

In recent years, transportation has had an increasing influence on product costs. Transportation costs can make up a substantial share of the price of an item—on an average, approximately 20%. Over 10% of the total labor force in the U.S. is employed in transportation and transportation related industries. In view of the tremendous amount of equipment (terminals, trucks, ships, pipes, aircraft, and so forth), the capital investment in transportation is substantial. For the average business, transportation costs are exceeded only by the costs of materials and labor. The significance of transportation to any given organization is indicated by the ratio of transportation costs to total product costs.

Largely because of technological change and the division of labor, the modern organization can be characterized as a collection of functional specialities (purchasing, finance, production, marketing, transportation, and so forth). Greater functional efficiency in an operation or a set of operations has been the outgrowth of specialization. Paradoxically, the functional efficiency offered by specialization is often accompanied by challenges to organizational effectiveness, in the form of greater operational complexity and functional interdependence. Organizational problems do not confine themselves within the boundaries of functional specialties.

[2]The term "transportation" will henceforth be used to mean transportation/physical distribution.

The complexity and functional interdependence of the modern organization are the general subjects of systems and integrative approaches to management. Such approaches seek to translate functional efficiency into organizational effectiveness. Only recently have serious attempts been made to fully integrate transportation into a systems approach to management. This belated recognition has been necessitated by the significant influences of *sensitivity*, *cost*, and *reliability*.

Functional interdependence refers to the omnidirectional flow of influence among organizational functions, and between internal functions and the external environment. The degree to which one function is influenced by behavior in another is called its *sensitivity*. Because transportation serves as the physical linkage among functions both internal and external, it can be conceived as the medium through which physical sensitivity is transmitted. Physical sensitivities among organizational functions generally involve transportation. Characteristically, transportation maintains high sensitivity between purchasing, production, inventory control, physical supply, and sales.

It is not uncommon for transportation to represent 20–40% of the final cost of a product. This is easy to understand when the total flow of materials is considered. Figure 9.1 illustrates that flow and the numerous links, each of which represents a transportation requirement. Multiple suppliers, multiplant locations, regional distribution centers, and numerous selling intermediaries further increase the significance of transportation costs. Thus an important organizational goal is to control transportation expenditures. Many organizations encounter difficulties in doing so. Transportation methods are numerous, cost structures are extremely complex, influencing variables are both internal and external, and interdependence with other functions is usually quite sensitive. Still, transportation represents an important area for potential cost reductions and efficiencies.

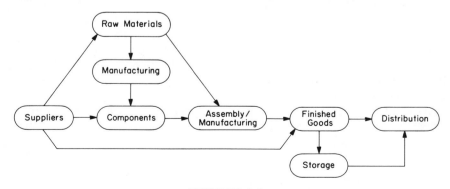

FIGURE 9.1

Another direct result of functional specialization and interdependence is the requirement for highly reliable service from transportation. The reliability demanded by an organization is usually measured by the criticality of raw materials, component parts, and finished goods. Reliability requirements have caused many organizations to increase their control over the transportation function. Efforts toward control can be directed to internal variables, usually entailing closer interfunctional coordination and planning. Or efforts may be designed to control both internal and external variables, through internal coordination and actual ownership of transportation equipment and facilities. Reliability is also related to costs in that costs generally vary directly with material urgency. Another important aspect of reliability in transportation is its temporal relationship with organizational service requirements. Material criticality is defined both in terms of availability and the lead time to availability. Criticality factors influence the method and cost of transportation.

Sensitivity, cost, and reliability influences have changed transportation from an isolated activity to a major organizational function. Attention is being paid to its interdependence with other functions and its importance as a cost center which represents significant savings potential. Thus more emphasis is being placed by upper management on interfunctional coordination, planning, and cost control.

Both production and marketing oriented organizations depend on the physical flow of materials. Effective management of the physical flow of materials is the main concern of the transportation function. The role of transportation as an interdependent function is illustrated in Figure 9.2. Usually in coordination with transportation functionaries, a purchase order authorizes a supplier to initiate the physical flow of materials. Raw

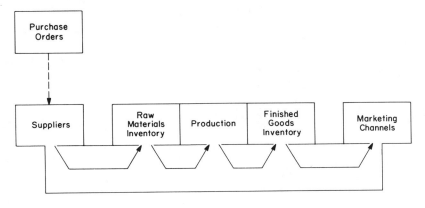

FIGURE 9.2

materials, components, and finished goods are transported to a specified location and usually become part of inventory until use or other disposition. Movement from the raw materials inventory through production and to finished goods inventory is accomplished by a transportation medium called materials handling. In a continuous production system, many materials handling activities become part of the production process. Movement of finished goods through marketing channels, perhaps via several intermediaries, is the final transportation activity.

Transportation does not contribute tangible value to the product; it adds value only in terms of time and place. However, inadequate transportation service can cause ineffectual purchasing, expensive inventory control, interrupted production, and erosion of customer satisfaction.

Transportation can be viewed as a function common to all organizations. Depicted in Figure 9.3, the function is described in terms of inputs, restraints, movement factors, and outputs. The importance of individual descriptive elements may vary from organization to organization, but the existence of each is characteristic of the decision process. Inputs include purchase and shipping orders, both of which define performance require-

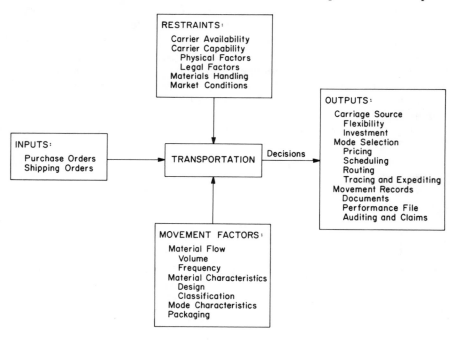

FIGURE 9.3

ments. Restraints, such as carrier availability and capability, limit decision prerogatives in the application of movement factor considerations. Common functional outputs concern carriage source selection, mode selection, and maintenance of movement records. The remainder of the chapter will delineate the transportation function.

TRANSPORTATION INPUTS

Transportation exists as a service to other organizational entities. Material movement demands placed on transportation originate as performance requirements from other functions internal or external to the organization. These requirements become inputs to the transportation decision process. Inputs define demand by describing material characteristics and stipulating movement requirements, such as commodity name, major design features, unusual properties, origin and destination, receiver, desired (or required) delivery date, and payment method. The most common inputs containing such information are purchase orders and shipping orders.

PURCHASE ORDERS

Purchase orders originate from purchasing and procurement. They authorize suppliers to furnish goods and services, and they specify acquisition terms. Acquisition terms contain information pertinent to transportation, including material characteristics, movement requirements, and the assignment of responsibility for providing transportation. That responsibility may be assigned to the seller or the buyer, or shared by both. Before they become part of the purchase order, transportation terms are usually coordinated with procurement, transportation, and the supplier.

An advance copy of the purchase order is normally provided to transportation for use in planning for material flow, manpower, and equipment requirements. It also serves as a source of information for preparing initial historical records, labels, markings, and movement documentation. Specific uses of the purchase order in transportation depend on whether the buyer or the supplier has responsibility for providing movement services. The purchase order represents an internal demand for goods or services, and it is an input to the function which provides the movement necessary to satisfy demand. Thus, transportation is a vital consideration in a procurement action. Transportation specifications should be developed with the same care given to the material being purchased.

SHIPPING ORDERS

A shipping order can originate from a product sale or from a desire to redistribute material among storage locations or plant sites. Like purchase orders, shipping orders provide information concerning the commodity and movement requirements. The lead time between receipt of shipping orders and delivery may be short compared to the duration of purchase actions because of established channels of distribution.

In the usual organization, product sales are represented by incoming customer orders. These orders may be received by mail, telephone, or other electronic means from either customers, salesmen, or other organizational entities. Orders are usually screened and verified for clerical accuracy, complete information, and material availability. Information provided by a customer order is then used to originate a multi-use form which functions to authorize, trace, and control the transaction throughout the organization. Copies of the form, normally called a shipping order at this point, are transmitted to physical supply and transportation. Physical supply (warehousing) uses the form as a guide to picking, packaging, and marking material. Transportation uses its copy for preparing movement documentation and performing initial transport planning.

Obviously, effectiveness in the order filling cycle is extremely important to the organization in general and to the transportation function in particular. The responsiveness of transportation often depends on the organization's ability to process incoming orders quickly and provide necessary advance information to the transportation and warehousing functionaries. The activity of handling customers' orders to effect minimum cycle time is called *order processing*. Automated order processing systems offer the advantage of reducing the lead time between order receipt and advance notification to transportation. In addition, such systems often perform such functions as clerical verification of incoming orders, internal trailing of orders, and preparation of shipping orders. In more sophisticated systems preparation of labels and shipping documentation is automatic. Order processing concerns the flow of information which interacts with the flow of material.

RESTRAINTS

Restraints characterize the decision environment and influence movement factor considerations. They simplify decision making by limiting the alternatives available. Major classifications of restraints affecting transportation decisions are carrier availability, carrier capabilities, the material handling system, and market conditions.

CARRIER AVAILABILITY

Carrier availability is a function of the transportation volume demanded, the service levels required, and the procurement source selected. As a general rule, the number of transportation alternatives available and the service levels provided increase as demand by an organization increases. There are three sources from which an organization may purchase transportation services: private carriage, contract carriage, and common carriage. The degree of control an organization has over availability varies with the source. It should be noted that availability requirements act as a restraint on selection of a purchased source, but the actual decision involved in such a selection is an output of the transportation function.

Private carriage offers the maximum of positive control over carrier availability. With private carriage, the organization takes responsibility for ownership, operation, and maintenance of the transportation vehicles and system. Since it is under internal control, the transportation function can quickly react to changes in input demands. Use of private carriage is usually limited to large organizations with round trip or multilocation movement requirements. Thus, a large food cannery might employ private carriage to move finished goods to an urban distribution center and use the return trip to supply empty containers to the production facility.

Contract carriage involves the purchase of a specified amount, type, and frequency of transportation service. It allows an organization to exercise control over carrier availability through contract terms. The carrier retains responsibility for system ownership, operation, and maintenance. Flexibility to meet demand fluctuations is limited, since a carrier is not usually under exclusive contract to a single firm. Contract carriage is common among organizations with consistent demand over a known time period for one-way movement services, and among organizations which require control over availability, but are unwilling to invest in private carriage. A producer of industrial products serving a limited market might select contract carriage.

With *common carriage*, the influence of an organization over availability is limited to that of a single customer. Common carriers must provide service to all customers without discrimination. Common carriage is used by organizations not requiring significant control over carrier availability and by those unwilling to invest in private or contract carriage. Organizations with geographically dispersed markets, each with an independently fluctuating demand, might favor common carriage. As an example, it would be appropriate for a small job shop producing labels for the apparel and textile industries.

CARRIER CAPABILITY

Regardless of the source selected by an organization for purchasing transportation services, the ability of a carrier to satisfy movement requirements is subject to physical and legal influences. Primary physical factors are vehicle or conveyance limitations and geographical limitations. Legal factors can be classified as internal and external to the entity.

Physical Factors

Transporting vehicles and conveyances have physical load limitations determined by cargo weight, volume, dimensions, density, package size, or commodity specification. Consideration of such factors during product design and procurement is known as transportability planning. Transportability planning minimizes the probability of being limited to special and expensive vehicles or conveyances. Various vehicles, rail cars, vessels, aircraft, and containers have physically limiting characteristics. Similarly, special conveyances such as parcel post, air express, and bus service have limiting package size and content restrictions.

Transportation attempts to mitigate the disadvantages of distance and location while capitalizing on the existence of numerous geographically dispersed supplier and consumer markets. The costs of transportation are significantly influenced by geographical limitations. Obviously, geographical barriers may limit mode selection or the number of available operating carriers. Costs usually increase with the difficulty in reaching a location. Geographical limitations control the evolution of transportation networks to which an organization is bound. This has occurred in the United States in two ways:

1. Geographical segmentation
2. Intermodal layering

Space is generally segmented by circumscribing physical barriers. Transportation networks have developed with links roughly parallel to existing barriers. Bodies of water simultaneously acted as directional barriers and movement media. This principle can be exemplified by observing transport links in the Southeast, most of which run in a north-south direction parallel to the Appalachian Mountains and the Atlantic Ocean. Interregional connecting links are usually few because they must go through or around barriers.

Partly because of geographical segmentation, the evolution of transportation networks has been characterized by intermodal layering. Early railroads connected markets already served by river, canal, and ocean transportation. Contemporary roadways follow the rails to facilitate duplicative motor service. While not hindered by the same geographical restrictions, air cargo service has been limited by stringent facility requirements and near total reliance on intermodal connections. Thus, air cargo service is developing as a captive of other modes and their limitations. Similarly, with the current development of containers, ocean container service is generally available from the same links as breakbulk service, while air containers serve the same links as bulk freighters.

Motor and air service have given flexibility to water and rail restraints by allowing expansion of market areas and extension to some submarkets. However, service flows are still restricted by the layered evolution of the transportation network. Network limitations on carrier capability are usually major considerations in facility location and distribution channel decisions.

Legal Factors

The primary legal restraints on transportation which are internal to the organization are terms of purchase or sale. While there are several classifications of terms, the two most important to transportation are F.O.B. (Free on Board or Freight on Board) origin and F.O.B. destination. F.O.B. terms stipulate the time and place of legal transfer of title to property. A purchase of raw materials under F.O.B. origin terms means the purchaser assumes title to the property when it is shipped from the place of origin; therefore, the purchaser is responsible for transportation. F.O.B. destination means the purchaser assumes title to the property after the shipment is received; therefore, the seller is responsible for transportation. F.O.B. terms do not prevent either principal in an exchange from agreeing to arrange for transportation, but that agreement does not alter the legal time and place of title transfer.

F.O.B. terms have a major influence on the control an organization has over its transportation expenditures. Minimum control is achieved by purchasing F.O.B. destination and selling F.O.B. origin, while maximum control is achieved by purchasing F.O.B. origin and selling F.O.B. destination. Of course, the optimum amount of control (and it may be very small) depends on the organization, product, and willingness to assume liability for settlement of in-transit damage claims with the carrier.

No other sector of business is subject to the intensity of external legal restrictions that transportation is. To some extent, all modes of transportation involved in interstate for-hire service are regulated by the federal government. In addition, each state regulates intrastate transportation through various commissions or agencies. Private and contract carriage are less regulated than common carriage.

Federal regulations can be separated into two general categories: (1) *safety regulation*, affecting all common, contract, and private carriers engaged in interstate commerce; and (2) *economic regulation*, governing most common and contract carriers engaged in interstate commerce. Table 9.1 identifies the major federal regulatory bodies by category and function. Safety regulations impose standards on vehicles, operator qualifications, equipment use, commodity restrictions, and packaging requirements. Economic regulations control carrier entry into, operation within, and exit from the transportation service market. Regulation is greatest with common and contract carriage and least with private carriage.

Table 9.1
Federal Regulatory Bodies

BODY	CLASS	FUNCTION	CARRIERS REGULATED
DOT (Department of Transportation)	Safety	Highway and traffic safety (National Highway Administration), aircraft and airport safety, pilot certification (Federal Aviation Administration), rail and pipeline safety (Federal Railroad Administration), marine safety (Coast Guard).	All interstate
ICC (Interstate Commerce Commission)	Economic	Grants operating authority; governs publication and filing of rates or changes; governs carrier accounting systems; authorizes mergers, consolidations, reorganizations, and abandonments; governs rail vehicle interchanges.	Common and contract rail, motor, water, pipeline, and freight forwarders in interstate commerce.
FMC (Federal Maritime Commission)	Economic	Governs rate filing procedures, controls service agreements between carriers, grants certifications and licenses.	Offshore and foreign water carriers, ocean freight forwarders
CAB (Civil Aeronautics Board)	Economic	Grants operating authority; approves rates; approves mergers, consolidations, or agreements; governs competitive practice; promotes effective movement of mail.	Domestic and international air carriers

To be effective, management must grasp the impact of physical and legal restraints on carrier capability. They are of particular importance because they influence the ability of the organization to meet its transportation requirements reliably. Physical factors tend to sensitize decisions related to supplier location, plant and warehouse locations, market segmentation, and market channel structure. Legal factors influence how transport is effected by influencing the long range decisions involved in private carrier use and the short range decisions of mode and carrier selection. The law must also be considered with regard to packaging and mode limitations on certain hazardous materials.

MATERIALS HANDLING

The physical flow of material between the transporting vehicle or production line and the place of use, storage, or other conveyance is the role of materials handling. It is a restraint on transportation decisions because ineffective handling systems can:

1. Decrease transportation load factors (utilization), thereby increasing unit cost of movement

2. Increase transit times

3. Increase vehicle holding time, which often results in additional charges

4. Decrease storage space utilization, increasing holding cost

5. Require more manpower, increasing labor cost

Materials handling tasks are found in physical supply, production, packaging, and transportation. Because of their direct interface, the physical capabilities of materials handling and transportation systems must be compatible.

Compatibility normally means using standardized multi-use handling equipment in similar tasks throughout the organization regardless of functional location. The recent revolution in the materials handling specialty is the direct result of the increasing complexity and interdependence among functions which rely on movement of materials. Handling equipment includes pallets, ramps, platforms, dollies, rollers, conveyors, monorails, specialized conveyors, tugs, lift trucks, and an assortment of special purpose devices. Since it provides movement effectiveness through interfunctional compatibility, some equipment is difficult to classify by function. For instance, the rigid container (usually steel, constructed to fit some vehicle) is useful for purposes of packaging, materials handling, and transportation. Regardless of the level of sophistication in equipment, the purpose of materials handling is to facilitate a system of interfunctional compatibility which minimizes restraints on other decisions.

MARKET CONDITIONS

Short run market fluctuations have little effect on the aggregate supply of transportation services. The number of carriers entering and leaving the total market over a short period of time tends to balance (although the failure rate of newly entering carriers is high). Also, legal controls and the vast number of carriers have a damping effect on short run fluctuations.

Long range market dislocations have a different impact. Pessimistic long range economic forecasts tend to cause common and contract carriers to collectively eliminate marginal links in the transportation network. Therefore, as links to small submarkets are abandoned, major market areas become smaller and more concentrated. The first evidence of such a phenomenon is general deterioration of service levels. Thus, a consumer of the transportation services of common and contract carriers will be restricted to fewer accessible suppliers and commercial markets. An example of this process is small shipment service over the past several years. Small shipments (less than 500 pounds) now represent less than 5% of rail revenue ton miles. The natural beneficiary, motor service, no longer solicits such traffic because of the low return it represents. The lack of LCL (less carload) and LTL (less truckload) links limits an organization in reaching its suppliers and markets.

MOVEMENT FACTORS

Movement factors are information elements which define the operational environment of transportation decisions. They describe the relationships between the material to be moved and transportation capabilities. The source of a movement factor may be internal to transportation, or it may be another functional area such as purchasing, production, or marketing. Regardless of the source, movement factors must be identified and analyzed before effective transportation decisions can be made.

The number of factors necessary for management to consider will vary from organization to organization, but several of major significance are:

1. Material flow characteristics such as volume and frequency
2. Material or product characteristics
3. Characteristics of the alternative transportation modes
4. Packaging characteristics

MATERIAL FLOW

The demand placed on transportation is largely derived from the physical flow of material through the network. The significance of flow considerations in an organization is dependent on the following:

1. The type of organization (production or marketing oriented)
2. Product characteristics
3. Product mix (homogeneous or heterogeneous items)
4. The type of production operation (continuous or intermittent)
5. Demand characteristics for the material (constant or irregular)

While material flow can be described in various ways, for transportation purposes it is commonly evaluated in terms of two measures: volume and frequency.

Volume

Flow volume refers to the number and size of shipments made during a planning period. A shipment may involve the movement of a single item, such as a large generator; many items, similar or unrelated; or a bulk product, such as grain. Planning periods depend on probable future demand for transportation and the selected source of the transportation services. Constant demand and the use of private or contract carriage would suggest a long planning period. Constant or intermittent demand with the use of common carriage permits a shorter planning period.

Single product volume may limit the alternative methods of transportation. Because of minimum charges, shipments of low volume single products by water and rail may not be economical. In addition, water and rail carriers generally do not solicit small shipments. Large volume and extradimensional shipments may exceed the loading capacity of vehicles or the size limitations of parcel post and package services.

Multiple item shipments are usually adaptable to consolidated or unitized shipping increments. Individual items can be grouped into volumes suitable for the most advantageous method. In some cases, carrier provided vehicles or containers may be staged at a firm to await the accumulation of capacity shipment volume. Shipment consolidation tends to increase holding costs, but reduces unit transportation costs and transit time.

Shipments of bulk products require specialized transportation services capable of moving large volumes of homogeneous material. They also require the close coordination of storage, materials handling, and transportation. Storage and materials handling may be the responsibility of the material owner, the carrier, or both. For instance, grain may be stored by the grower awaiting favorable market conditions. Upon sale, the grain is moved by a motor vehicle to a carrier operated storage facility at a railhead or seaport loading area. There, the grain will remain in temporary storage until volume is sufficient or vehicles are available. Pipelines also maintain temporary storage and handling facilities.

As a general rule, unit transportation cost decreases as shipment volume increases. Volume is also a criterion for selecting among modes, since a mode may specialize in a specific size parcel. Volume may also influence storage, packaging, and materials handling costs. Since storage cost is usually charged per cubic measurement, large volume material has an important impact on storage costs. While some volume materials require little or no packaging (oil or grain), they do require specialized and expensive handling equipment. Volume material may be limited to modes which require extra protective packaging to insure safe movement. It is also important to note that volume shipments usually have longer transit times.

Frequency

Flow frequency is the distribution of transportation demands over time. It is dependent upon the production schedule and inventory restraints. A production schedule is predicated on consumer demand, resource availability, and plant capacity. Inventory policy is influenced by the production schedule, holding costs, order costs, stockout costs, and storage limitations.

Movement frequency is usually dependent upon the production and inventory systems. A continuous production process requires constant supplies of raw materials or components to maintain acceptable plant equipment utilization, and consistent demand for finished goods to justify continuous production. Inventory policy and movement frequency interact to ensure adequate supplies of material inputs to production and sufficient stocks of finished goods to satisfy market demands. Generally, movement frequencies are inversely related to inventory levels. Frequency enters into the inventory total cost function as transportation costs (usually a part of order cost) and transit times (lead times). Movement frequency can also be used as a hedge against stockouts by reducing transit times through expeditious use of premium transportation sources.

Intermittent and job shop production processes are more responsive to short-run demand, and their inventory decisions are essentially deterministic. Movement frequencies are more sensitive to discrete demand levels concentrated around order points and delivery dates. Greater movement frequency is required to respond to the demand for raw materials and components necessary for production startup. Movement frequencies will also be greater in response to customer demand during a peak demand period or on a predetermined delivery date. Since large inventories are not maintained in intermittent and job shop processes, transportation frequency provides the cushion normally provided by inventory.

In satisfying production and inventory restraints, movement frequency must be considered a relevant cost factor in the transportation decision process. The manager must determine the marginal cost advantage of serving production and consumer demands by high frequency movement support for low inventory levels in comparison with low frequency movement support for high inventory levels.

MATERIAL CHARACTERISTICS

Material or product characteristics affect the transportation decision in two main ways: (1) the design or inherent qualities of the material influence the number of available transportation modes, or may require special shipment preparation, and (2) material characteristics determine the transportation commodity grouping, called classification, to which a product is assigned. A commodity classification is ultimately used in formulating cost information for many movements.

Design

Material or product design refers to the physical makeup, content, or other characteristics of an item. Design considerations have major influences on packaging, warehousing, materials handling, and transportation. In fact, the future costs in these areas are important factors during the development of a product. The design considerations which most often affect transportation decisions are product size, shape, fragility, hazard, value, and shelf life.

Material size and shape are factors in establishing the compatibility of the product with a transportation mode. Small stackable items are well suited for container service, but extradimensional items are not; vehicles and large machinery are usually not compatible with air freight service. Product size and shape also affect materials handling procedures. Most transportation vehicles are designed to move loads that are rectangular solid in shape. Packaging can be used to conform the product to vehicle shapes, increasing space utilization and promoting handling efficiency.

Product fragility, value, and hazard are considerations for mode selection and packaging design. Many carriers will not accept extremely fragile or valuable items without agreement to reduce liability. Hazardous qualities of a product may restrict it to a few modes, or the acceptable quantity of such an item may be severely limited. Fragile, valuable, and hazardous items are usually subject to packaging regulations. Packaging specifications for hazardous materials vary with different modes, and it is the shipper's responsibility to be aware of and satisfy all regulations.

Susceptibility to spoilage or short shelf life may override other determinants of movement frequency and mode selection. Thus, with fresh bakery or meat products, the product characteristics rather than economic quantities dictate movement frequency. These characteristics may also create transit time restraints capable of being met by only a limited number of transportation modes.

Transportation costs usually reflect special material characteristics. Extra charges in addition to regular line-haul transportation charges are applied to services that accommodate special material characteristics. The organization may incur additional internal expense for packaging, materials handling, and the use of premium transportation. A common or contract carrier may levy additional charges for providing such special services as:

1. Environmental controls (refrigeration, icing, freezing, or heating)
2. Special equipment
3. Extra or special personnel
4. Feeding and watering of livestock

Charges for such special services are called accessorial or ancillary charges. Carriers may also make additional charges for products requiring terminal services such as storage, transfer, and weighing.

Classification

Commodity or freight classifications serve to group materials into homogeneous categories according to transportability and expense of movement. They are used in determining the prices for many transportation services.

Classifications are found in separate publications applicable to commercial rail and motor transportation. For movement by rail, the *Uniform Freight Classification* applies; motor classifications are found in the *National Motor Freight Classification*. Each publication contains: (1) a list of commodities identified by item numbers, (2) a rating and minimum weight for each listed commodity, (3) rules of application, and (4) exceptions.

The rating of a product is not the rate or charge for movement. It is a ranking of the product among all groupings according to considerations which influence the cost of transportation. Ratings are used in conjunction with price lists, called tariffs, which contain rates. Ratings and rates are factors for determining transportation charges. As a general rule, when classification ratings are used to determine charges, higher ratings will result in higher prices.

Rail freight rates between a given origin and destination are published in tariffs and usually are quoted in cents per hundred pounds. Rates may be class rates or commodity rates. Class rates apply on all items moving between specified origins and destinations. Commodity rates apply only to specifically named items moving between established points. Commodity rates are quoted for heavy-volume, bulky, low-value, and long-haul items. Class rates are more generally applicable, but the vast majority of rail traffic (in ton-miles) moves under commodity rates.

Classification ratings are specified for two load quantities. The Uniform Freight Classification has separate ratings for products shipped in less carload (LCL) and carload (CL) quantities. Similarly, the National Motor Freight Classification has separate ratings for less truckload (LTL) and truckload (TL) quantities. Each classification defines carload or truckload quantities in terms of minimum weights. Carload and truckload ratings are usually lower than less carload and less truckload ratings.

Commodity classifications may be redetermined if the organizations or carriers involved can justify such a change. Potential classification is a significant factor in new product development, particularly when extensive use of common carriage is anticipated. The classification will determine the cost of transportation in support of production and marketing, which may be an important factor in long term profitability.

MODE CHARACTERISTICS

Transportation modes can be divided into primary and special. Primary modes are motor, rail, water, pipeline, and air. The major special service modes include parcel post, express service, freight forwarders, and intermodal services. Transportation managers within the organization must be acquainted with differences in the service capabilities of modes. All modes have a role to play, since each has its advantages.

Motor

Motor transportation features the flexibility to penetrate virtually any market served by the existing highway system. It offers a wide range of services, equipment, and schedules. Movement can be effected without rehandling for pickup and delivery (door to door service). Less truckload quantities may be moved economically. Transit times are usually good to excellent and predictable.

Unlike railroads, the for-hire trucking industry is made up of contract carriers as well as common carriers. Motor carriers are flexible and responsive to service needs and economical for short hauls. Truck rates are generally lower than rail rates on small shipments and short hauls. Up to fairly long distances, trucks usually give more rapid service than railroads. Trucks can operate on a flexible time schedule, leaving and arriving according to customer desires.

Rail

Service area flexibility offered by common carrier rail transportation is limited by existing trackage. Very large quantities may be moved cheaply. Service is discriminatory toward carload shipment (less carload shipments account for less than 1% of rail revenue). Transit times are long and variable. Massive bulk shipments are economical by rail transportation through the use of unit trains, in which trainload quantities are moved. Extractive commodities are prime users of unit trains.

Since delivery is from terminal to terminal, rail shipments frequently require other modes for movement to and from the terminals. Rail is best suited for raw material transport rather than finished products. In general, rail freight rates are lower than truck rates on large shipments for long distances. Rail rates are usually higher than water or pipeline rates. Nationally, rail transport is more flexible than trucks, but locally and regionally the situation is reversed. A truck can leave a shipper's door at any time and arrive at its destination at any desired time; rail shipments are bound by timetables and sometimes by the necessity of building up a complete train before departure.

Water

Water transportation provides the largest capacity at the lowest unit cost. Service is geographically inflexible and very slow. Its chief users are volume shippers. Recent service expansions have included the use of containers and lighter aboard ship (LASH) equipment. Rigid containers of several standard sizes can be used to consolidate small shipments, protect cargo, and improve vessel utilization. A lighter is a small barge which can reach points inaccessible to large vessels. The LASH can receive cargo in a shallow port, return to the mother ship, and discharge cargo in a similar manner at the ultimate destination.

In addition to river, canal, intracoastal, and lake transport, the domestic water system includes coastwise and intercoastal ocean water transportation. Less power is needed to propel on water than on land, so costs are lower. However, large sections of the country are entirely without navigable waterways. Water transportation is slower, with less frequently scheduled service. Delays due to weather must be anticipated. Goods usually must be transported to and from water by land carriers, which involves extra handling expense.

Water carriage is suited to movements of heavy, bulky, low value per unit items that can be loaded and unloaded efficiently. It is desirable when speed is not important, the items are not susceptible to shipping damage or theft, and accompanying land movements are unnecessary or limited. However, vessels can only go where there is enough water to float them.

Pipeline

Pipeline transportation is a highly specialized mode almost exclusively dedicated to the petroleum industry. Geographical flexibility is extremely limited. Great volumes of a commodity can be moved without packaging and at a very low operating cost per mile. Pipelines and the commodity they move are often owned by the same organization or group of organizations.

Pipeline routes are unidirectional, closed systems with no flexibility. Storage tanks and pumping stations are needed at terminals for continuous operation. The capacity is limited by pipe diameter and pressure. Great quantities can be moved over time by continuous flow at low speed. Transportation is limited to gases, liquids, and solids in slurry suspension.

Air

The fastest and most expensive mode, air transportation, is subject to the flexibility restraints of a limited number of port facilities and dependence on other modes for pickup and delivery. Air express service augments air transportation and delivery service. Air transportation is usually limited to small quantities of cargo. Containers specifically designed for aircraft are now being used for small shipment consolidation, improved handling efficiency, greater aircraft utilization, less airport handling, and greater intermodal compatibility.

Speed of movement is the primary advantage of air shipments. Air transportation is high speed from terminal to terminal, but requires service to and from terminals; terminal delays and congestion may reduce the time benefit. Air carriage is suitable for high-value and highly perishable traffic. The speed advantage may reduce overall costs by requiring smaller inventories and less warehouse service. All major commercial airlines are common carriers.

Parcel Post

A service of the United States Postal Service, parcel post transportation is available between essentially all points in this country. Carriage is limited to small packages, and many commodities are not accepted. Transit times are quite variable. Of primary benefit to users is the door-to-door service at relatively low cost.

Package Services

Besides parcel post, small shipment service is available through carriers such as United Parcel Service (UPS), Federal Express, and commercial bus companies. They compete with parcel post but do not offer as extensive market coverage. Package services are growing in popularity because of specialized attention they are able to provide to large customers. Some offer pickup and delivery services, guaranteed reliability, and most important, competitive rates.

Freight Forwarders

Freight forwarders act as transportation intermediaries. As agents for several shippers, they consolidate shipments for specific destinations and purchase services from carriers, usually at lower volume rates not available to individual shippers. Freight forwarders provide a single point of contact and responsibility for the shipper, regardless of the number of different carriers involved in pickup, line-haul transportation, or delivery. The freight forwarder is a purchasing agent for transportation services.

The primary function of freight forwarders is the consolidation of small shipments of several or numerous shippers into large shipments which move at lower rates. The forwarder sells his service directly to a shipper. The shipper pays no more than he would have to pay for a small-lot movement. However, the shipper does not have to deal with the basic or primary carriers, and may receive better pickup and delivery services.

Intermodal Services

Container on flatcar (COFC), trailer on flatcar (TOFC), and truck on train are examples of intermodal or combination services. Their purpose is to combine the most advantageous characteristics of modes. For instance, TOFC service features the low cost of rail movement and the extensive local distribution capability of motor transportation. Expanding use of shipping containers is increasing the importance of intermodal service. The development of durable, standardized, interchangeable containers will facilitate traffic movement through the various transportation modes.

PACKAGING

The role of packaging[3] in transportation is to minimize the influence of material characteristics on mode selection. Each mode of transportation offers different types of movement hazards such as vibration, shock, exposure, and long transit time. Packaging could be used to reduce in-transit damage to an absolute minimum. Such efforts usually prove impractical because of the added volume and transportation charges and the expense of designing the package. Realistically, the package is designed to afford the product an optimum level of protection and transportability.

Both the contents and surrounding materials must be protected from damage during storage, handling, and transportation. Protective packaging can mitigate requirements for special services such as environmental controls or special equipment. Packaging preservation may add shelf life to a commodity and permit the use of slower, less expensive modes. Unitizing and container packaging techniques can be used to reduce pilferage. The responsibility for packaging a product for shipment, stenciling or labeling shipping instructions on the container, and delivering it to the carrier commonly belongs to the shipping department.

Packaging can modify the shape of a commodity and give it added strength to allow stacking, thus enhancing transportability. But packaging adds size and weight, which increases transportation costs. Packaging design is usually accomplished with some transportation mode in mind, so that light materials would be used for expensive modes. Cost-benefit or breakeven analysis is often used to determine the amount and quality of packaging. In addition to transportation cost and safety, the analysis should include factors such as the value of the material, intended storage environment, package reusability, package appearance, and other marketing considerations.

[3]Technically, packaging can be distinguished from packing. Packing refers to material in a container to preserve or protect the contents. Examples of packing are oil, paper, sawdust, and excelsior. Packaging refers to the exterior containers, such as a box, crate, or can. The term "packaging" is normally used to describe the entire area of packing and packaging.

TRANSPORTATION DECISIONS

The transportation manager is responsible for making decisions by combining inputs, restraints, movement factors, and his own judgment. His decisions, in the form of outputs, will control the cost effectiveness of the flow of material and become inputs or restraints to other functions. Ultimately, his decisions will control the amount of time and place value created through transportation.

TRANSPORTATION OUTPUTS

Since transportation adds time and place utility to an item but no physical value, it is a cost center rather than a profit center. The objective of transportation is to minimize the costs of providing services that create acceptable time and place values (service levels). To attain its objective, transportation management must select for each item or group of items a type of carriage and then a specific mode; thereafter it must maintain adequate movement records (documentation).

CARRIAGE SOURCE

The choice of a source of transportation services is essentially a make or buy decision. Private carriage (make) represents an internal supply source, common carriage (buy) is a source external to the firm, and contract carriage (lease) is an intermediate alternative source with both internal and external controls. Ultimately, the decision is based on a comparative evaluation of the benefits and disadvantages. The criteria for evaluation vary among firms according to their size, production orientation (continuous or intermittent), market position, planning horizon, and so forth. However, there are two major factors that are common to the evaluation in most firms. They are the firm's internal demand for movement flexibility and the availability of investment funds.

Flexibility

Flexibility in transportation is the amount of control an organization has over the frequency of service, patterns of distribution, and expediting of urgent requirements. Frequency of service refers to the availability of transportation equipment at the proper time and in sufficient quantity to satisfy an organization's needs. Patterns of distribution concern the ability of a carrier to transport goods over a route which satisfies the organization's requirements. Expediting is the organization's ability to make short notice changes to mode, route, delivery instruction, or priority for a specific shipment. The amount of flexibility desired by an organization is usually reflected in whether its primary source of carriage is private, contract, or common carriage.

With private carriage the organization is owner and operator of the transportation equipment. It has complete managerial control over the entire transportation function. Purchase of such service assumes the organization will have a continuous demand for flexibility. Service frequency can be unilaterally manipulated to satisfy supply and distribution demands. The organization has constant control over equipment availability and scheduling. Patterns of distribution can be modified according to market fluctuations without the impairment of external institutional relations. Expediting to satisfy an emergency requirement involves only the temporary rearrangement of the priority of a movement. Normally, the private carriage purchased by an organization is a single mode, which is most often motor. Thus, the inherent flexibility of private carriage is usually limited to the capability of an individual mode. Of course, few organizations use private carriage exclusively, and commercial modes are available for supplemental purposes.

Contract carriage involves an agreement between the organization and a carrier for scheduled service between specified points. Demand for flexibility is assumed to be continuous for the duration of the agreement. Service frequencies and distribution patterns are stipulated by contract, but terms are generally broad enough to allow limited variation. Equipment scheduling is a carrier function. Because the carrier may serve other organizations under different agreements, expediting is frequently difficult and expensive.

Common carriers control their own service frequencies and patterns, subject to stringent governmental regulations. Scheduling is limited by competition for available carrier equipment. The organization's movement flexibility is under external control. This does not mean that there is no flexibility, but only that control over it is exercised by the carrier. In marketing his service, the common carrier seeks to satisfy customer demands, one of which is movement flexibility. A common carrier serves many customers, each having different demands. To achieve satisfactory movement flexibility, an organization must rely on several different modes and carriers. As with contract service, expediting is difficult and expensive. Unlike private and contract carriage, the use of common carriage does not require a commitment to a single primary mode.

Investment

Transportation competes with other functions in an organization for available investment funds. But unlike many other functions, the transportation requirements in most organizations can be met with or without significant long-term investments. Each purchase source has a different investment requirement, and the investment decision is dependent on potential benefits and the availability of funds.

Heavy long-term investment in equipment is characteristic of private carriage. Equipment includes transportation vehicles, compatible materials handling equipment, maintenance equipment, and facilities. Funds must also be committed for operating and maintenance personnel, insurance, fees, and training. These commitments are only somewhat offset by savings through reduced packaging requirements, lower inventory levels, and fewer stockouts because of improved transit times, reduced shipment documentation expense, and on-vehicle advertising. Allocation of funds for such a long-term investment requires great confidence in one's forecasting and planning abilities.

Investment requirements for contract carriage are not as severe in terms of funds and time. Since the carrier retains responsibility for equipment ownership and operations, the organization pays only for services covered by the contract in increments stipulated in the schedule of payments. The contract also specifies the period of obligation, terms of agreement, and liability limitations. Most benefits accrue as a result of predictable and consistent service. The limited investment requirements for contract carriage allow a shorter planning horizon.

No long-term investment is necessary to finance common carrier service. Transportation funds are expended on a pay-as-you-go basis. Payments are made in advance, collect, within a specified period, or according to a credit arrangement. Common carrier service can satisfy an organization's movement requirements without causing the transportation function to compete for scarce investment funds.

MODE SELECTION

The choice of the most economical means of transportation capable of satisfying movement requirements is called mode selection. An objective of transportation is to add as much value as possible with the least increase in cost. The minimization of transport costs does not always optimize performance or profits. Sometimes, a higher price mode will decrease some other cost considerably more than it increases transport costs.

Private and contract operations are usually, though not always, motor. Mode selection is of primary importance when common carriers are used. Transportation restraints or movement factors may eliminate certain modes or necessitate selection of one mode. Relevant considerations involved in mode selection are:

1. Transportation pricing

2. Scheduling
3. Routing
4. Tracing and expediting

Pricing

Cost determination for common carrier service can be an extremely difficult task, primarily because of the volume and complexity of pricing mechanisms. Transportation prices can be classified into the two categories of *line-haul rates* and *special services charges*. Line-haul rates are listed in publications called tariffs or circulars, and usually specify a charge or rate for shipment in cents per hundred pounds. Most rates are subject to redetermination through negotiations between the shipper and carrier. Transportation costs are primarily a function of four basic elements

1. Distance a shipment must travel
2. Weight of the shipment
3. Nature and type of product
4. Mode of transportation utilized

Of the over fifty distinct types of rates, three of the most common are *class, exception,* and *commodity*. Class rates are based on the ratings for items found in the applicable commodity classification. They are cost oriented in that they are tied to the average cost to the carrier. Class rates tend to vary with weight and distance and are generally the highest. A firm purchasing transportation services based solely on class rates is probably overspending. Exception rates, as the name suggests, are applicable for exceptions to class rates. An unusual requirement for movement of a commodity, such as special equipment, can justify an exception. Exceptions rates take precedence over class rates, and may be higher or lower. Commodity rates are established for specific high-volume commodities moving between specific points. They are generally lower than class and exception rates.

Special service charges (accessorial charges) can be expressed as part of the line-haul rate or as a separate charge. They cover such services as *diversion, reconsignment, transit privileges, protection,* and *terminal services*. Diversion is a change in destination initiated by the shipper, usually during transit. It allows last minute changes in marketing decisions, such as redirecting shipments of fresh meats to prevent spot shortages. Reconsignment involves a change in the documented receiver or consignee.

Transit privileges offered by many rail and motor carriers over certain routes permit the shipper to stop a shipment at an intermediate point for processing, partial loading, or partial unloading. One rate covers the entire movement, which usually results in lower total transportation charges than the combination of charges for two separate movements.

Protective services provided by some carriers include icing, refrigeration, and extra packaging. Terminal services which may result in additional charges are pickup and delivery, demurrage, and detention. Not all carriers offer pickup and delivery services. Those that do usually limit such services to metropolitan areas in the proximity of a carrier operated terminal facility. Demurrage charges are penalty fees for retention of rail equipment for loading or unloading beyond a stated free time. Detention charges are similar fees for retention of motor carrier equipment, but the free time is much shorter.

Transportation rates and charges have been under varying degrees of government regulation since the turn of the century. There have been many attempts to automate and simplify transportation pricing. Some success has been possible for applications to a limited number of commodities and service points. Comprehensive simplification has been hampered by pricing inconsistencies and the tremendous number of possible rate combinations.

Scheduling

An important method for effecting maximum equipment utilization is scheduling. Scheduling requires internal coordination among transportation, purchasing, and sales. Acquisition and customer delivery lead times must allow for time consumed in transportation equipment ordering and shipment consolidation. Sufficient equipment and a optimum quantity of material prepared for shipment should be available simultaneously. Proper scheduling can help prevent lead time extensions, late customer deliveries, and excessive inventory holding times while permitting the selection of the most economical transportation mode.

Routing

Routing depends on the transportation service level required for specific commodities. It makes individual service requirements compatible with expected carrier performance. An organization's routing policy is determined by carrier dependability, equipment quality, rates, services offered, transit times, and claim procedures.

Routing policy can control carrier and mode selection through service requirements for a specific commodity. The transportation "pipeline" can be used as an extension of the inventory system for commodities such as grain by selecting a dependable carrier in a slow mode operating over indirect routes. Transit times may be long enough to allow a constantly moving inventory or permit shipment before sale.[4] Products requiring consistent service lead to standardization in routing.

Tracing and Expediting

Tracing is the initiation of a search routine, normally requested by the manager of transportation to locate a shipment lost or delayed in transit. Expediting is a procedure to provide priority handling and movement of a shipment. Expediting can begin before a shipment is tendered to a carrier or after it is in transit. The carrier provides periodic status reports concerning the progress of the shipment.

Many carriers maintain special organizational entities for handling, tracing, and expediting actions. Requests for tracing and expediting action must provide the carrier with sufficient information to identify the shipment, such as commodity, shipper, consignee, route, vehicle number, and document number. The nature of some shipments requires that they be moved by traceable means and that they can be expedited. Mode selection may be limited in those cases; for instance, parcel post and routine express shipments cannot be traced or expedited because few shipment records are retained by the carriers.

MOVEMENT RECORDS

The physical flow of material is documented through the flow of information relevant to each shipment. The information can be operational, such as tracing action, expedite requests, and status reports. It can also be historical. Movement records contain documented information necessary to evaluate performance effectiveness and reconcile financial inconsistencies. Organizations have various methods for structuring movement records. Whether automated or manual, most record systems contain transportation information classified by (1) mode, (2) carrier, (3) carrier within mode, (4) geographic region, (5) customer or consignee, (6) commodity, and (7) a document number. The broad categories of information retained in movement records include documents, performance files, and auditing and claims files.

---

[4]Transit time is the total time (including all movements, storages, and transfers) from the time the items are shipped until they reach the user.

Documents

Application of automated documentation procedures to transportation has been slow, laborious, and of doubtful effectiveness. This has been true for several reasons, such as:

1. There is no universally acceptable shipping document.
2. Intermodal compatibility is not yet a reality.
3. Mechanization is complex (fully automated documentation procedures would require access to all rates, and there are in excess of 40 trillion possible rates[5]).
4. It is difficult to coordinate documentation requirements for international shipments.

Thus, most transportation documentation is still manually prepared with clerical assistance from local automated procedures. The most important documents generated are the *bill of lading, waybill,* and *freight bill.*

A bill of lading (B/L) is an order for transportation services. The bill of lading serves three functions: (1) a receipt for the material, (2) evidence of title, and (3) a contract for carriage. It is prepared by the shipper (consignee) from information on the purchase order, requisition, or packing slip. Since it stipulates the terms of performance and liability limitations, the bill of lading is a contract between the shipper and carrier. When signed by the consignee it becomes a receipt for goods and a proof of delivery. The bill of lading file is usually the most important movement record in the organization.

The carrier's waybill is prepared by the initial carrier from information on the bill of lading. A waybill is used to document every stage of a movement. At each transit point, or each time custody of the shipment changes, the waybill is often the key to tracing and expediting. The carrier sometimes assigns his own unique numerical identifier (called a "pro" number or "pro" bill, since the number is one of a progression over a specified time), and it is necessary that the shipper and carrier maintain a method for cross referencing bill of lading numbers and "pro" numbers. Often the waybill also functions as an arrival notice or an on-hand notice at the delivering carrier's terminal or agent location.

The freight bill, prepared from information on the bill of lading, serves as the carrier's billing document or invoice.

---

[5]"Expensive Guesswork Eliminated in Choosing Best Freight Rates", *Industrial Distribution* **64**: 91–92 (March 1974).

Performance File

Most organizations maintain a file on all carriers to evaluate transportation effectiveness. Called a carrier performance file, it contains information helpful in carrier selection, scheduling, and routing. The file normally contains historical data on a carrier's availability, lead time, equipment quality, transit time, and claims actions.

Auditing and Claims

It is not uncommon for an organization's transportation bill to be overstated. Although most of the excess charge can be reclaimed, that seldom occurs. Responsibility for erroneous charges for transportation service rests with both shipper and carrier. Common causes for such charges are improper freight classification, invalid tariff application, simple arithmetic errors on invoices, damage, and shortages. Financial inconsistencies can be reconciled by *auditing* freight charges and initiating *claims* actions.

When auditing freight charges the organization simply duplicates the task of the carrier's billing (rate) department. The auditing requires very specialized expertise. The carrier usually employs a freight rate analyst with years of experience dealing with thousands of rate structures. In addition, he probably maintains current files of tariffs, classifications, and related publications. If the organization does not possess this expertise and it is too expensive to acquire, there is another very useful option. Commercial auditing firms are available which employ a staff of analysts. These firms will audit an organization's freight bill for a price based on a percentage of overcharges they reveal. Overcharges (and undercharges) are reconciled by submitting a claim to the carrier. The auditing and claims function also encompasses the responsibility for handling loss, shortage, and damage actions.

CONCLUSION

The transportation function provides time and place utility. Organizations have accepted that premise for many years. Only recently have organizations begun to view transportation as a function which can be controlled for the benefit of cost effectiveness. The old view of transportation as a technical clerical task lingers because the function is so dispersed throughout many organizations. It can be found (totally or partially) in purchasing, inventory, or marketing. It is influenced by both internal and external variables, including institutions such as regulatory agencies. Perhaps the old view is retained because the interdependences between other functions and transportation are complex. Even inefficient transportation systems can be effective at a premium cost, and owing to the complexity of the situation the cost may not be evident.

It should be recognized that transportation represents a primary area for cost savings. Through management effort, inefficient systems can be made efficient without sacrificing organizational effectiveness. Attainment of such results requires a recognition of the importance of both functional specialization and functional interdependence. It also requires a comprehensive understanding of the environmental framework of the transportation function. Included in that framework are the inputs which initiate the decision process, the restraints on the decision process, the important movement factors, and the decision outputs.

QUESTIONS

1. What significant influences have increased the importance of transportation for many organizations?
2. What two types of utility are created by transportation?
3. Define the transportation/physical distribution function.
4. What are the basic inputs to the transportation function? Relate any personal experiences you have had with the purchase of transportation services.
5. From what three sources can an organization purchase transportation services? What source is the most flexible?
6. What federal bodies regulate transportation?
7. Name the primary transportation modes. Which mode tends to have the lowest unit cost? The highest?
8. What is a freight forwarder and what function does he perform?
9. What basic elements determine transportation charges?
10. List the three most common line-haul rates.
11. What are the three most common transportation documents?
12. What is the purpose of a waybill?
13. What are the three basic outputs of the transportation function?
14. What are the advantages of viewing transportation as a function?
15. Select a product you have purchased lately and try to determine the logistics it has followed prior to your ownership.

Case 1: Set Point

Smash, Inc., a manufacturer of tennis racquets, is located in Suffolk. The company has been growing rapidly, and gross revenues are expected to exceed $5 million.

As Smash has grown, its transportation problems have compounded. Raw materials, mainly wood and metal alloys, come in from a few local suppliers. Shipments out consist of a large number of small shipments to shops and tennis centers, plus some large ones to schools and universities. At present the total annual cost of transportation is about half a million dollars.

The transportation department at Smash is made up of a supervisor and one clerk. It is under the control of the production manager. Smash is organized along functional lines with managers for marketing, finance, and production. For quite some time there has been considerable friction between the marketing and production managers about transportation problems. The marketing manager contends that in terms of value to the company he is the largest user of transportation. If he is unable to control the methods of transportation, sales will be lost. The production manager attempts to justify his controlling of transportation in terms of volume. He also argues that his experience in the area of transportation (about 10 years) enables him to schedule shipments more efficiently. Finally, he notes that the major concern of the marketing department is increased sales, and therefore it would give only secondary attention to transportation and other cost controls.

Just recently, at the request of the marketing manager, several small orders were air freighted to customers at a cost of about 50 cents per ton mile. Had these orders been scheduled routinely and sent by truck, the cost would have been less than 10 cents per ton-miles. Consequently, any profits to be realized were lost on these shipments. The production manager was disturbed because all the costs of transportation come from his budget.

1. Who should control the transportation department? Why?
2. Should some orders be air freighted to maintain customer goodwill?
3. What alternative structural changes in the organization might reduce the conflict between marketing and production?

Case 2: Bernie's Interview

Bernie Rich had been a staff transportation advisor to the Executive Vice President of the National Material Traffic Organization for five years. In his experience he had accumulated what he considered a substantial knowledge not only in the field of transportation, but also in allied disciplines. Bernie perceived his career had reached a plateau with National, particularly since his boss, LaVerne Hanks, seemed adamant that Bernie should strictly limit his efforts to transportation. Therefore, Bernie began a search for new employment opportunities.

Two weeks ago Bernie had an interesting interview with Enviro, Inc., a New Jersey based producer of air filtration devices. The position open was new. It was for a Director of Logistics who reported directly to the Vice President for Materials Management, Mr. Gary Julian. During his conversation with Mr. Julian, Bernie jotted down the following notes:

1. Mr. Julian was formerly the production manager at National.
2. There was some question about what logistics would include. Mr. Julian was mainly interested in ensuring on-time deliveries of raw materials.
3. Finished goods delivery was handled by the shipment clerk, Juan Bales, who worked for the production manager.
4. The Vice President for Marketing, Luther Dailey, was responsible for all purchasing and sales. Since federal and state regulations currently require the use of Enviro's products, sales forecasting and purchase planning were not considered important. Several governmental specifications are written around Enviro's products, which are protected by patent.
5. Mr. Julian did not seem to appreciate Bernie's interest in disciplines related to transportation.

Although he did not expect it, Bernie was invited for a second interview, at which time a final selection would be made. Bernie had decided he wanted the job. However, he was worried about the final interview, especially since it would be with both Mr. Julian and Mr. Dailey. To prepare for the interview he felt it would be helpful to outline his conception of the new job, the responsibilities, and internal relationships.

1. Suggest an outline for Bernie.
2. What should it include or exclude? Discuss in detail.
3. Should Bernie try to change Mr. Julian's concept of materials management? If so, should he do it before or after he accepts the position?

Case 3: A Big Change

Glasgow Manufacturing is a medium size manufacturer of farm equipment located in the coastal plains of North Carolina. It is a family owned operation which has become an important supplier of regional agricultural needs. Major product lines include peanut harvesting equipment, tobacco harvesting and curing machinery, tractors, and various small farm implements. Except for tractors, production is job-shop oriented. Tractors are assembled by a simple line process. Raw materials are purchased from vendors throughout the eastern United States on short term contracts; tractor components are supplied by a single vendor in Germany on an extended contractual basis.

To satisfy expanding demand Glasgow is building a distribution warehouse in Montgomery, Alabama. Completion is expected within six months. The Vice President for Finance, who also handles all purchasing and marketing, is Mr. Franks, and he wants to build another warehouse in the midwest. Additionally, he wants to explore market opportunities in Africa and South America.

The President and owner, Mr. Lee Glasgow, is rather uncertain about the future of his company. Production has always been his primary interest. He feels that if production is effective, everything else will take care of itself. However, he has noticed some difficulty in coordinating the efforts of his staff, particularly in this time of rapid change in agribusiness. While he knows he is making money, Mr. Glasgow does not know exactly how. The staff organization is depicted in Figure 9.4.

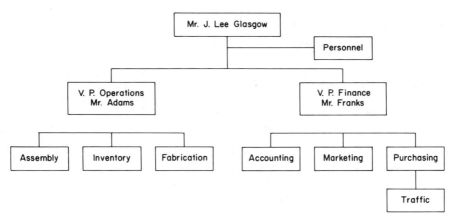

FIGURE 9.4. Glasgow Manufacturing Company.

To complicate matters, Mr. Glasgow plans to retire next year and offer the company for stock ownership. Since he wanted to leave his company in sound condition, Mr. Glasgow hired Biggarly, Carper, Lillard, and Associates, a materials management consulting firm. They were to evaluate current operations and recommend a five year plan. After four months of study, recommendations of the consulting firm were on Mr. Glasgow's desk. One of the major recommendations was to establish a physical distribution department integrating the current and projected flow of material.

1. Evaluate the consultant's recommendation. Should it be implemented?

2. What other recommendations would you make to Mr. Glasgow?

Case 4: You Pick It

United Distributors, Inc., stocks a large amount of low cost material. Orders are received from retail customers and are filled from material in stock. The warehouse is large, covering approximately 210,000 square feet. The company stocks approximately 9000 individual line items, and approximately 450 orders are processed a day. The warehouse occupies a single floor and is a manual operation. The existing technique for picking items is to have individual warehousemen pick the items and forward the complete order to the packing section. Mr. Wilson, the warehouse manager, believes that this is the best system because it ensures that material remains segregated by customer, thus avoiding any mixing of orders. As the physical distribution center manager, you have been approached by a staff of efficiency experts. In their opinion the current manpower utilization in the warehouse is less than satisfactory. They are recommending that the existing system be changed to a bulk order picking system.

1. What factors must be considered in deciding what picking system to adopt?
2. What picking system would you recommend?

Case 5: Take Your Choice

The Knerr Storage Company is in the physical distribution business. Mostly small items are received, stored, and issued. The items are received in large lots and usually issued in small quantities. There is a highly seasonal fluctuation in demand for the majority of items carried. The current storage technique of assigning a specified block of warehouse space to each item has recently come under criticism by the new warehouse manager. He has requested permission to change the system to a random storage system, which he claims will improve warehouse space utilization.

Your boss (the physical distribution manager) has asked you to brief him on the advantages and disadvantages of both the preassigned and random storage techniques. He has also asked you to recommend which technique should be used and to support your recommendations.

Case 6: Unidentifiable

The receiving department of International Distribution, Inc. is currently experiencing difficulty in identifying material. The major problem appears to be the identification of metal products, such as steel plate, pipe, angle iron, and bar stock. These items are usually received in less than truckload quantities of mixed freight. The metal products are physically difficult to handle because of their size and weight. The marking of the material is difficult because of the smooth surface on which the identification tag must be placed. The bill of lading from the commercial carrier is of no assistance, because the freight is normally billed as "freight all kinds".

The present procedure is to unload the truck and lay the material on an open hard stand, release the truck, and then identify the material and its ultimate destination. The receiving supervisor feels that this technique is necessary because he has only two hours "free time" to unload and release a truck before a detention charge of $25 for every additional 30 minutes is charged by the trucking company. The inventory manager is upset by the existing procedure because he claims that unloading the truck before identification of material results in the loss of identification tags. Without the identification tag, it is almost impossible to route the material.

During a recent storm much of the material unloaded and placed on the hard stand lost its identification. The inventory manager has just returned from a tour of the hard stand receiving area. He requested the receiving manager to identify and mark all material with waterproof marking *before* unloading the material from the trucks in the future. He stated that any detention charges incurred would be small compared to the savings on unidentifiable material.

1. What action would you take?
2. What factors should be considered?

Bibliography

Alfandary-Alexander, Mark. *An Inquiry into Some Models Of Inventory Systems*, Pittsburgh, Pennsylvania: University of Pittsburgh Press, 1962.

Aljian, George W. (Ed.). *Purchasing Handbook*, New York: McGraw-Hill, 1973.

American Management Association. *Company Approaches to Production Problems: Inventory, Warehousing, Traffic*, New York: American Management Association, 1955.

_____. *Key Consideration to Inventory Management*, New York: American Management Association, 1953.

American Production and Inventory Control Society. *Management of Lot-Size Inventories*, Washington, D.C.: American Production and Inventory Control Society, 1963.

_____. *Material Requirements Planning by Computer*, Washington, D.C.: American Production and Inventory Control Society, 1971.

Ammer, Dean S. *Materials Management*, Homewood, Illinois: Richard D. Irwin, 3rd edition, 1974.

Arrow, K. J. et al. *Studies in the Mathematical Theory of Inventory and Production*, Stanford, California: Stanford University Press, 1958.

Baily, P. J. *Design of Stock Control Systems and Records*, London: Gower Press, 1970.

Baily, Peter and David Farmer. *Managing Materials in Industry*, London: Gower Press, 1972.

Ballot, Robert P. *Materials Management*, New York: American Management Association, 1971.

Ballou, Ronald H. *Business Logistics Management*, Englewood Cliffs, New Jersey: Prentice-Hall, 1973.

269

Barrett, D. A. *Automatic Inventory Control Techniques*, London: Business Books Limited, 1972.

Bierman, Harold et al. *Quantitative Analysis for Business Decisions*, Homewood, Illinois: Richard D. Irwin, 1969.

Bowersox, Donald J. *Logistical Management*, New York: Macmillan, 1974.

Bowman, Edward H. and Robert B. Fetter. *Analysis for Production and Operations Management*, Homewood, Illinois: Richard D. Irwin, 1967.

Briggs, Andrew J. *Warehouse Operations Planning and Management*, New York: John Wiley and Sons, 1960.

Brown, Robert G. *Decision Rules for Inventory Management*, New York: Holt, Rinehart and Winston, 1967.

_____. *Smoothing, Forecasting, and Prediction of Discrete Time Series*, New York: Prentice-Hall, 1963.

_____. *Statistical Forecasting for Inventory Control*, New York: McGraw-Hill, 1959.

Buchan, Joseph and Ernest Koenigsberg. *Scientific Inventory Management*, Englewood Cliffs, New Jersey: Prentice-Hall, 1963.

Buffa, Elwood S. and William H. Taubert. *Production-Inventory Systems: Planning and Control*, Homewood, Illinois: Richard D. Irwin, 1972.

Carroll, Phil. *Practical Production and Inventory Control*, New York: McGraw-Hill, 1966.

Davis, Grant M. and Stephen W. Brown. *Logistics Management*, Lexington, Massachusetts: Lexington Books, 1974.

D'Anna, John P. *Inventory and Profit: The Balance of Power in Buying and Selling*, New York: American Management Association, 1966.

England, Wilbur B. *The Purchasing System*, Homewood, Illinois: Richard D. Irwin, 1967.

England, Wilbur B. and Michiel R. Leenders. *Purchasing and Materials Management*, Homewood, Illinois: Richard D. Irwin, 6th edition, 1975.

Enrick, Norbert Lloyd. *Inventory Management*, San Francisco, California: Chandler, 1968.

Fabrycky, W. J. and Jerry Banks. *Procurement and Inventory Systems: Theory and Analysis*, New York: Reinhold, 1967.

Fetter, Robert B. and Winston C. Dalleck. *Decision Models for Inventory Management*, Homewood, Illinois: Richard D. Irwin, 1961.

Forrester, Jay W. *Industrial Dynamics*, Boston: M.I.T. Press, 1961.

Fourre, James P. *Applying Inventory Control Techniques*, New York: American Management Association, 1969.

Greene, James H. *Production and Inventory Control Handbook*, New York: McGraw-Hill, 1970.

_____. *Production and Inventory Control*, Homewood, Illinois: Richard D. Irwin, 2nd edition, 1974.

Gross, Harry. *Make or Buy*, Englewood Cliffs, New Jersey: Prentice-Hall, 1966.

Hadley, G. and T. M. Whitin. *Analysis of Inventory Systems*, Englewood Cliffs, New Jersey: Prentice-Hall, 1963.

Hanssmann, Fred. *Operations Research in Production and Inventory Control*, New York: John Wiley and Sons, 1962.

Hedrich, Floyd D. *Purchasing Management in the Smaller Company*, New York: American Management Association, 1971.

Heinritz, Stuart F. and Paul V. Farrell. *Purchasing: Principles and Applications*, 5th edition, Englewood Cliffs, New Jersey: Prentice-Hall, 1971.

Heskett, James L. et al. *Business Logistics*, New York: The Ronald Press, 2nd edition, 1973.

Hobbs, John A. *Control Over Inventory and Production*, New York: McGraw-Hill, 1973.

Hoffman, Raymond A. and Henry Gunders. *Inventories: Control, Costing and Effect upon Income and Taxes*, New York: Ronald Press, 2nd edition, 1970.

Holt, Charles C. et al. *Planning Production, Inventories, and Work Force*, Englewood Cliffs, New Jersey: Prentice-Hall, 1960.

_____. *Operations Research in Production and Inventory Control*, New York: John Wiley and Sons, 1962.

Jenkins, Creed H. *Modern Warehouse Management*, New York: McGraw-Hill, 1968.

Johnson, Lynwood A. and Douglas C. Montgomery. *Operations Research in Production Planning, Scheduling, and Inventory Control*, New York: John Wiley and Sons, 1974.

Killeen, Louis M. *Techniques of Inventory Management*, New York: American Management Association, 1969.

Lee, Jr., Lamar and Donald W. Dobler. *Purchasing and Materials Management*, New York: McGraw-Hill, 2nd edition, 1971.

Lewis, C. D. *Scientific Inventory Control*, New York: Elsevier North-Holland, 1970.

Lipman, Burton E. *How to Control and Reduce Inventory*, Englewood Cliffs, New Jersey: Prentice-Hall, 1973.

Magee, John F. *Physical Distribution Systems*, New York: McGraw-Hill, 1967.

———— and David M. Boodman. *Production Planning and Inventory Control*, New York: McGraw-Hill, 1967.

Mathews, Lawrence M. *Control of Materials*, London: Industrial and Commerical Techniques, 1971.

McGarrah, Robert E. *Production and Logistics Management*, New York: John Wiley and Sons, 1963.

McMillan, Claude and Richard F. Gonzalez. *Systems Analysis: A Computer Approach to Decisions Models*, Homewood, Illinois: Richard D. Irwin, 2nd edition, 1968.

Mills, Edward S. *Price, Output, and Inventory Policy*, New York: John Wiley and Sons, 1962.

Mize, Joe H. et al. *Operations Planning and Control*, Englewood Cliffs, New Jersey: Prentice-Hall, 1971.

Morse, Philip M. *Queues, Inventories, and Maintenance*, New York: John Wiley and Sons, 1958.

Mossman, Frank H. and Newton Morton, *Logistics of Distribution Systems*, Boston: Allyn and Bacon, 1965.

Mudge, Arthur E. *Value Engineering: A Systematic Approach*, New York: McGraw-Hill, 1971.

Naddor, Eliezer. *Inventory Systems*, New York: John Wiley and Sons, 1966.

National Association of Accountants. *Techniques in Inventory Management*, Research Report No. 40, New York: National Association of Accountants, 1964.

New, Colin. *Requirements Planning*, New York: John Wiley and Sons, 1973.

Niland, Powell. *Production Planning, Scheduling, and Inventory Control*, London: Macmillan, 1970.

Orlicky, Joseph. *Material Requirements Planning*, New York: McGraw-Hill, 1975.

————. *The Successful Computer System*, New York: McGraw-Hill, 1969.

Oxenfeldt, Alfred R. *Make or Buy: Factors Affecting Decisions*, New York: McGraw-Hill, 1965.

Peckham, Herbert H. *Effective Materials Management*, Englewood Cliffs, New Jersey: Prentice-Hall, 1972.

Peterson, R. and E. A. Silver. *Decision Systems for Inventory Management and Production Planning*, New York: John Wiley and Sons, 1977.

Plossl, George W. and Oliver W. Wight. *Material Requirements Planning by Computer*, Washington, D.C.: American Production and Inventory Control Society, 1971.

_____. *Production and Inventory Control*, Englewood Cliffs, New Jersey: Prentice-Hall, 1967.

Prabhu, N. *Queues and Inventories*, New York: John Wiley and Sons, 1965.

Prichard, James W. and Robert H. Eagle. *Modern Inventory Management*, New York: John Wiley and Sons, 1965.

Putnam, Arnold Q. et al. *Unified Operations Management*, New York: McGraw-Hill, 1963.

Raymond, Fairfield E. *Quantity and Economy in Manufacturing*, New York: McGraw-Hill, 1931.

Reisman, Arnold et al. *Industrial Inventory Control*, New York: Gordon and Breach Science Publishers, 1972.

Sampson, Roy J. and Martin T. Farris. *Domestic Transportation: Practice, Theory, and Policy*, Boston: Houghton Mifflin, 1971.

Scarf, Herbert E. et al. *Multistage Inventory Models and Techniques*, Stanford, California: Stanford University Press, 1963.

Sims, E. Ralph. *Planning and Managing Materials Flow*, Boston: Industrial Education Institute, 1968.

Smykay, Edward W. *Physical Distribution Management*, 3rd edition, New York: Macmillan, 1973.

Starr, Martin K. and David W. Miller. *Inventory Control: Theory and Practice*, Englewood Cliffs, New Jersey: Prentice-Hall, 1962.

Stelzer, W. R. *Materials Management*, Englewood Cliffs, New Jersey: Prentice-Hall, 1970.

Stockton, R. Stansbury. *Basic Inventory Systems: Concepts and Analysis*, Boston: Allyn and Bacon, 1965.

Sussams, J. E. *Industrial Logistics*, Boston: Cahners Books, 1972.

Taff, Charles A. *Management of Physical Distribution and Transportation*, Homewood, Illinois: Richard D. Irwin, 5th edition, 1972.

Tersine, Richard J. *Materials Management and Inventory Systems*, New York: Elsevier North-Holland, 1976.

Tersine, Richard J. and Cyrus A. Altimus, Jr. *Problems and Models in Operations Management*, Columbus, Ohio: Grid, 1974.

Thomas, Adin B. *Inventory Control in Production and Manufacturing*, Boston: Cahners, 1970.

Tyler, Elias S. *Materials Handling*, New York: McGraw-Hill, 1970.

Van DeMark, R. L. *Inventory Control Techniques*, Dallas, Texas: Van DeMark, 2nd edition, 1972.

————. *Managing Material Control*, Dallas, Texas: Van DeMark, 1970.

————. *Production Control Techniques*, Dallas, Texas: Van DeMark, 1970.

————. *New Ideas in Materials Management*, Dallas, Texas: Van DeMark, 1963.

Van Hees, R. N. and W. Monhemius. *Production and Inventory Control: Theory and Practice*, New York: Harper and Row, 1972.

Wagner, Harvey M. *Statistical Management of Inventory Systems*, New York: John Wiley and Sons, 1962.

————. *Principles of Operations Research*, Englewood Cliffs, New Jersey: Prentice-Hall, 1969.

Warman, J. *Warehouse Management*, London: William Heinemann, 1971.

Welch, W. E. *Tested Scientific Inventory Control*, Greenwich, Connecticut: Management Publishing Company, 1956.

Westing, J. E. et al. *Purchasing Management: Materials in Motion*, New York: John Wiley and Sons, 3rd edition, 1969.

Whitin, T. M. *Theory of Inventory Management*, Princeton, New Jersey: Princeton University Press, 1957.

Wight, Oliver W. *Production and Inventory Management in the Computer Age*, Boston: Cahners, 1974.

Willets, Walter E. *Fundamentals of Purchasing*, New York: Appleton-Century-Crofts, 1969.

Zimmerman, Hans-Jurgen and Michael G. Sovereign. *Quantitative Models in Production Management*, Englewood Cliffs, New Jersey: Prentice-Hall, 1974.

Index

275